Women at War in the
Borderlands of the
Early American Northeast

The study of borderlands—places where different peoples meet and no one polity reigns supreme—is undergoing a renaissance. The David J. Weber Series in the New Borderlands History publishes works from both established and emerging scholars that examine borderlands from the precontact era to the present. The series explores contested boundaries and the intercultural dynamics surrounding them and includes projects covering a wide range of time and space within North America and beyond, including both Atlantic and Pacific worlds.

This book was published with support provided by the William P. Clements Center for Southwest Studies at Southern Methodist University in Dallas, Texas.

Women at War in the Borderlands of the Early American Northeast

Gina M. Martino

The University of North Carolina Press CHAPEL HILL

© 2018 The University of North Carolina Press
All rights reserved
Set in Espinosa Nova by Westchester Publishing Services
Manufactured in the United States of America

The University of North Carolina Press has been a member of the
Green Press Initiative since 2003.

Library of Congress Cataloging-in-Publication Data
Names: Martino, Gina M., author.
Title: Women at war in the borderlands of the early American Northeast /
    Gina M. Martino.
Other titles: David J. Weber series in the new borderlands history.
Description: Chapel Hill : University of North Carolina Press, [2018] |
    Series: The David J. Weber series in the new borderlands history |
    Includes bibliographical references and index.
Identifiers: LCCN 2017057353 | ISBN 9781469640990 (cloth : alk. paper) |
    ISBN 9781469641003 (ebook)
Subjects: LCSH: Sex role—Northeastern States—History. | Sex role—New France—
    History. | Women soldiers—Northeastern States—History. | Women soldiers—
    New France—History. | Women—Northeastern States—History. | Women—
    New France—History.
Classification: LCC HQ1075.5.N7 M37 2018 | DDC 305.40974—dc23
    LC record available at https://lccn.loc.gov/2017057353

Jacket illustration: *Madeleine de Verchères Defends Fort, 1692* by J. D. Kelly.
Used by permission of the Canadian Anglo-Boer War Museum
(http://angloboerwarmuseum.com/Boer001_menu.html).

Portions of chapter 1 were previously published as "'As Potent a Prince as
Any Round About Her': Rethinking Weetamoo of the Pocasset and Native
Female Leadership in Early America," *Journal of Women's History* 27:3 (Fall
2015): 37–60. Copyright © 2015 The Johns Hopkins University Press. Used
here with permission.

John Easton letter, May 26, 1675, to Josiah Winslow (Mss C 357). R. Stanton
Avery Special Collections, used with the permission of the New England
Historic Genealogical Society, www.AmericanAncestors.org.

Josiah Winslow to Weetamoo, June 15, 1675, Winslow Family Papers II,
1638–1760, used with the permission of the Massachusetts Historical Society.

To my fellow members of the "Original Five,"
Rich, Nancy, Annie, and Tommy.
Thank you for everything.

Contents

Illustrations and Maps

Acknowledgments

I am deeply moved when reflecting on the support I have received in writing this book, from family and friends to teachers and colleagues. In influencing its development, Kirsten Fischer deserves a place of honor as a mentor and friend. I can never thank her enough for her unwavering support, thoughtful and constructive criticism, and excitement in seeing this project evolve. I am grateful to Lisa Norling for suggestions that helped me refine my approach to gender analysis in this book. I also benefited greatly from Barbara Welke's advice to keep the scope of the project as wide as it is—especially during those moments when writing a narrower history became so very tempting. Finally, I thank Chris Corley for seeing potential in my first efforts as a young historian and for introducing me to early modern history.

This book would not exist without the generous assistance of numerous institutions. The University of Minnesota provided several short- and long-term grant and fellowship opportunities in the project's early stages. A Michael Kraus Research Grant from the American Historical Association allowed me to spend extra time conducting research in Ottawa. And in the final phase of my research, a University of Akron Faculty Research Grant offered the opportunity to return to the archives once more. As the manuscript became a book, the William P. Clements Center for Southwest Studies at Southern Methodist University and the University of Akron helped underwrite production costs. In researching this book, I drove thousands of miles from the Midwest to archives and libraries throughout the northeastern borderlands. I thank the staff at the Massachusetts State Archives, the Massachusetts Historical Society, the New Hampshire Historical Society, the Phillips Library at the Peabody Essex Museum, the New England Historic Genealogical Society, and the Library and Archives Canada. Special thanks are owed to Marie Lamoureux of the American Antiquarian Society for her help tracking down an image used in this book. Staff at the University of Minnesota's Wilson Library and the University of Akron's Bierce Library brought remote sources closer to home through Interlibrary Loan and OhioLINK.

At the University of Minnesota and Minnesota State University, Mankato, I found friends and colleagues whose generosity of time and thoughtful comments were invaluable in helping the book reach its current form. In particular, members of the Early American History Workshop at the University of Minnesota (now the Early Modern Atlantic Workshop) offered vital suggestions on early versions of this project. I am especially grateful to Tony Brown, Sarah Chambers, Anna Clark, Boyd Cothran, Demetri Debe, Caitlin Gallogly, Ed Griffin, John Howe, Lori Lahlum, Rus Menard, Jean O'Brien, Eric Otremba, Don Ross, and Kathleen Vandevoorde for their ideas and encouragement.

I arrived at the University of Akron to the warm welcome of a group of historians who have become good friends and inspiring colleagues. I owe a special debt of gratitude to Lesley Gordon for believing in my scholarship and for sharing her insights as an editor. Connie Bouchard's energy, enthusiasm, and sage advice were exceptionally helpful during the manuscript's final stages of development. My department chair, Martin Wainwright, is a resolute advocate with a generous spirit, and I am fortunate to have him in my corner. I am also grateful to Steve Harp for his timely words of wisdom over the past several years. Thanks to Kevin Kern for his friendship and gentle reminders that Tuesday trivia nights are ideal for taking the occasional and much-needed break. And I will always be thankful to Mike, Emily, Zoe Resmer, Isaac, and Paula Levin for giving me a home base in Akron.

I offer Kym Rohrbach and Wade Wilcox my gratitude for years of encouragement, generosity, and friendship. Wade (an archaeologist by training) also deserves my thanks for conversations about gender and the production of weapons in Indigenous polities that inspired the book's opening pages. I have also benefited greatly from the hard work and sense of fun that the department's student staff members bring to the office, particularly Britt Davies, Robin Guiler, Devon Kahl, Janean Kazimir, Jill Koesling, and Bridget Sciscento.

Working with graduate students at UA is one of my great joys, and I am honored to have the opportunity to teach and learn with them. While writing this book, Angela Riotto acted as an excellent sounding board for all things military and Pat Troester went above and beyond to help me decipher nautical terminology. Thanks also to Kat McDonald-Miranda for sharing her expertise in Latin. Finally, studying early American history with Kat, Matt Nowak, and Amanda Sedlak-Hevener gave me a timely burst of scholarly energy as I was preparing my manuscript for submission.

Over the years, colleagues from across the country have contributed to the project's development at seminars, conferences, and by reading early versions of part or all of this book. I am thankful to John Brooke, Cole Jones,

Ann Little, Lucy Murphy, Kira Thurman, and Hilary Wyss for sharing their ideas. Kevin Vrevich, Josh Wood, and Grace Richards invited me to present a chapter at the Ohio Seminar in Early American History and Culture at Ohio State, where members' comments and questions were essential to refining a central argument of the book. I am especially appreciative of the perceptive and constructive comments offered by the reviewers for the press, self-identified reader Edward Countryman and the second, anonymous reader of the manuscript. My dear friend and fellow early Americanist Joanne Jahnke Wegner dropped everything to read the entire manuscript at a critical time in its development. It is a far better book for her help.

I am delighted that this book is part of the David J. Weber Series in the New Borderlands History at UNC Press. Series editors Andrew Graybill and Benjamin Johnson have been energetic champions and excellent sources of advice. I am deeply grateful to Andrew for volunteering to do a full read of the final manuscript. My editor at the press, Chuck Grench, has been a strong supporter of this project from the beginning, and I thank him for his guidance and efforts to produce a quality book. Jad Adkins has answered my many emails about even the smallest details with professionalism and delightful good humor. Thanks also to the rest of the staff at UNC Press for helping with every aspect of this book. Ezra Zeitler was a joy to work with and created the book's wonderful maps. Any mistakes are my own, but I share the rest of this book with all of you.

Since I began this project, I have seen my family grow in numbers, scattering geographically yet always remaining close. Thank you to Santi, Geneva, and (my *abijado*) Matías Vallejo for being part of this funny family. Gene, Nora, Kara (Lattu), and Rachel Reckin have enriched my life by sharing outdoor adventures and a love of learning over the years. My grandparents— Martino and Reckin—and my large, extended family of aunts, uncles, and cousins have been lifelong sources of encouragement and enthusiasm for my work. I also thank my grandmother, Juanita Reckin, for her unconditional love, her curiosity, and her delight in life. She would have been thrilled (but unsurprised) that I became a historian, and I wish I could have handed her this book. Thanks also to Jim Hougas and the rest of the Hougai: Estelle, Helen, Eddie, and my goddaughter, Greta. Annie Martino Hougas and Tommy Martino, you are the best siblings I could have wished for and I am so grateful for your presence in my life. I never laugh more than when I'm with you two. Mom and Dad, I am incredibly lucky that I get to have you as my parents. Thank you for being there every day.

Women at War in the
Borderlands of the
Early American Northeast

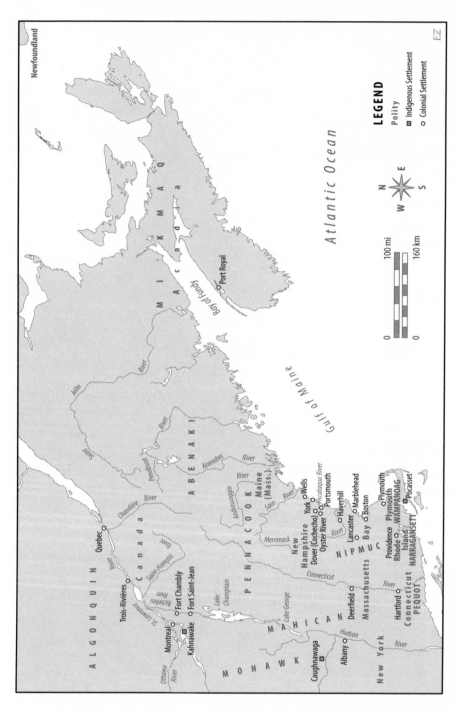

Newfoundland

Atlantic Ocean

LEGEND

Polity

■ Indigenous Settlement

○ Colonial Settlement

N
W — E
S

| | 100 mi |
| 0 | |

| | 160 km |
| 0 | |

M I K M A Q

A c a d i a

Bay of Fundy

Port Royal

St. John River

Gulf of Maine

A B E N A K I

Pennobscot River

Chaudière River

Kennebec River

Androscoggin River

Saco River

P E N N A C O O K

Maine (Mass.)

New Hampshire

Wells
York
Dover (Cochecho)
Oyster River
Piscataqua River
Portsmouth

Merrimack River

Haverhill

Lancaster
Marblehead
Boston

Massachusetts Bay

N I P M U C

Providence
Plymouth
Rhode Island
NARRAGANSETT

Plymouth

WAMPANOAG

Pocasset

Connecticut River

Deerfield

Hartford

Connecticut

PEQUOT

A L G O N Q U I N

Canada

Quebec

Trois-Rivières

Saint-François River

St. Lawrence River

Richelieu River

Montreal

Kahnawake

Fort Chambly

Fort Saint-Jean

Lake Champlain

Lake George

M A H I C A N

M O H A W K

Caughnawaga

Albany

Hudson River

New York

Ottawa River

Northeastern borderlands region, c. 1630–1700

Introduction

Among the Vanguard

The inhabitants of Caughnawaga awoke to the noise of musket balls slamming into the village's palisade on the morning of August 18, 1669. A coalition of Native polities from the east—some carrying New England supplied firearms—had undertaken a campaign to strike a blow against this prominent Mohawk community in an ongoing war. Although Caughnawaga's residents had little time to spare after waking, life in a borderlands village on the eastern edge of the Mohawk nation's territory demanded military readiness. Caughnawaga's people quickly rallied. According to Jesuit missionary Jean Pierron's account of the assault, "the men at once took gun and hatchet in hand," and this initial stand at the palisade afforded the women of Caughnawaga time to begin their role in the battle, dividing into two groups, each with a critical mission. The first group of women began casting musket balls, keeping the defenders of the palisade supplied with ammunition. The other group had a grimmer task. They were to prepare for a possible breach of the town's fortifications, "arm[ing] themselves with knives and defensive weapons." If the enemy overran the palisade, Caughnawaga's men and women would fight together, hand-to-hand against the eastern coalition in defense of their village. Ultimately, Caughnawaga's defenders repelled the siege after hours of fierce fighting, and the attackers retreated.[1]

As the successful defense of Caughnawaga shows, attempting to maintain a tenuous grasp on land and power in the borderlands of the early American northeast required the participation of whole communities. Despite social and cultural differences between Iroquois, English, French, and Algonquian peoples, the Mohawk women's combat support at Caughnawaga would not have seemed out of place in European and Native communities throughout the northeastern borderlands. A region roughly encompassing New England, the southern reaches of the modern province of Quebec, Acadia, and areas controlled by dozens of Native polities, the northeastern borderlands experienced almost continuous warfare throughout much of the seventeenth and eighteenth centuries. Although men served as the primary combatants in these conflicts, women performed a variety of vital military and economic wartime roles as defenders of fortified towns, spies, military leaders, and administrators—both alongside and in the absence of men. Across the northeastern borderlands, gender ideologies that delineated appropriate roles for women within their families and communities supported a diverse range of women's martial activities.

Women's war making in these conflicts was neither accidental nor incidental. Indeed, women's active military participation was widely accepted—sometimes even expected—by their communities and allies. When Mrs. Joseph Mason of Brookfield, Massachusetts, described as "a lively & Intelligent woman," related to colonial officials the story of a raid on her town and her brief captivity in 1693, she seemed determined to defend her failure to fight, asserting "that if she had any weapon she thinks she might have made her escape."[2] In some Algonquian polities of southern New England, female sachems wielded political and military authority and were respected by Native and colonial leaders alike. One New Englander even noted during King Philip's War (1675–76) that Weetamoo of the Pocasset was "as Potent a Prince as any round about her, and hath as much Corn, Land, and Men at her Command."[3] At the same time, nonelite Native women served their polities as combatants and spies, and participated in ritual torture. Elite women in Canada and Acadia led defenses of the colonies' seigneuries, one woman declaring in 1699 that Canada's women were "eager" to "manifest their zeal for the king's glory should the occasion arise" in the wars against the Iroquois.[4] Her words seem accurate in light of the Ursuline Mother Superior Marie Morin's memoirs, which approvingly described ordinary French women as "Amazons" who "ran armed like the men" to fight, Morin adding that she "had seen this many times," a phrase suggesting both frequency and a broader cultural acceptance of women's wartime activities.[5]

Such stories of women's war making in the northeastern borderlands have largely been forgotten today, a few familiar accounts set aside as anomalous, as curiosities lacking historical context or consequence. Most of these examples come from a small number of major narrative histories from the seventeenth and eighteenth centuries. Yet, a wealth of sources including personal papers, government documents, and newspapers testify to the importance of women's activities in these wars. Indeed, women's participation in warfare and their presence in fortified, vanguard communities that formed the region's unstable perimeters were central to a society's survival and to contests over autonomy and imperial authority. Acutely aware that their lives, livelihoods, and the continued existence of their communities and polities were bound up in the successes or failures of colonial and expansionist projects, French, English, and Indigenous women sought to advance their own polities' agendas while countering opposing ones. They would do so not as passive helpmates but as invested actors.[6]

Ideologies of gender that predated the conflicts between Native and European polities in the northeastern borderlands created space for women to act as leaders and combatants in war. Far from discrediting these women's often violent actions, political and religious leaders in the borderlands praised and even materially rewarded women's war making. Accounts of women's martial activities asserted that the women acted with the blessing of God, their nations, and their husbands. These positive portrayals served as propaganda that sought to further local and imperial agendas. Even as European metropoles exported and attempted to reorder these gender roles and existing colonial military institutions in the early eighteenth century, they were neither immediately nor wholly successful. Women's war making—and the memories of their wartime roles—persisted in one form or another beyond the imperial climax of the Seven Years' War (1756–63) and contributed to the nascent nationalism of those empires' successors.

Of course, the acceptance and encouragement of women's war making did not mean that women received carte blanche to rampage across the northeastern borderlands. Violent acts performed outside of the accepted boundaries of warfare, such as the murder of a member of one's own group, retained their criminality.[7] Few sources reported disapproval of women's participation in the border wars, but of these accounts, most involved activities deemed treasonous, disorderly, or "unnatural." Unsurprisingly, European authors refrained from celebrating nonallied Native women's wartime violence aimed at those authors' own societies. Nor did Native women's vital military and social roles in ritual torture and adoption ever seem acceptable to European observers. Women of French descent suspected of treason in New France and Acadia were banished from those colonies, and authorities in New England investigated, but did not charge, women involved in violent war-related riots that many New Englanders supported. These few exceptions aside, women who performed wartime violence in the service of their polities did so to broad social acceptance and even acclaim.

IT IS IMPORTANT to understand how people waged war in the northeastern borderlands during this tumultuous era, characterized by unending conflict punctuated by short stretches of uneasy peace. In such conditions, the threat of war—combined with fumbled or hostile cultural encounters—

produced what historian Louise Dechêne evocatively dubbed "ambient war."[8] A sense of dread saturated the atmosphere of the towns, fields, and forests of the northeastern borderlands, even in times of peace (which often simply meant a chance to regroup, as past enemies continued to distrust one another while preparing rhetorically and materially for anticipated future wars). The outbreak of a new round of hostilities was frightening, though unsurprising, as most conflicts began and ended with predictable flurries of diplomatic activity, smaller skirmishes, and treaty making. Initial aggressions soon gave way to lengthy wars, with seemingly interminable stretches of nerve-wracking inactivity interrupted by raids and invasions. Military strategy in the borderlands, often patchwork and unstable, relied on a shifting combination of remote, fortified vanguard settlements, military outposts, teams of rangers and raiders, allies, and larger offensive invasion forces. The diversity of opinions regarding how best to protect and expand territory was a major source of disagreement, both within leadership circles and between residents and leaders.[9] Confidence in the firmness of political and religious identities as well as in the loyalties of neighbors and allies crumbled under the weight of shared suspicion. Lines between civilian and soldier, military and family life blurred and even disappeared as desperate communities, colonies, and nations struggled for survival, one generation after another.

At first glance, it would be easy to assume that this environment of social and spiritual tumult contributed to widespread anxiety over emerging reports of women wielding hatchets and firearms, killing adult men and even small children in often grisly scenes. Indeed, historians have shown that the language and ritual of warfare among both European colonists and Native nations in the region reflected deep commitments to the cultural and social connections between masculinity and warfare.[10] After all, in the early modern European societies of the Atlantic world, women's violence was inseparable from issues of social order and religion. The concept of the "little commonwealth" or "miniature monarchy" thrived as a model for order at the familial level during this period. With God's blessing, men played the role of king, ruling over orderly subjects in this idealized household in much the same way the sovereigns of Europe claimed to rule over their larger domains.[11] Native polities, too, tended to gender war making as a masculine activity, although women served as sachems during wars and often assumed formal wartime roles in the ritual torture and adoption of captives that concluded a raid or battle.[12] Despite the reputed rigidity of ideologies that favored men as the primary combatants in war, significant space remained within these systems for women to assume critical wartime roles.

Yet, until now, women's participation in these border wars—and the context in which it occurred—has remained largely unexplored. Studies of women's martial activities in early America more often focus on the rare cross-dressing women who joined militaries—particularly navies—and on literary representations of Amazons.[13] That said, one aspect of colonial women's wartime experiences has appeared in many studies, and that is the searing experience of captivity.[14] Although I consider the extensive scholarly literature on captivity in the northeastern borderlands—as well as the experiences of several captives—captivity is not my primary focus. Captivity was not the only way women in the northeastern borderlands experienced war, though it may be the best documented, thanks to published narratives and French recordkeeping. Fear of captivity was a constant companion in the northeastern borderlands; however, the experience of captivity—particularly in those instances of extended internment—represented relatively rare, extreme situations. I focus on women as active participants in war rather than as its human spoils. To highlight this difference, I have used the terms "war making," "participation," and "martial activities" in this book, which convey the complex process of making and unmaking so central to these conflicts. Both women and men made war in the traditional sense of the phrase, yet they also constructed expansionist policies, propaganda, and the gender ideologies that determined the identities of appropriate military combatants. These terms also demonstrate that women had other roles to play beyond the captive and the cultural broker.

In writing this book, I have built on a body of scholarship that has demonstrated the importance of gender as a contested category in the borderlands of North America. This work has revealed how inhabitants of these liminal spaces used their awareness of similarities and differences in gender cultures to forge peaceful relationships and to escalate violence.[15] Indeed, the ability and inability of communities in the northeastern borderlands to make sense of other cultures of gender and violence proved critical throughout the seventeenth and eighteenth centuries. And the misunderstandings of other cultures' motivations for warfare often proved disastrous, as many Europeans failed to understand Native cycles of warfare based on retribution and captive taking.[16] At the same time, studies emphasizing cultural similarities help explain otherwise baffling examples of intercultural cooperation and mutual respect. They also provide a sense of change over time, as groups that previously sought common ground increasingly turned to violence as cultural differences began to form the foundation of many European and Native relationships in North America.[17] Unpacking the nature of the significant roles women played in the conflicts of the northeastern borderlands requires a combination of these approaches, examining periods when the importance of both similarities and differences overlapped as well as eras when one or the other predominated.

Central to understanding how women's war making functioned in these contests for power is the recognition that early modern gender ideologies included significant space for women's martial activities and differed greatly from later models of feminine behavior based on notions of separate spheres. Historians have noted the dynamic nature of public and private life in the early modern period, describing fluid or overlapping spaces in which both men and women participated as public actors. As members of shifting coalitions acting with varying degrees of unity and method, these public actors enforced order and instigated change.[18] Studying England and its American colonies, historian Mary Beth Norton has offered a valuable framework for understanding the intersection of public action and early modern gender ideologies, identifying three primary spheres of action in the seventeenth century.[19] In the formal public sphere, men—and some women of higher rank—wielded secular and church authority. Rank often proved a more potent force for social organization than gender, and women of rank might exert authority within the formal public sphere. The informal public sphere was more community based and included both men and women who sometimes violently disagreed with decisions made within the formal public sphere. The private sphere more frequently referred to something secret or personal, rather than to a specific domestic sphere of women or families. According to Norton, changes in English political thought following the Glorious Revolution of 1688 challenged older, rank-based models of authority and encouraged the development of more fully gendered spheres of action.[20] English colonists at war would incorporate these ideas selectively and slowly, as military success and survival continued to require the participation of women. For its part, an increasingly militarized New France took its ideological cues from the French imperial metropole, where scholars have found that French women maintained more significant public roles and political power than their English counterparts.[21] These differences aside, in the wars of the northeastern borderlands, women participated as public actors, and most limitations to their martial contributions were functions of social status and military need.

Questioning the timelessness of gender ideologies is essential to this study in another sense, as many of the stories told in this book involve women behaving in ways that are vulnerable to being read as transgressive or overly heroic. My aim is not to present triumphant heroines or suffering victims for modern consumption. Nor is my goal to search for some form of pro-tofeminism within seventeenth- and eighteenth-century celebrations of women's violence and leadership in the border wars. Rather, I argue through-out that even women's most violent wartime behavior upheld existing gen-der roles as women fought to preserve—not to overturn—existing social orders. As a result, most women's violence in the wars of the northeastern borderlands fell well within what historian John Smolenski referred to as a "range of permissible exchanges of violence."[22] Illuminating women's roles in these conflicts—and the policies and cultural ideas that resulted in their participation—means that viewing women's wartime actions (and others' reactions to them) through an early modern mind-set is critical. Acquiring this perspective demands a reconsideration of early American women's war making within period-appropriate gendered spheres of action as well as a stronger appreciation of the differences between ideal, acceptable, and trans-gressive behaviors.

This book is a borderlands history that situates women's active partici-pation in the wars of the northeastern borderlands within a larger context of transnational conflict and transatlantic dialogues. It draws inspiration from studies of contested territories that demonstrate the staggering range of intercultural relationships and power dynamics that emerged in diverse geographic regions. Significantly, as scholars continue to uncover new ways in which Atlantic perspectives can inform borderlands histories, the land, the shoreline, and the sea have been revealed as sites of contestation for In-digenous and European polities alike. As such, maintaining an awareness of the region's connections to the Atlantic world is essential to understand-ing the ways in which polities sought access to land and trade through peace and war.[23]

In struggling for control of the northeastern borderlands, residents and policy makers of this complex region oriented themselves and their expan-sionist strategies in a dizzying variety of compass directions. Canadians faced the St. Lawrence River from their long lots, which lined the river's northern and southern banks. Peering toward the west, they watched the river bring both furs and Iroquois attacks as it flowed eastward. Eventually, the massive waterway emptied into the Gulf of St. Lawrence and greeted arriving ships during the months that ice did not isolate Canada from the rest of the French Atlantic. Gazing to the south, French colonists saw fortified English towns creeping up the coast of Maine and dotting the Connecticut River Valley, encroaching upon the territories of Native allies and threatening French access to the continent and the sea. New England's colonists seized land to the west and northeast for their expanding population and to further their military and economic objectives. They also sought greater control over the resources of the Gulf of Maine and the North Atlantic. The strategically important colony of Acadia, perhaps the heart of this borderland region, served as both a meeting place and a buffer. The Indigenous Mi'kmaq and French and English colonists fought, traded, and established communities in Acadia, a French-claimed colony that divided the Gulf of Maine from the Gulf of St. Lawrence. Control of Acadia could tip the balance of power in the northeastern borderlands and the northwestern Atlantic. Native nations operating within the northeastern borderlands worked through both established and newer political and economic systems. Pursuing their own agendas, Indigenous polities welcomed goods through expanded trade networks while also making war against and forging diplomatic ties with their counterparts on both sides of the Atlantic.

A greater awareness of the northeastern borderlands as a contested space with transatlantic connections helps explain the important roles Euro-American and Native women played in the region's conflicts. European and Native cultures did not hurriedly create ideological space for women's war making as a response to borderlands encounters. Rather, European colonists and Indigenous peoples preserved and adapted existing traditions of women's war making while fighting to control the northeastern borderlands. At the same time, men and women throughout the region sought to understand both similar and unfamiliar female martial traditions through their own cultural lenses. Native women who took part in the region's wars negotiated the gender expectations of their own societies while employing their understanding of relationships established in the borderlands. For example, one influential female sachem projected her authority by fusing her own polity's symbols of power with carefully selected sartorial signifiers worn by her peers among England's elite.[24] Euro-Americans, who brought ideologies that supported women's war making with them when crossing the Atlantic, straddled the roles of residents of a borderlands region at war and colonial subjects beholden to metropoles an ocean away. Without this perspective, how can we fully understand the letter of a young Canadian woman who received a pension by framing her military exploits as part of a larger war that stretched from Europe to the Great Lakes of North America? Why did colonists publish approving reports in London and Paris that depicted Euro-American women performing gruesome acts of war in the northeastern borderlands? How these discourses of women's war making both persisted and adapted to challenges from cultural encounters in the northeastern borderlands—and from across the Atlantic—is a key question this book seeks to answer.

THE AVAILABILITY OF sources and the timing of critical events shape the contours and content of every book, a phenomenon that is perhaps particularly evident in comparative and borderlands studies. Following the direction in which sources from different comparative groups point inevitably results in chronological and geographic boundaries that fail to align neatly. Yet, by acknowledging and even embracing this lack of tidiness, we can reach a closer understanding of times and places that were defined by disorder. Such an approach can also reveal more about the ways in which people attempted to preserve and create old and new orders. In writing this book, which spans over two hundred years and analyzes French, English, and Native women's war making, I have become particularly aware of the challenges of unstable source bases and asynchronous political, military, and cultural developments. New Englanders have left the most thorough sources pertaining to the border wars. The region's higher literacy rate, robust printing industry, and the growing availability of newspapers in the eighteenth century offer a depth and breadth of sources unavailable in other polities. The relative consistency of New England's military strategy and targets also allows for the construction of a smoother narrative. In New France, where the literacy rate was much lower and printing presses absent, researchers are much more at the mercy of changes in the relationship between colony and metropole. The royal takeover of Canada in 1663—combined with a sharp decline in missionary-penned accounts—marks a shift in the book, as it transitions from a cultural history of women's participation in war to a political history based on diplomatic correspondence and bureaucratic records.

Sources also dictate which groups are included in comparative studies. I originally intended to include a third, fully comparative group: Native polities. After all, much of this book engages with Native people and polities, and through the course of my research, I collected a substantial number of sources related to Native women's participation in the border wars. Within this collection, however, no single nation left behind sufficient sources to support a detailed study in the mode of the book's analyses of New England

and New France. Forming a composite experience for all Native women was equally impossible. In a study so concerned with how specific policy decisions of individual governments reflected and influenced women's participation in war making, reducing dozens of sovereign, diverse Native polities into a homogeneous "Indians" section seemed both incongruous and irresponsible. When sources permit, I do include Native perspectives. However, Europeans produced most accounts of Native women's war making, often revealing more about the observers than the observed. Thus, I more frequently use these sources as windows into the societies of New England and New France.

In establishing the geographic boundaries of this study of the northeastern borderlands, I found that many of the same natural features contested as valuable transportation corridors and strategically important points of access also frequently functioned as borders to defend or to breach. The most significant of these—the St. Lawrence River, Lake Champlain, the Hudson River, and the gulfs of Maine and St. Lawrence—roughly established the northern, western, and eastern extents of the northeastern borderlands in early America and in this study. More difficult to ascertain was a southern border, as areas claimed by Connecticut and Rhode Island are also part of the larger New England region. Certainly, the Pequot War of the late 1630s, a central event in the colonization of Connecticut, played a considerable role in the development of English and Indigenous war making in the region. The influence of the Pequot War on ideas about gender and warfare was also considerable, and it figures into my larger analysis of the early phases of militarization in the seventeenth century. The southern reaches of New England are also known for the presence of powerful female sachems in the seventeenth century. Indeed, nearly all sources that detail women's martial activities from the 1620s to the onset of King Philip's War in 1675 describe female sachems, although these interactions were primarily with Plymouth and Massachusetts Bay. Notable female sachems who later led their polities in King Philip's War ruled coveted territory situated between Rhode Island and Plymouth, fighting near or to the north of their polities in a war that would fundamentally shift the focus of future wars toward the northeast and west. Thus, in choosing to situate this boundary along the southern border of present-day Massachusetts, sources relating to women's war making have shown the way, pointing northward to the primary military contests over the northeastern borderlands.

Chronologically, I have divided the wars of the northeastern borderlands into two major phases, separated roughly by key treaties and an increased transatlantic imperial presence that by the early eighteenth century sought to transform the institutions and practices of warfare in the region. The first phase of these conflicts opened approximately in 1630, the beginning of a decade marked by the arrival of Jesuit missionaries, authors of the first accounts of women's war making in New France, and by the escalation of hostilities between the Iroquois Confederacy and the Franco-Native alliance. Further south, English colonists had already founded Plymouth Colony in 1620, followed by the Massachusetts Bay Colony and the colonies of southern New England beginning around 1630. Accounts of cultural encounters and legal records from these early years offer the first descriptions of the martial roles of female sachems, and the alliances that colonists formed with both female and male sachems would shape the future political and military dynamics of the region.

For much of the seventeenth century, European colonists attempted to gain a foothold in northeastern North America. During this period, English and French colonists found vital Native allies and made dangerous enemies while simultaneously becoming a part of and influencing the existing military, economic, and political dynamics of the region. By the second half of the seventeenth century, each became embroiled in major wars— New France's Beaver Wars of the mid-seventeenth century, fought with its allies against the Iroquois, and New England's King Philip's War, against a coalition of many of the region's Indigenous polities. Both wars were fought against Native coalitions determined to reduce or eliminate their European foes' presence in northeastern North America. In the aftermath of these wars, the French and English crowns asserted greater control over their colonies in the region.

Following these initial imperial interventions, most wars involving New England and New France were fought—at least in part—as American theaters of European imperial wars, though parallel clashes and alliances with Native nations remained important and increased the complexity of all conflicts. Indeed, the tidiness of the "American theater" paradigm fails somewhat when considering the conflicts that mark the end of the first phase of the border wars, King William's War (1688–97) and Queen Anne's War (1702–13). These conflicts, known in European historiography as the Nine Years' War and the War of the Spanish Succession, might best be viewed from the perspective of the inhabitants of the northeastern borderlands as episodes of a larger "Twenty-Five Years' War." Although the Treaty of Ryswick officially ended hostilities between England and France in 1697, the French and the Iroquois did not make peace until 1701, and New Englanders became increasingly paranoid about the alleged existence of a plot hatched between Jesuit missionaries, the Abenaki, and Catholic Mohawks in 1700.[25] When hostilities officially resumed in 1702, English and French imperial troops and officials joined colonial forces in Queen Anne's War, which included a newly neutral Iroquois Confederacy and the English conquest of Port Royal in Acadia. The war also ushered in a more imperial militarism that—at least in theory—relied less on families' shared defenses of provincial, fortified outposts and more on professionalized male soldiers and dedicated military installations.

This useful division also serves as the foundation for the book's loosely chronological, two-part structure. The wars of this first phase significantly influenced settlement patterns and military policies and set precedents for women's active wartime participation that lingered into the next century. Part 1 examines how the intersection of preexisting gender roles and expansionist policies in the northeastern borderlands encouraged women's war making in the seventeenth and early eighteenth centuries. In New England, government-sponsored, fortified towns blurred lines between military and domestic, settler and soldier. Barred from evacuating, women took on active roles in the wars, keeping watch, administering forts, and fighting alone and with their husbands. I also explore how New Englanders responded to Native women's participation in the wars. Engaging in a variety of wartime roles including ritual torture and serving as sachems and spies, Native women often challenged but sometimes fulfilled New Englanders' expectations of appropriate female behavior. Finally, I examine how English women exploited cultural and legal loopholes to lead popular protests and vigilante groups against colonial leaders and foes.

In New France, where the seigneurial system magnified official distinctions of status, women of rank led their troops when under attack and used their financial resources and influence to raise armies. Nonelite women, who lacked a formal role in New France's wars, were more often described as running to join the battle, sometimes dressed as men. I also explore how French Jesuits and Ursulines conveyed accounts of allied Indigenous women's actions in their personal journals and publications during the wars of the mid-seventeenth century. I argue that French missionaries, privileging rank over gender and ethnic or national origins, similarly portrayed nonelite French and allied Native women in war: as expressing European and Christian values.

In addition to the more material roles that women played in the expansionist contest for the northeastern borderlands, elite men and women in both New England and New France appropriated reports of women's often violent actions, employing the stories for political and religious purposes at the local, colonial, and imperial levels. Using these accounts, authors attempted to establish female role models, finance religious missions, and overthrow colonial governments. In New France, Jesuits paired accounts of New World Amazons—both French and Native—with appeals for donations from wealthy French women. Officials in New England also used stories of fighting women as positive examples: to promote morale and to score political points in England.

The second phase of the border wars began with a period of relative calm following the French peace with the Iroquois in 1701 and the Treaty of Utrecht in 1713. Colonial wars in the late seventeenth century were frequently disastrous and poorly managed. As a result, the French and English monarchies began to assert greater control over their colonies. During this interval, changes in military strategy and imperial involvement that appeared during Queen Anne's War slowly reshaped the nature of war in New England and New France. At the same time, the Iroquois and Abenaki sought to preserve and expand their presence in the region, sparking smaller-scale conflicts and exploiting the antagonistic relationship between the French and the English. Throughout these decades, all parties continued to prepare for another seemingly inevitable large-scale conflict. This arguably peaceful stretch came to a close in 1744 when King George's War marked the opening of sixteen years of conflict in the region that resulted in the French surrender of most of its North American territories at the end of the Seven Years' War in 1763.

The changes I examine in the book's second part speak to larger shifts in regional and transatlantic history that eventually altered the identities of appropriate combatants in war. New ideologies regarding gender emerged, as well as colonists' changing relationships to their monarchs, combining with substantial alterations in military strategy to transform women's participation in the border wars. In New France, peace with the Iroquois and increased English naval attacks resulted in a new military focus on fortified coastal areas of the colony. This strategic shift away from the St. Lawrence reduced the need for women to defend the colony physically. At the same time, imperial policy increasingly wove Canada and Acadia into the military and bureaucratic fabric of the French Empire. Secular and religious officials arriving from France sought to fortify the colony, linking colonial women's sexual contact with soldiers in coastal towns to treason and military failure. Yet, women's decreased role in physical war making, as well as imperial concerns over their sexuality, did not signal a rejection of women's participation in the new French military society. Indeed, women would assume key roles in trade and in financing the fortification of New France in the early to mid-eighteenth century.

A lull in the fighting in 1730s New England offered women new opportunities to petition legislatures for compensation for service in earlier wars. These appeals raise complex issues regarding women's political and legal identities as subjects, as wives, and as individuals. They also emerged at a time when home and front began to separate in response to a greater British military presence. When war erupted again in 1744, debates over the effectiveness of the king as a benevolent, paternal protector figure resulted in rhetoric that painted both male and female colonists as suffering, helpless subjects. Thus, women's participation in mid-century conflicts appeared as more a consequence of poor military planning than as a contribution of integral members of fortified communities.

In the decades following the border wars, accounts of women's war making became tools for creating memory and identity beyond the eighteenth century. New Englanders writing during the late eighteenth and early nineteenth centuries retold—and altered—these stories when creating new local, state, and national identities after the American Revolution. In many cases, alterations to these stories reflected a new emphasis on motherhood and domesticity, adopting and driving separate spheres ideology by the nineteenth century. And as authors increasingly portrayed colonial fighting women as vital, more capable actors from an earlier era, they helped define a new gendered order for a nascent nation with its own aggressive colonial agenda.

THROUGHOUT THIS BOOK, I have made numerous linguistic choices, each with the goal of bringing clarity to the reader of a project that ranges across three centuries, dozens of polities, and draws on the works of both English- and French-speaking authors. When possible, I have identified Native polities by name (i.e., Pocasset). I have also chosen to follow the examples of many historians of American Indians in employing the noun "Indian" when a nationality was not available. I have retained the terms "Native" and "Indigenous" (always capitalized) for use as adjectives. When speaking of New France, which included parts of the interior of North America as well as the Caribbean, I use the word "Quebec" to refer to the city, "Canada" (the term used in the colonial period) to refer to much of what is now the province of Quebec (which was then the extent of that region), and "Acadia" to refer to the French colony of the same name. When speaking of Canada and Acadia collectively, I use the admittedly imperfect term "New France."

Although the historiographies of the United States, Canada, and many European countries employ different names for many of the conflicts discussed in this study, I have chosen to use those terms most familiar to an American reading audience. Thus, I have adopted King William's War rather than the Nine Years' War or the War of the Grand Alliance (1688–97), Queen Anne's War rather than the War of the Spanish Succession (1702–13), Dummer's War rather than Ralé's War or Greylock's War (c. 1723–26), King George's War rather than the War of the Austrian Succession (1744–48), and the Seven Years' War, which has become the common term in the United States for the French and Indian War (1756–63). As France adopted the Gregorian calendar in 1582, well before the events described in this book, I have used modern dates for both New France and New England, converting English years when necessary. Unless quoting from a modern translation or transcription, I expanded archaic contractions but otherwise maintained authentic spellings.

PART I | Encountering Martial Women

CHAPTER ONE

Necessary to Abide

Gendered Spheres and Spaces in New England's Wars

On April 27, 1706, at least eight people in an unfortified home in Oyster River, New Hampshire, were killed during an attack on their settlement. It was the worst raid on a frontier community since the infamous Deerfield incursion that killed forty-nine people in 1704. This assault marked the beginning of a period of renewed attacks on fortified communities after a quieter 1705.[1] And casualties in the town would have been much higher had it not been for an extraordinary event that took place at a house nearby. As chronicler Samuel Penhallow related in 1726, "not a man" remained in the garrison house at the time of the attack. According to Penhallow, a number of women in the house at the time "assum'd an Amazonian Courage seeing nothing but Death before them, advanc'd the Watch-box, and made an Alarm." The women then adopted a classic military strategy, manipulating their enemy's perception of the strength of the garrison's forces. Posing as men, they "put on Hatts, with their Hair hanging down, and fired so briskly that they struck a terror in the Enemy, and they withdrew, without firing the house, or carrying away much Plunder."[2] That Penhallow described the women as firing "briskly" was a testament to their effectiveness and the respect Penhallow accorded them. In early New England, the term suggested positive masculine qualities such as courage and a no-nonsense martial capability.[3]

Two months after the women of Oyster River repulsed that 1706 invasion, the Massachusetts government approved a remarkable amendment to an earlier law that banned the desertion of officially designated "frontier towns."[4] The addendum to the 1695 law specified that "during the time of the present war, all persons with their families" must "abide" in their appointed garrisons. Any "person capable of bearing arms" who deserted faced fines from five to twenty pounds. A second amendment required that "all male persons in the frontiers capable of bearing arms" carry their weapons at all times, even in the fields and at church. Unrelated families had frequently lived together, sometimes alongside small numbers of provincial troops who had found themselves assigned to such unfashionable posts. Although inhabitants had sheltered in fortified homes when attacks seemed likely, these living arrangements had not been mandated by provincial law. The amendment that passed following the Oyster River incident suggests that Massachusetts had gained a greater understanding of the dangers faced by colonists in unfortified homes. It also highlights the emphasis placed on fortified communities as simultaneously family spaces and military installations.[5]

In northern New England, the home and the front were at times indistinguishable, and families who settled in towns near the frontier occupied a complex and shifting set of social, military, and cultural roles. The presence of families in fortified communities that marked this first line of defense was considered critical to the overall security of the entire colony. As recipients of government assistance in strengthening designated homes in which all residents could shelter, male members of families in frontier towns had significant obligations to the colony, such as helping with the upkeep of the town's defenses and serving in the local militia. Relying on fully occupied, fortified frontier towns on the outer edges of the colony to protect more established settlements closer to Boston, officials in New England required the presence of whole families for a number of reasons. Leaders believed that the family structure bolstered the godliness of the frontier's inhabitants and their willingness to fight for a Protestant New England. The official discouragement of absentee landholding also added men to the militia, while colonists who brought their entire families were more likely to remain permanently in these communities. Laws forbidding families from deserting these settlements sought to obviate flagging morale that accompanied the loss of outposts and ensuing refugee crises. Because there is not an adequate term in use that captures the complexity of the functions and duties of men and their families on the frontier, I have adopted the term "settler-soldier" to convey this role more succinctly. I use this term for its ability to convey male colonists' mutually reinforcing roles as land-hungry agents of expansionism encroaching upon already settled ground and foot soldiers making war to advance a larger colonial project.[6]

Officials also indicated that women's presence in frontier towns was critical, particularly during periods when settlements were at greatest risk. In the fortified towns of New England, female colonists would take on their husbands' role of settler-soldier when necessary, administering garrisons, petitioning the government, and fighting alone, together, and alongside their spouses. Indeed, as historian Steven Eames has observed of fortified towns, "during actual attacks there was little semblance between the militia as delineated by statute and the regular community fighting for survival."[7] As such, the inherently public nature of garrison towns, with their extreme lack of privacy, and the blurring of boundaries between military and household, settler and soldier, and duty to family and duty to colony and crown, challenges modern perceptions of masculine public and feminine private spheres. Part of a broader early modern system of formal and informal public spheres, garrison houses and fortified communities functioned well within those realms of action. Women's participation as public actors in New England's wars rarely operated within the more masculinized formal public. Instead, their war making often fell into the realm of the informal public—the sphere most conducive to female action—due to desperation, historical precedents for women's wartime participation, and laws mandating the presence of women and families in homes that combined military and domestic functions.[8]

The government's response to the raid on Oyster River indicated that it had confidence in the strength of fortified houses and the ability of inhabitants of either sex to defend those structures. Male settler-soldiers remained the primary defenders of these communities, their military obligations within the formal public sphere officially expanded to include areas outside their homes. The tightening of restrictions in the new law was not a negative reaction to the women's defense of the garrison house in Oyster River. As the amendment suggests, men's absence from garrison houses while working in the fields was necessary to the community's survival. Rather, the location of families in unfortified homes, such as the one in which eight to ten people died that day, was unacceptable. A successful defense mounted by either men or women was far more likely in a fortified home. Leaders believed that the presence of whole families in designated garrison houses was vital to both colonial morale and to the defense of New England—regardless of whether the arrangement was convenient or even reasonable for families whose houses and fields lay further from the town's designated strongholds.

Despite the strategic and political importance of officially designated frontier towns, the belief in a fixed line of settlement often proved illusory. Any household might come under attack when towns meant to serve as bulwarks fell. Because early modern gender ideologies provided space for women's war making, women living in previously safe communities defended those towns as members of the informal public sphere with universal male approval, even if the head of household did not have settler-soldier

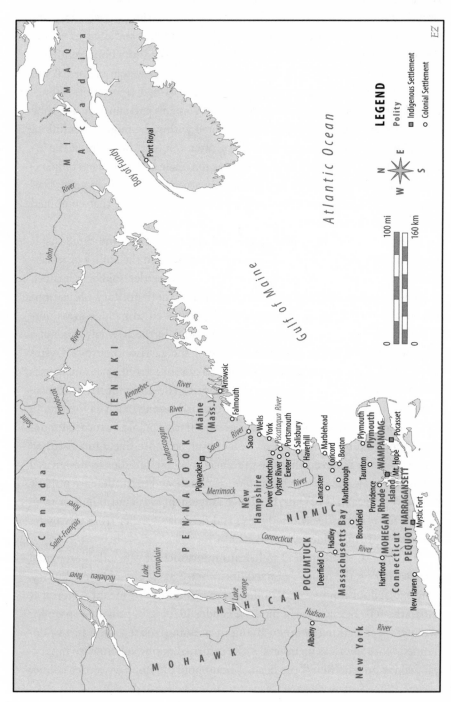

Southern extent of the northeastern borderlands, c. 1630–1700

status. Reflecting the diversity of the region's women and their experiences, this chapter examines women's war making within the context of the formal and informal public spheres in New England from three angles.

First, it explores policies and ideologies that placed women in fortified frontier communities—the most common site of women's participation in these border wars and the frequent intersection of the informal public and formal public spheres. It also investigates how, although tolerant and even encouraging of New England women's often gruesome wartime actions, English writers and policy makers used early modern gender spheres to understand—and misunderstand—Indigenous women's participation in these conflicts. Finally, this chapter analyzes how English women operating within the informal public sphere in small towns and larger cities successfully challenged wartime leadership and decisions through collective violence, often with the support of their male neighbors.

Gendering Fortified Communities

English colonization of the northeastern borderlands favored an approach by which prospective landowners founded towns radiating outward from the main settlement at Boston as if creating an island of security. Although Boston and its neighboring settlements faced possible destruction in King Philip's War, the system of frontier towns largely protected the area around Boston in later, broader conflicts. Settlers frequently brought their entire families to these new remote towns, which enemies of New England saw as relatively easy pickings. A nervous colonist gazing north would have known that her town was separated from the heart of New France along the St. Lawrence River Valley by vast stretches of land controlled by Native polities frequently allied with the French. Fortified towns in or along the edge of the northeastern borderlands served increasingly as important vanguards of the English expansionist project following King Philip's War. At the same time, New England's own geography encouraged northward settlement in the direction of French-controlled and French-allied areas.[9]

The policies and institutions that developed in the late seventeenth century to support New England's war making rested upon a combination of preexisting martial practices and gender ideologies as well as the experience of colonization earlier in the century. Indeed, the lasting military and cultural influence of the first significant war involving English colonists in the region appears almost outsized compared to its duration and geographic scope. The Pequot War of 1636–37 began when a coalition of English,

Narragansett, and Mohegan polities took advantage of the suspicious deaths of a handful of English traders to reduce the influence of the powerful Pequot and seize their land in the southern Connecticut River Valley.[10] The conflict is particularly famous for the massacre of hundreds of Pequot noncombatants when English troops, along with various Indigenous allies, set fire to Mystic Fort in 1637. That massacre—and the decision by English leaders to sell members of defeated polities into slavery—introduced new norms of brutality that all sides eventually adopted, even against noncombatants. A war that established future conflicts between English and Indigenous polities as contests infused by disputes over the masculinity of the primary combatants, the Pequot War sowed distrust and encouraged divisive notions of dangerous gender difference and ruthless domination.[11] True intercultural cooperation soon seemed out of reach. As historian Katherine Grandjean has observed, the war "left in its wake a human landscape shattered by suspicion, fear, and additional violence," arguing that the period between the Pequot War and King Philip's War (1675–76) was not a peaceful interlude. Rather, conditions in New England perhaps more closely resembled the state Louise Dechêne hauntingly termed "ambient war," as the Pequot War's violent legacy fermented over four decades.[12]

English colonists' willingness to enslave and commit extreme forms of violence against combatants and noncombatants in the Pequot War likely increased the need for women's participation in future conflicts that relied heavily on captive taking as well as numerous raids on settlements. It was against this backdrop that colonists' growing reliance on towns that served as both vanguards and bulwarks defended by settler-soldiers and their families prompted a greater investment in the fortification of traditional public spaces (and homes that would function as public spaces). Although some towns continued to build palisades around their core buildings, forgoing these defenses in favor of designated fortified homes became increasingly popular in the 1660s and 1670s. Some of the houses were ordinary homes with fortifications added later, but others were designed with defense in mind. More effective garrison houses had watchtowers that allowed inhabitants to spot attackers, while a palisade, thick door, and shutters provided additional structural defenses. In repelling an attack, homes with two stories and loopholes in sturdy walls were particularly effective. Colonists also spread sand and ash on the floor of second stories to protect the ground level from roof fires.[13] As the incident at Oyster River demonstrated, well-fortified buildings protected by colonists of either gender were rarely worth attacking, although crops and outbuildings were frequent targets of raids.

A rare surviving officially designated garrison house, the so-called McIntire Garrison House near York, Maine, was built in the late seventeenth or early eighteenth century, likely during King William's War or Queen Anne's War. Later owners added new siding, shingles, doors, and windows to this garrison house. (*Source:* Library of Congress, Prints & Photographs Division, HABS ME, 16-BERN.V, 1–2.)

Garrison houses and their owners served as the heart of any frontier community's militia and, by extension, as the foundation of New England's defensive strategy. Dominating the administrative and leadership positions located within the formal public sphere in these towns, owners impressed inhabitants when volunteers were scarce, assigned inhabitants to fortified houses, and made decisions regarding provisioning.[14] Fortified structures and the vanguard communities they protected were so critical to military and settlement policy that colonies refused to allow the inhabitants of such towns—including women—to flee when under attack. These restrictive policies emerged during King Philip's War, when the Massachusetts General Court made its stance on the subject clear in October 1675. A new law required "all inhabitants to attend their places in such fortiffication or garrison as they are appointed unto, and in case of alarum or invasion, to appear at and for the defence of such places." Those who disregarded the new law risked a fine of five shillings per day or even the loss of an abandoned property. The court also ordered that particularly endangered frontier towns "judged not able of themselves to bear the distress of the warr" should send women and children to safer towns. Crucially, the court required a certain number of women, "so many as are necessary to abide," to remain on the front lines. This law effectively impressed these women into—at the very minimum—a kind of noncombatant defensive service. It also placed women in situations that would demand their assumption of more violent martial roles as public actors, blurring distinctions between the formal and informal public spheres in fortified communities.[15]

The decision to forbid women from leaving designated frontier towns in King Philip's War anticipated similar developments in later conflicts. The 1706 amendment that passed following the attack on Oyster River and the original 1695 law, which prevented the desertion of fortified communities, were at the center of sometimes devastating policies that kept families in vulnerable situations. Both statutes require additional scrutiny from historians, particularly in their use of the word "person" and various pronouns. It is also important to establish who was subject to this law and its amendments. Certainly male freeholders were, particularly when acting as settler-soldiers in the formal public sphere, as they owed the government service due to the "considerable sums of money . . . expended in the defence and for preservation" of their towns. The first two sections of the law demanded that all freeholders in designated frontier towns acquire a special license from the governor and council before "remov[ing] from thence with intent to sojourn or inhabit elsewhere." Selectmen and chief military officers in the towns were required to report any cases of abandonment. Freeholders who left faced forfeiture of their property, which was sold to pay for "defence of such town or plantation and support of the garrisons within the same." A third section required the return of freeholders "able and fit for service" who had lived in any frontier town since "the beginning of this war" and who had already fled to safer ground. Unless they returned or paid for another "able, sufficient person" to take their place, they, too, faced forfeiture.[16]

Although freeholders were the mainstay of the colonial settler-soldier strategy, the 1695 law placed restrictions on all men, including those who did not own land. Section 4 pertained to any "male person of sixteen years of age or upwards, being an inhabitant of or belonging to any of the said frontier towns . . . and not having any lands or tenements in such town." This section applied to male residents without land as well as the sons of landowners over the age of sixteen. As they had no land to forfeit, these men faced a ten-pound fine for failure to acquire a license from the governor and council.

Men who neglected to or were unable to pay the fine were to be impressed into service until their debts were paid off.[17] Taking aim at the heart of a model of masculinity that prized land ownership and military prowess, lawmakers sought to bind a man's existing or future ability to hold land to his performance of formal martial duties in designated frontier towns.[18]

Women and children—not specifically mentioned in the 1695 law—lived in these vanguard communities, making war as public actors in the incidents described in the histories, diaries, and legal documents of the time. Only when a major invasion by an enemy force seemed imminent were women and children withdrawn temporarily from the outermost towns. Because these brief retreats were limited to periods when officials feared a full invasion, they reinforced the idea that families belonged in fortified communities during the stretches of irregular warfare that dominated these border skirmishes. Even so, not all women and children were allowed to flee invasions. In June 1704, fear of an impending invasion prompted the governor of Massachusetts to issue an order "that two or three Hundred Men . . . go Eastward for Enforcing the Frontiers for about a Months Space, And that the Women & Children that can be spared with the Cattle drawn in."[19] This order is particularly revealing, as it sent some of the women and children away with livestock while declaring another group of women and children indispensable wartime actors. Certainly, officials knew from experience that those who could not "be spared" had a history of taking up arms and would likely do so again. It was in these moments of crisis, when lawmakers mandated women's presence in fortified communities readying for battle, that the adaptability of gendered martial roles within formal and informal public spheres was most evident.

When facing imminent attacks, colonists' terror and desperation warred with their sense of duty and their fear of violating harsh colonial laws. Joanna Rossiter Cotton described this atmosphere of dread and confusion while awaiting death or captivity with her pregnant daughter in the coastal frontier town of Salisbury, Massachusetts. In the immediate aftermath of the March 1697 raid on Haverhill, Joanna Cotton wrote to her brother-in-law, the Rev. Increase Mather, pleading for the prayers of prominent New England clergymen. Her letter depicted a community on the verge of collapse, its inhabitants weighing the truth of rumors from Maine that "it is far wors at the eastward" and despairing that "all the rest of the towns are in eminent danger of destruction with out the lord doth wonderfully appeare beyound all expectation." With the more remote vanguard towns and their inhabitants in disarray, it seemed inevitable that Salisbury would soon fall. Certainly, Joanna Cotton warned, "thay cannot continue long thus opressed," as Salisbury's inhabitants struggled to feed their families with rotting food while paying high taxes to avoid forfeiting their land. Some families considered "removing" illegally to safer towns, their incentive to stay weakened as impressment undermined the town's militia system, draining the town of soldiers "forced to leave thear one [own] families to be a prey to the heathen." Signing her letter, "your Afflicted sister in law," Joanna Cotton could only hope "that god would be plesed to save us in this day of trouble and distress."[20]

The policies that Joanna Cotton described and that colonial laws formalized were designed to keep sufficient numbers of colonists in fortified communities, which in turn created significant hardships for families. This was particularly true when conditions and even laws required families to live together in garrisons. Claustrophobia-inducing conditions and a lack of privacy defined life in a garrison house facing an attack. One such home in Maine boasted two stories and was nearly two thousand square feet in total. Garrison houses such as this one might hold anywhere from twenty-five to one hundred people when inhabitants fled to their assigned safe houses.[21] In a tract directed to the inhabitants of frontier towns, Cotton Mather empathized with terrified families, exhorting them to "Consider your uneasy condition, when you are Thrust and Heap'd up together in Garrisons, where the Common Comforts of your Lives must needs have an Extreme Abridgment brought upon them." He then acknowledged that the inhabitants' "continual Fear of Incursions from Armed men, must needs bring in upon you Poverty like an Armed man," noting that "Ever now and then, we hear of some who in Planting their Corn, alas, have their Fields water'd with their blood."[22] Mather's text then went on to give advice on issues such as chastity, temperance, and regular prayer, suggesting that embracing these virtues would help to defend the frontier.

Although Mather's *Frontiers Well-Defended* provides valuable information about the conditions facing frontier families as well as insight into what was considered proper Christian behavior, examining the words of frontier town inhabitants provides perhaps more immediate perspectives. Representing the town of Lancaster, John Houghton pled with Governor Phips and his council for assistance in February 1694. His petition illustrates the harsh conditions and flexible gender roles of the vanguard community, stating that "by being so long Nessessitated to live in Garisson where *neither men nor women* can doe but very litle towards the supply of theire familyes: theire being so mutch time spent in watching warding & many allarrums that have been amongst us & that which is more the dayly feares we were expossed to in the Dangers which atended us in our labours."[23] Houghton's petition and Joanna Cotton's letter offer rare glimpses into the lives of frontier families, moving beyond Mather's empathetic but prescriptive text. Houghton's petition also sheds light on men's and women's shared defensive roles in these public spaces and offers insight into how and why men such as Mather ultimately accepted and encouraged women's war making.

Policies mandating the close quarters that settler-soldiers such as John Houghton reported led directly to women's participation in New England's expansionist wars. In discouraging—even forbidding—men from sending their wives and children to safety, colonial governments interfered with the rights of husbands in their family governance. Yet, such interference was well within the purview of the government of a society in which family, religion, and rule were fundamentally intertwined. According to early modern theories regarding the family, fathers served as heads of their own godly "little commonwealths" or "miniature monarchies." Ruling these basic units of social organization, fathers ideally worked in concert with higher levels of authority to maintain spiritual and civic order throughout colony and kingdom. As subordinates of the father, wives—under the legal doctrine of coverture—and children, as minors, were covered by the wide umbrella of the father's legal personhood.[24] A settler-soldier's wife—along with his other dependents—also became enveloped by the father's role as a settler-soldier. The concept of the "deputy husband," as described by historian Laurel Thatcher Ulrich, is helpful in sorting out wives' roles within this system. The idea that a woman might assume some of the responsibilities of an absent or deceased husband is common in many patriarchies. But despite this conceptual familiarity, it is critical to remember that Ulrich's deputy husband was a product of early modern societies that understood the world in terms of the formal and informal public spheres, rather than societies that associated the public sphere with men and the private sphere with women. As a public actor and a member of a family at war, the wife of a settler-soldier learned to perform routine military duties—and in some cases wartime administrative tasks—in the course of living in a fortified community.[25]

The image of the deputy husband taking on her husband's duties solely in his absence is complicated by reports of women fighting alongside men. Cotton Mather approvingly recounted that in 1692, defenders of both sexes at Storer's garrison in Wells, Maine, repelled an attack. In his account, Mather wrote that Wells's women assisted the men with ammunition and "took up the Amazonian Stroke" and "with a Manly Resolution fired several Times upon the Enemy."[26] Although the women of Wells acted as assistants to men while performing essential combat services, the incident does suggest that the role of deputy husband was quite flexible. Rather than merely filling a husband's shoes during his absence, the wife of a settler-soldier might also be expected to assist her husband if he needed an extra set of hands. Perhaps the term "deputy husband," which describes a woman empowered to act as a substitute for an absent superior, might be replaced by "assistant combatant." These words maintain the unequal nature of the partnership while emphasizing both actors' public roles and expanding the range of scenarios in which such partnerships functioned.

In addition to fighting alongside their husbands, a woman might also petition the government on behalf of a busy, though present husband. Lydia Scottow petitioned the governor on behalf of her husband, Captain Joshua Scottow, just after King Philip's War. Scottow noted that her husband defended their garrison with the help of only four men. She asked for six or eight more men to "defend the place, & prevent the Barbarous Enimy, to make Inroade in & march further into the Country."[27] As demonstrated by John Houghton's petition claiming that both men and women were too busy attending to security matters to care for their families, the wife of a settler-soldier may have assisted a present yet overwhelmed husband on a regular basis.

The role of settler-soldier might even pass to a woman upon the death of her husband, albeit without the clear mandate for physical combat.[28] And if these widows' complex public roles were not firmly situated within the formal public sphere, neither were they located solely within the informal public sphere. One widow, Elizabeth Stover of Cape Neddick, Maine, discharged martial duties ordinarily performed within the formal public sphere, even as she turned to a man to act as an intermediary when dealing with the upper echelons of the colonial government. In February of 1696, James Convers petitioned Lieutenant Governor William Stoughton for fifteen pounds and seventeen shillings on behalf of Stover. According to the petition, Stover, "(in the beginning of this present Warr) lost her husband, and she, with much deficoulty & Charge maintained her fort at Cape Nuddick, about two Years." Eventually, her neighbors and sons left the area, and "she was forced to quitt the (then) best fort in the Easterne parts, which was within one Week Seized by the Enemy, her houses one of stone an other of wood within the Wals burnt." For two years, Elizabeth Stover had administered her garrison as a public actor working closely with male representatives of the formal public sphere, distributing supplies and food to soldiers and receiving receipts for reimbursement. The petition recounted how her son-in-law traveled to meet up with her to deliver a debenture signed by the treasurer, but lost the note on his journey. By 1696, Stover had already traveled to Boston on more than one occasion with a man she hired to help her recover her money. Convers wrote that he assisted Stover in this latest attempt as "she being weary, left the matter with your pette-tioner."[29] The House of Representatives awarded Stover the money in March of 1697, validating women's administrative roles in garrison houses and for-tified communities.

Elizabeth Heard, a widow from Cochecho, New Hampshire, featured prominently in Cotton Mather's history *Decennium Luctuosum* as a virtuous woman whose commitment to expansionism protected both her vanguard community and the larger colonial enterprise. Relaying an account from John Pike, minister at Dover, New Hampshire, Mather credited Heard with helping to preserve New England's northeastern periphery. Heard, "a Widow of Good Estate," avoided capture in a 1689 attack on Cochecho with the help of an Indigenous man who recognized her as the woman who shel-tered him in an earlier attack on his people. After making her way to an-other garrison, she learned "that her own Garrison, though one of the first that was assaulted, had been bravely Defended and mentaned, against the Adversary." Mather praised Heard for returning to live in "this Gentle-womans Garrison," which was "the most Etxreme [*sic*] Frontier of the Province . . . and more uncapable of Relief." As a result of returning to her garrison, Mather argued, through "her presence and courage, it held out all the War, even for Ten Years together; and the Persons in it, have Enjoy'd very Eminent preservations." He noted that she had refused offers from friends in Portsmouth to live "in more safety." Her absence, he claimed, "would have been a Damage to the Town and Land: but by her Encourage-ment this Post was thus kept; and She is yet Living in much Esteem among her Neighbours."[30] The stabilizing presence of a settler-soldier's widow served as an example to all, reinforcing the importance of fortified commu-nities as simultaneously martial and familial spaces that were essential to New England's expansion and defense.

The cases of Elizabeth Heard and Elizabeth Stover demonstrate how the status, responsibilities, and property of a settler-soldier could pass to a widow in these vanguard towns. In one instance, a wealthy widow of ele-vated rank who owned a stake in a remote community operated as a powerful, more formal public actor. Mary Goodyear Lake was well connected, the daughter of a former New Haven deputy governor, Stephen Goodyear. Her husband, Captain Thomas Lake, was the son of an English baronet, and one of their sons later inherited the baronetcy. In 1673, Thomas Lake and his partner, Thomas Clarke, received permission from the Massachusetts government to establish a town on Maine's Arrowsic Island. An attack during King Philip's War in 1676 destroyed the nascent settlement and resulted in the death of Thomas Lake. Undeterred, Mary Goodyear Lake and Major Thomas Clarke successfully petitioned the General Court the following year for the return of "two gunns" that they required for rebuilding the settlement on Arrowsic.[31] It is unclear whether Mary Lake ever visited Arrowsic, though she clearly took an interest in it as an investment, if not as a home.

Mary Lake's continued investment in Arrowsic had legal ramifications for decades. In asserting his right to the troublesome and vulnerable site in 1731, Sir Bibye Lake traced his claim to the land through his grandmother, Mary Lake, recounting how after the 1676 attack, Thomas Clarke returned to the site with Mary Lake's "Concurrence & assistance." In his petition, Bibye Lake wrote that Clarke and his "late Grandmother Endeavoured with a very great Expence to Resettle the Premmes [premises] and to repair and Rebuild the severall Settlements ruined or destroyed by the Indians." Lake described how the pair had "proceeded therein untill such time as a New Warr broke out." By the time resettlement was possible after 1713, Mary Lake had died, and Bibye Lake partnered with Clarke's descendants in later colonization attempts. Bibye Lake's successful claim to Arrowsic rested upon the fact that although his grandfather died, his grandmother refused to abandon the colonial project. It was her active work restoring Arrowsic in the years between King Philip's War and King William's War (1688–97)—not merely her inheritance of the claim—that ultimately established her grandson's right to the land alongside the claims of Thomas Clarke's descendants.[32]

The concept of the deputy husband is useful in understanding how a husband's role of settler-soldier affected wives and widows, though it does not fully explain the participation of a daughter. Because a husband's status covered an entire family, female children of settler-soldiers also had defensive duties. In one instance in February 1676, a fifteen-year-old "maid" was carried off by Indians while "set to watch upon an hill."[33] William Hubbard reported that there had been several attacks on homes in the area during the preceding weeks. It is likely that the young woman's family was on edge and sent their daughter out to take her turn on the watch. In another incident, father and daughter fought and died side by side. In August of 1723, Aaron Rawlins and his daughter, age twelve, held off an attack while vainly awaiting assistance from neighbors who watched helplessly as the events unfolded. Rawlins was eventually killed by stray bullets, his daughter beheaded when their attackers finally entered the home. According to Jeremy Belknap's account (based on the collected testimony of witnesses), she was killed for putting up a defense "which evidently appeared by her hands being soiled with powder."[34]

Servants, fictive children in the settler-soldier's family, also appear to have been trained in the use of firearms for defense. A female servant in John Minot's Dorchester home (located a few miles south of Boston) saw a Native man approach the house while she minded her employers' children. Realizing that he could not enter through the shut door, the Native man attempted to come in through the window. The servant hid Minot's two children under brass kettles, "ran up Stairs and charged a Musket and fired at the Indian" after his shot missed. Shot in the shoulder, he "was just coming in at the Window" when the servant "made haste and got a Fire-shovel full of live Coles and applied them to his Face, which forced him to flie and escaped."[35] He was later found dead five miles away and was identified by his burned face. This example is particularly interesting in that, along with the story of the young woman carried off while keeping watch, it suggests that the role of settler-soldier covered both real and fictive children of the household. Despite the fact that wives were called upon to assist in defense more frequently, all members of the household might be required to help defend New England.

Government policies placed women in garrison communities, although the physical structures and technologies employed in defending those towns assisted women in taking on public, active roles in New England's wars. Perhaps the most important technological factor that contributed to female participation in these conflicts was their use of guns. Indeed, women's familiarity with firearms was essential to the contest for the northeastern borderlands. It is true that the male monopoly on gun ownership was a powerful nod to patriarchy.[36] Yet, the consistency of stories praising women's able handling of firearms hints at a remarkable degree of cultural flexibility with regard to gun possession and use. A rare, surviving account ledger from Exeter, New Hampshire, recorded that Philip Moodey purchased half a pound of gunpowder for his mother from merchant Nicholas Perryman in April 1722, as tensions between New England and the Abenaki increased during the first skirmishes of Dummer's War (c. 1723–26). It would be a mistake to assume that the ledger's author had found the purchase unusual, thus prompting him to note that the intended recipient of the powder was a woman. In fact, the ledger shows that Philip Moodey also bought powder and shot for his brother, Josiah, and even purchased a quantity of garlic for probable relative Jonathan Moodey in 1724. Married to a settler-soldier, Philip Moodey's wife presumably had access to the household powder her husband purchased in his own name. That the purchase of gunpowder for a man's mother warranted the same treatment as the purchase of garlic for a man suggests a broader acceptance of women's possession of firearms.[37]

Tactically, gunpowder weapons provided women with two distinct advantages in war making. When defending a garrison, firearms allowed women to drive off an attack from the relative safety of a fortified house—as the raids on Wells and Oyster River prove. Occasionally, women living in unfortified homes successfully defended themselves with guns, as the account of the servant in John Minot's house demonstrates. In an incident from 1724, a woman living in Oxford in "a House that lay under a Hill" shot an Indian in the stomach as he and his three companions attempted to break in through the roof.[38] They retreated at this point, perhaps because the woman reportedly had three other loaded firearms, sufficient to take on each remaining assailant at close range. The second advantage rested on the poor accuracy and unreliability of early modern guns. The appearance of the flintlock musket in the late seventeenth and early eighteenth centuries marked an improvement over earlier matchlock muskets. Still, even flintlock muskets left much to be desired, suffering from poor accuracy, slow loading time, and frequent misfires.[39] When confronted with an armed enemy, women might benefit from a wild shot or the time it took to reload.

The element of surprise was critical to a successful raid, and doorways featured heavily in stories of women defending their homes as members of the informal public sphere. Doors could be shut and weight placed against them to delay or prevent entry. As a narrow point for enemy entry, doorways were an ideal location for an ambush. In some cases, the opening of a door marked the first time combatants saw each other face to face. Perhaps the most dramatic—and literal—example illustrating the importance of doorways occurred on October 1, 1675, when a group of fifteen women and children gathered in Richard Tozer's home at the Salmon Falls settlement near present-day Dover, New Hampshire. Two Indians, known to the colonists as Andrew and Hope-hood, son of Robin Hood, attacked the house. An eighteen-year-old woman, described as a "young maid," saw the two men approaching the house, shut the door, and kept it shut while the other fourteen ran out the back door to a nearby house that was better fortified. She continued holding the door shut until "the Indians had chopt it in pieces with their Hatchets."[40] Upon entering, they wounded the young woman with their hatchets and chased after the escaped colonists. All of the occupants of Tozer's house arrived at the garrison house, with the exception of two children. The injured young woman was able to make her way to the stronghold and eventually recovered.

When surprised by attackers at doorways, women sometimes resorted to fighting with household implements. In such instances, the fascinating blurring of homes and martial spaces is at its most dramatic. One of the most colorful examples of this phenomenon is the tale of the twice-captured Hannah Bradley. Bradley was first taken from Haverhill in the infamous 1697 raid that also resulted in Hannah Dustan's better-known captivity, which ended when Dustan killed and scalped ten Indians in the middle of the night with the help of two other captives during their escape. After returning home to Haverhill following her less violent redemption, Hannah Bradley spent several more years in the town before it was attacked again in February 1704. This time, Bradley grabbed the pot of soap she had been boiling and threw it on two of her assailants, killing one and maiming another before finally being subdued and carried away again.[41] In 1708, Susannah Eastman Swan found herself working with her husband to hold their front door shut during another raid on Haverhill.[42] Seeing that her husband was close to surrendering, Swan grabbed a nearby spit and skewered the first attacker as he came through the door. It is tempting to see doorways in these accounts as metaphors or as transition points marking the end of the rough outside world and the beginning of a feminized domestic space. However, no textual evidence exists to support the idea that the doorway or threshold developed gendered or sexualized meanings in wars of this period. The strong association between gender and domestic spaces and spheres was a later phenomenon.

Women's martial activities in towns such as Wells and Oyster River—as well as their work keeping watch and petitioning the government—reflect the space available to women in New England's wars. Although male settler-soldiers and expeditionary forces acting within the formal public sphere remained New England's primary defenders throughout the seventeenth and early eighteenth centuries, women were essential public and martial actors in the fortified communities that served as the vanguard of English expansionism in the northeastern borderlands. Located at the intersections of the fort and the home, the settler and the soldier, and the local and the imperial, women made war as public actors in towns where the informal and formal public spheres blurred in a region perpetually at war.

Native Women Encounter
Formal and Informal Public Spheres

The Reverend John Pike of Dover, New Hampshire, regularly recorded in his diary instances of English women and children killed and captured. On one occasion, he also noted the return of soldiers from an expedition to the area near the Pigwacket fort in October 1703. In this entry, Pike observed that the expedition "brought in 6 Indian scalps & 5 Captives, all squaws and children (both killed and taken) except one old man."[43] On all sides, the capture and killing of women and children brought financial rewards in the form of forced labor, ransom money, and scalp bounties. These acts also served to weaken one's respective enemies while simultaneously functioning as revenge for the deaths of loved ones. Such reports from colonists suggest that Native women participated in attacks on New England's settlements and soldiers. In addition to the wartime leadership roles that female sachems assumed, such as commanding troops and conducting diplomacy, other Indigenous women acted as spies, staged ambushes, and participated in ritual torture. These women's actions, and the settings in which they took place, produced significant anxiety in New England.

Laws establishing scalp bounties hint at the confusion Native women's assumption of martial roles produced among English colonists.[44] A September 1694 law offered fifty pounds for the scalps of "every Indian, great or small" killed in an offensive capacity abroad as well as five pounds "for every Indian that shall be slain in the defence of any house or garrison attacked."[45] Certainly, the higher rewards for volunteers who left the shelter of fortified towns to raid Indigenous communities indicates a policy intended to encourage colonists' offensive military roles while simultaneously destabilizing the targeted communities for ensuing generations. Significantly, the law also defined the military value of Indigenous people engaged in activities that breached the boundaries of places New Englanders had designated as both homes and military spaces. As these laws were, at least in part, designed to encourage colonial men to venture away from the relative safety of their vanguard towns, the reward for killing Indigenous combatants of both genders in colonized spaces was much lower: five pounds. A later law that placed bounties on Indigenous scalps during the war passed in October of 1697, elaborating on the gendered precedent set in June 1694. Again encouraging colonists raiding abroad to target adult women as combatants, the government placed identical bounties of fifty pounds on both men and women. A colonist who killed a child while raiding would receive a much smaller reward of ten pounds, demonstrating lawmakers' conviction that Indigenous women should be classified as full combatants rather than grouped with children.[46] Although there is little evidence that women participated in the joint Indigenous-French raids of this period, nervous colonists clearly believed that they might.

As with English women in garrison houses, lines between combatants and civilians in Native societies were never absolute. Any woman might become a combatant, and any fortified settlement was at once a home and a military space. The leaders of a combined group of Pennacook and Saco grasped these nuances and used this knowledge to engineer a devastating midnight attack on the settlement of Cochecho, New Hampshire. The June 27, 1689, raid was—at least in part—an act of patient retaliation for Major Richard Waldron's betrayal of Indigenous men who agreed to participate in a friendly mock battle following King Philip's War. The group included men from the Pennacook nation, which had not gone to war against the English, as well as men from other nations who had fought against the English. These Native men had taken refuge with the Pennacook and were the target of Waldron's betrayal. After surrounding the Native participants in the mock battle, Waldron and his fellow officers attempted to separate Pennacook from non-Pennacook Indians. Those whom Waldron deemed non-Pennacook—and therefore hostile—he shipped to Boston, where they were hanged or sold into slavery.[47]

John Gyles, a captive taken two months after the raid on Cochecho, wrote of the attack in his memoir. Gyles had heard that two Native women infiltrated the garrison following a feast meant to inaugurate several days of trade in Cochecho. The women likely had been preselected for their abilities, their plea for shelter strengthened by inclement weather. Their task was to "take Notice of the Numbers, Lodgings, and other Circumstances of the People in his Garrison, and if they could obtain leave to Lodge there, to open the Gates and Whistle."[48] Perhaps indicative of the careless practices officials sometimes associated with fortified communities, the "Gates had no Locks but were fastned with Pins" and the residents of Cochecho neglected to keep a watch. Both Gyles and the Reverend Jeremy Belknap noted in their accounts that many of Cochecho's residents argued against allowing the women to stay overnight but were overruled by Major Waldron.[49] The inhabitants' resistance may have been the result of discreet warnings given by friendly Indigenous women in the days leading up to the attack. Ultimately, the overconfident, unsavory Waldron dismissed the women as potential combatants and allowed them to infiltrate the town.

That evening, wrote Gyles, "the Squaws went into every Apartment, and observed the Numbers in each and when the People were all asleep, rose and opened the Gates and gave the Signal."[50] The attack resulted in the deaths of Waldron and twenty-two others, as well as the captivity of twenty-nine residents of heavily damaged Cochecho. The incursion's success can only be attributed to the Native leaders' nuanced understanding of the complex nature of vanguard communities. As spaces where martial identities shifted and structures functioned as shelters and strongholds, these settlements offered unique opportunities to opponents able to exploit the subtle cracks in the foundation of New England's expansionist program.

An account from Boston merchant Nathaniel Saltonstall illustrates the confusion and horror that Indigenous women's war making stirred up among colonists. Saltonstall reported that in March 1676, "a great Number of Indian Women" ambushed two Englishmen in the woods between Marlborough and Sudbury in Massachusetts. According to Saltonstall, these women were "armed with Clubs, pieces of Swords, and the like." He emphasized that through "their numbers," the women "over-mastered the two poor Travellers, that had nothing but small sticks to defend themselves." The women "beat out their brains, and cut off their privy members, which they carried away with them in triumph." Although Saltonstall was quick to praise English women who killed Indigenous men, he and his contemporaries were—understandably—less inclined to honor the martial skills of Native women. Yet, in addition to lamenting the deaths of his countrymen, Saltonstall's narrative offered a highly gendered, colonialist interpretation of the attack as the work of Indigenous Others, of women whom he claimed had "utterly abandoned at once the two proper Virtues of Womankinde, Pity and Modesty." He argued that it was "vain" to expect Indians to behave civilly when—as he saw it—"the most milde and gentle sex" in those societies "delight in cruelties."[51] Curiously, a group of Englishwomen in Marlborough threatened several English-allied Indians—including women and children—who had taken shelter in Marlborough while on their way to Boston.[52] This attack occurred in the same month and area as the Marlborough incident, though it is unclear which occurred first. It is possible that one of the attacks was in response to the other.

The image of Indigenous women emerging from the forest and setting upon two Englishmen clearly troubled Saltonstall. Their attack on the men while in the grip of what appeared to be a violent frenzy evokes exotic images of disorderly pagan rituals performed in an uncharted, unholy wilderness. That the Native women went on to castrate their victims only added to Saltonstall's perception that the gendered and moral order had been upended at the hands of a people who were, perhaps, too savage to civilize after all. It likely was also reminiscent of reports that Indigenous women participated in the ritual torture of captives in their camps and settlements. English colonists were particularly troubled by women's participation in ritualized torture. A formal aspect of war making in many Native communities, ritual torture appeared wild and uncontrollable to New Englanders. English observers did not understand that, although the act of seeking out battle was largely gendered male in Native societies, once men returned with captives, war making continued within the village with the critical assistance of women and even children. Women's assumption of the role of torturer appeared to showcase the perceived disorder to European colonists of Native gender roles and families. In fact, it demonstrated quite the opposite: an orderly transfer of formal war-making roles to the larger community.[53]

The confusion New Englanders felt regarding Native women in less formal combat roles—as well as those roles *perceived* as less formal—largely did not translate to their attitudes toward female sachems in the seventeenth century. Among their many roles as leaders of Native polities, female sachems signed international treaties, participated in land deals and disputes, and commanded troops.[54] Although it is possible, as one study suggests, that early New England's officials lacked the power to shape Indigenous leadership and were forced to tolerate female sachems' authority, English leaders knew that their own nation had been ruled by queens, and they referred to female sachems as "queens" and occasionally "princes" in an attempt to understand their roles within a European notion of rank and the formal public sphere.[55] When Nathaniel Saltonstall referred to the Pocasset sachem Weetamoo as "Potent a Prince as any round about her," he drew on the early modern European notion of a prince as sovereign.[56] Similarly, both Elizabeth I of England and her subjects referred to her as a prince in speeches, correspondence, and publications.[57] A glossary printed in one of the reports sent to London during King Philip's War included an entry for the commonly used term "squaw sachem," stating simply that "A Squaw Sachem is a Princess or Queen."[58] Even had colonists possessed the ability to shape Native leadership in this early phase of colonization, a preference for male leadership would not preclude women of appropriate status from assuming political and military roles in a rank-based society.

Acceptance of Native and European female leadership as a function of rank and kinship was one element within a broader scheme by Europeans and Indians to understand each other by emphasizing social and cultural similarities. This was particularly true when trying to make sense of unfamiliar political systems and hierarchies, as each group tried to adapt their own abstract languages of governance to the political systems of others. Despite inaccuracies in cultural and linguistic translation, this work was crucial to diplomacy between nations.[59] A shared belief in the right of a woman of rank to rule was evident in a meeting between Iroquois leaders and New York's Governor Lord Cornbury in 1702. Iroquois leaders reaffirmed their friendship with England after Queen Anne assumed the throne, telling the governor that "they were glad to hear that the sun shined in England again since King William's Death," and that "they did admire at first what was come to us, that we should have a squaw sachem." English observer John Talbot then paused to note in his writing that a squaw sachem was a "woman-king."[60]

Accounts of Native female leaders in North America dating back to the early seventeenth century reflect shared cultural assumptions of their right to rule and to perform military roles in addition to conducting diplomacy and land deals. Plymouth's Governor William Bradford reported that as early as 1621, ten colonists from Plymouth and three Native men went in search of a female sachem, the formidable "Queene" of the Massachusett. Forming alliances throughout southern New England, Plymouth had positioned itself in opposition to the Massachusett nation. Approaching the shores of Massachusetts Bay, they encountered a male sachem who described himself as an enemy of the Queene. He agreed to take the colonists to see that female sachem after they promised to protect him from her. The colonists hoped to conduct negotiations—and possibly trade—with the Queene, since she had reportedly been threatening the colonists.[61] This same female sachem of the Massachusett, known by 1637 as "Squa Sachem," appeared at the Massachusetts General Court that year regarding the sale of land that would become Concord and Charlestown.[62] In addition to these land deals, she also negotiated matters related to firearms. Although gun ownership was exclusively male in seventeenth-century New England, at least some female sachems—likely as a privilege of their rank—did own guns.[63] In 1643, the court granted the same Massachusett sachem "haulfe a pound of gunpowder" and agreed to repair her gun. The court also agreed to sell her an additional quantity of shot and powder later that year.[64]

In an episode spanning 1667–68, the General Court of Massachusetts seriously considered, though ultimately rejected, a female sachem's claim to domination over another Native polity. In August of 1667, the Narragansett female sachem Matantuck—then called Watowswokotaus—sent 126 warriors to the Nipmuc village of Quantisset to seize guns and other valuable items in payment of tribute. The Nipmuc approached the court in September in an attempt to reclaim their property and to declare themselves free of Narragansett control. Nipmuc leaders insisted that a treaty prevented the Narragansett from using force on another Native polity without first consulting the English. Matantuck refused to appear in court but sent deputies as well as a signed statement to an October 1667 hearing.[65] The General Court tentatively found that the Nipmuc were a free people due to lack of evidence and ordered the Narragansett to return the goods they had taken. The court also ruled that if Matantuck were able to prove that the Nipmuc did owe tribute, the court would help formalize the terms. Although she provided proof in the form of a letter from Roger Williams of Rhode Island, the letter and the Narragansett deputies arrived several days late to a scheduled May 1668 hearing. Meanwhile, the Nipmuc agreed to submit to the General Court and accept the presence of a Christian mission in their community.[66]

The English ruling against Matantuck's right to tribute was not related to her gender, nor did any party, Native or English, question her right or ability to dispatch troops and collect tribute due to her sex. Roger Williams's delayed letter strongly supported Matantuck, tracing her claim to power based on rank and kinship through her deceased husband, Mixanno, son of the powerful Narragansett leader Canonicus. Drawing a parallel with a more familiar form of political organization, Williams wrote of the Nipmuc's "plaine and cleare" position as subjects of Matantuck and the Narragansett, and he awkwardly but earnestly compared the Indigenous polities' hierarchical relationship to the way in which the "Inhabitants of Ipsich [Ipswich] or Newbrey [Newbury] &c are subject to the Government of the Massachusets Colony."[67] Williams's letter offers additional evidence that the General Court's unfavorable decision was not an attack on Matantuck's right to rule as a woman of rank. Instead, the judgment that denied Matantuck's claims resulted from the poor timing of the letter, the late appearance of the Narragansett at the May hearing, and—most significantly—English desire to control the Nipmuc. Matantuck, known as "Quaiapen" in later histories due to a misplaced comma in a 1675 Narragansett treaty, maintained control over her people and her position as a powerful sachem in New England. She eventually joined the Native coalition in King Philip's War and died in a well-publicized attack on her camp in July 1676.[68]

Younger than Matantuck—though both were leaders in the years between 1650 and 1676—Weetamoo of the Pocasset came to power a generation after female sachems first encountered English colonists.[69] Weetamoo is unusual among Native female rulers who left a strong presence in the historical record. Other sachems about whom greater numbers of documents survive, such as Awashunkes of the Saconet, who also ruled during King Philip's War, and Cockacoeske, who led the Pamunkey during Bacon's Rebellion, aligned their polities with English colonists and outlived the wars. Unlike Awashunkes and Cockacoeske, Weetamoo died opposing European colonization and dispossession. Documents describing her political and military leadership before and during King Philip's War offer unique opportunities to study the wide range of formal roles a female sachem might assume as a ruler in peacetime and as a ruler who helped forge and lead an anticolonial military coalition.

Appearing in colonial records beginning in the 1650s, Weetamoo quickly gained experience in diplomacy and land deals and proved eager to challenge unfair agreements in court. Some of these court appearances involved challenges to her husband Wamsutta, alias Alexander, who assumed the leadership of the Wampanoag Confederacy upon the death of his father Massasoit around 1661.[70] Representing his absent father in 1659—and possibly without his consent—Wamsutta and Weetamoo sold a large parcel of Pocasset land to some of Plymouth's most prominent men. In this instance, Weetamoo received a third of the proceeds from the sale.[71] Perhaps believing he had a right to sell Pocasset land as head of the Wampanoag Confederacy, Wamsutta then attempted to "freely Give" most, if not all, Pocasset land to a Rhode Islander named Peter Talman in early 1662.[72] Weetamoo and a Saconet man named Tatacomuncah appeared separately before the General Court of Plymouth later in 1662, asking assistance in reclaiming land they argued Wamsutta had unlawfully sold. In its responses, the court seemed sympathetic to their land rights but indicated it would wait for a "convenient time" to act.[73] It is likely that Wamsutta's unexpected death of a fever in 1662 helped preserve Pocasset lands. Following Wamsutta's death, his brother Philip took power as head of a Wampanoag Confederacy increasingly threatened by English encroachment.

Although Philip now led the Wampanoag Confederacy, Weetamoo continued to assert her authority as sachem of the Pocasset polity, a member-nation of the larger Wampanoag Confederacy. Philip's role as head of the Wampanoag was not that of an absolute monarch, and sachems who led its member-nations, such as Weetamoo, maintained a fair degree of autonomy. In 1662, in the wake of Wamsutta's death and Philip's succession, the General Court of Plymouth arbitrated a dispute between Philip and Weetamoo. The dispute appears to have been related to her alleged right to entertain

Narragansett visitors against his wishes. The court found in favor of Philip due to his position as head of the Wampanoag, but ordered him to return canoes and other items he had taken from her. The timing of this case suggests a power struggle between Weetamoo—a sachem and former wife of the head of the Wampanoag Confederacy—and Philip, the new Wampanoag leader who was just establishing power.[74]

English attempts to dispossess the Wampanoag and other polities of their land and sovereignty would only intensify over the next fourteen years. Philip became increasingly pessimistic after Plymouth, with the help of Massachusetts and Connecticut, forced him to sign a humiliating document of submission to Plymouth in 1671.[75] When Plymouth tried and executed three Wampanoag men—including one of Philip's chief councilors—in June 1675 for the murder of the English ally and Christian Indian John Sassamon, Philip began assembling a coalition for war.[76] As tensions between Philip and Plymouth grew, both sides scrambled for allies among the region's Native leaders. The most highly sought after ally in this period was Weetamoo, sachem of the Pocasset.

In addition to her legal, political, and diplomatic acumen, Weetamoo commanded the loyalty of troops numbering in the hundreds. Writing in 1677, historian and minister William Hubbard estimated that at the beginning of the war, Weetamoo commanded close to three hundred men who, Hubbard wrote, "belonged" to her and served "under her." In fact, Hubbard speculated that Philip himself brought only slightly over three hundred men.[77] The value of an alliance with such a powerful leader was not lost on Philip or his enemies, and both sides approached Weetamoo early in the war. One Massachusetts observer, the aforementioned Nathaniel Saltonstall, reported to his London audience that once Philip had decided to attack the colonists, he approached Weetamoo before any other sachems, "promising her great rewards" and meeting with her first because she was "as Potent a Prince as any round about her, and hath as much Corn, Land, and Men at her Command."[78] According to Saltonstall, Philip only sent messengers to other sachems asking for alliances after securing Weetamoo's assistance, believing, perhaps, that her support would ease the task of persuading other sachems to join his coalition.[79]

Saltonstall's estimation of Weetamoo's value as an ally helps explain the urgency both Philip and the English colonists displayed in their attempts to gain her support in the late spring and early summer of 1675. Representing Plymouth, Captain Benjamin Church traveled to meet with her in early June.[80] Weetamoo had remarried after Wamsutta's death, and her husband at this time, Petananuet, accompanied Church and spoke with him along the way. Petananuet—who served her as an advisor and junior partner—informed Church that he had recently returned from visiting a "Dance" that Philip had been hosting for several weeks in an attempt to gain support. Petananuet told Church that "Young Men from all Parts of the Country" attended the event. When Church reached Weetamoo, he found that many of her men had left to attend the dance. Although Church urged her to side with the English in the coming conflict, she declined to give a firm answer.[81]

Despite English efforts to woo Weetamoo, Increase Mather reported in July 1675, "that Squaw-Sachem of Pocasset [and] her men were conjoyned with the Womponoags (that is Philips men) in this Rebellion."[82] Chroniclers writing during and after the war disagreed about Weetamoo's reasons for allying with Philip's cause. Saltonstall believed that her alliance with Philip was driven by revenge for the death of her previous husband, and that Philip "perswaded [her] that the English had Poysoned her Husband [Wamsutta], and thereupon she was the more willing to joyn with him."[83] Church suggested that her men had attended Philip's dance against her will, implying that she may have had less choice in the matter than Saltonstall believed. Writing in December 1675, Deputy Governor John Easton of Rhode Island claimed that he had offered her an alliance and safety in his colony. Easton wrote that she seriously considered the offer, but before Easton was able to "send for hir," a group of English soldiers attacked some of her canoes in late June 1675. The soldiers apparently believed the canoes belonged to Philip, and Weetamoo's people retaliated, her allegiance perhaps decided by circumstance.[84] In addition to the reasons offered by chroniclers of the war, there is convincing evidence that she understood the dangers of English encroachment and believed that resistance was in the best interest of her people.

A letter written by John Easton to Plymouth's Governor Josiah Winslow on May 26, 1675, supports the claim that Weetamoo was motivated by a desire to resist dispossession.[85] In his letter, Easton reported that Weetamoo and her husband had approached him two days prior with a letter from Constant Southworth, Plymouth's treasurer. Weetamoo feared that Southworth meant to challenge the boundaries of Pocasset land. Her concerns were likely well founded, as Plymouth and Southworth's own family had strong interests in expanding into Pocasset territory.[86] Easton's letter to Winslow shows that Weetamoo had "great feare of opretion [oppression] from the English" several weeks before events led Philip and Church to approach her as an ally.[87] It also suggests that Plymouth colony continued to maintain that it was the threatened party despite the fact that officials high in the government were working to chip away at Pocasset land.

Rather than seeking to assuage Weetamoo's fears, Governor Winslow sent a letter on June 15, 1675, that was at once ingratiating and threatening, addressing it to "Weetamoo, and Ben her husband Sachems of Pocasset."[88] Despite elevating her husband—Petananuet, alias Ben—in rank, this salutation demonstrated that the governor of Plymouth understood that Weetamoo was the senior partner in the marriage.[89] Addressing them as "Friends and Neighbors," Winslow began by asserting that Philip's claims against the English were unfounded and that baser motives drove his preparations for war. The governor attempted to quash any rumors that "wee were secretly designeing mischief to him, and you," though she had already learned of Plymouth's plans to dispossess the Pocasset of a portion of their land in Constant Southworth's April 1675 letter. Winslow—likely acting on intelligence from Benjamin Church—wrote that he was willing to believe that Weetamoo was loyal to Plymouth and disregarded reports that her men were meeting with Philip as the actions of "giddy inconsiderate young men." In return for continued peace and future protection against Philip, Winslow demanded that she prove her allegiance by betraying Philip and providing Plymouth with "what intelligence you may have, or shall gather up."[90] Weetamoo clearly had more practical—and perhaps believable—motives for fighting against the English than revenge. In the end, however, it may be impossible to ascertain precisely which factors led to her decision to side with Philip against the colony.

Once Weetamoo committed to Philip's coalition, she made a loyal ally, second only to Philip himself in importance. Particularly in the earlier months of the war, authors spoke of Philip and Weetamoo in the same breath. For example, in November 1675, Governor Winslow referred to the conflict as the "Warr with the Indians of Mount hope and Pocassett," naming Philip's and Weetamoo's polities as the war's primary players.[91] When Captain James Cudworth reported on English actions in a July 20, 1675, letter to Winslow, he wrote of "march[ing] out with about an hundred and twenty men, to search for Philip and squaw sachem."[92] The English assault initially drove Philip and his followers from their base at Mount Hope to a cedar swamp in Weetamoo's Pocasset territory. Although English commanders had hoped to trap Weetamoo and Philip in Pocasset, the two sachems and their followers used their knowledge of the swamp to evade and eventually escape English forces, traveling at night by water. Rather than confining the conflict to Wampanoag territory, the events of late July led to a broader war, allowing Weetamoo and Philip to seek out new allies among the region's other nations.[93]

After their escape, Weetamoo brought "as mani of hir men as shee could get" to the neutral Narragansett.[94] Weetamoo and more than one hundred Pocasset took refuge with the Narragansett for several months in the summer and fall of 1675.[95] Hubbard suggested in his chronicle of the war that Philip had already begun sending women and children to the Narragansett in June 1675, though it is unlikely that Weetamoo was simply hiding out.[96] Indeed, it appears that her presence among the Narragansett was an attempt to seek an alliance between the new Native coalition and the Narragansett people while Philip met with potential allies further north and west.[97] Weetamoo also used this opportunity to strengthen her kinship ties to the Narragansett. She ended her marriage to Petananuet, who chose to side with the English for reasons unclear, and married the Narragansett sachem Quinnapin in August or September of 1675. Nathaniel Saltonstall reported to readers that his side had become pessimistic about the likelihood of an Anglo-Narragansett alliance due to Weetamoo's new marriage.[98] The marriage did partially tie the Narragansett to Philip's coalition, though it would ultimately strain the bonds of the Narragansett Confederacy.

Despite the potential obstacle presented by Weetamoo's marriage, English negotiators repeatedly requested that Weetamoo's Narragansett hosts turn her over to the English.[99] Along with the military victory that might result from persuading the Narragansett to betray Weetamoo, English leaders saw an additional financial incentive. Saltonstall admitted that if she were "taken by the English, her Lands will more then pay all the Charge we have been at in this unhappy War."[100] Governor Josiah Winslow described Weetamoo's Pocasset lands as some of the "best Land in the Colony."[101] Lost as a potential ally, her English enemies believed her wealth might be used to finance the entire war. In the end, one study argues, Weetamoo's presence and legitimate claims to kinship, as well as generational conflicts and resistance to colonial pressure, split the Narragansett.[102] Their aging head sachem, Ninigret, left the group with a number of his men and declared neutrality, while his younger relative, the sachem Quinnapin, joined forces with his new wife Weetamoo and several other sachems.[103]

Weetamoo's sanctuary with the Narragansett ended in a massacre, as Narragansett refusal to agree to English demands prompted a massive colonial military response.[104] English forces, led by a disaffected Native guide named Peter, attacked the Narragansett in the Great Swamp Massacre in December 1675.[105] Hundreds of Native soldiers and families burned to death or later died of exposure when English troops set fire to the fort in which they had taken shelter. Captain Benjamin Church reported that nearly one-third of the Narragansett at the fort had perished.[106] For the survivors, including Weetamoo and Quinnapin, the attack strengthened bonds between coalition members.

Following the massacre, King Philip's War increasingly became a Narragansett war. Indeed, one historian has argued that some colonists apparently considered the Narragansett to be their primary enemies.[107] Although the majority of accounts written during the conflict focused on Philip as the head of the Native coalition, the Narragansett did take on a larger role in the struggle in 1676. Gambling by leaving the primary theater of the war, Philip had traveled to the area near present-day Albany in fall 1675 seeking alliances and supplies. He spent the winter there before suffering a devastating defeat at the hands of the Mohawk, who likely saw a chance to strike a blow at rival polities from New England while maintaining an advantageous friendly relationship with the royal colony of New York.[108] This left Weetamoo and the Narragansett as the primary Native coalition players in New England for much of the remainder of the war. After the December massacre, Weetamoo, Quinnapin, several other sachems, and their followers responded by raiding at least two dozen towns over the next seven months, including Mary Rowlandson's Lancaster, Massachusetts, in February 1676.[109]

Weetamoo's time with Mary Rowlandson during the latter's infamous captivity is the best-documented and analyzed period of her rule and is our only window into the sachem's daily life.[110] This glimpse demonstrates how Weetamoo's power derived from her status, not her sex—even as Rowlandson's narrative sought to convey a very different perception of Weetamoo's situation. Rowlandson saw Weetamoo merely as one of her master Quinnapin's three wives or as "King Phillips wives Sister."[111] Mary Rowlandson's failure either to understand or respect Weetamoo's position is an intriguing example of the limits of Native and European common ground on the issue of gender and rank. In such situations, English captives often turned to the figure of a male master as a positive symbol of household and social order in their captivity.[112] Rowlandson likely did not see how Weetamoo could be at once a wife and her husband's equal in rank and so found Weetamoo's station and behavior frustrating, as she attempted to find familial and political order in what she saw as Quinnapin's household.

Mary Rowlandson's well-known captivity narrative disapprovingly lingered over details of Weetamoo's dress and behavior, reflecting Rowlandson's own beliefs regarding Weetamoo's rank and providing scholars with a rare opportunity to examine the sachem's self-presentation. Describing Weetamoo as a "severe and proud Dame," Rowlandson critically observed that Weetamoo vainly devoted "as much time as any of the Gentry of the land" to dressing each day. Her toilette, which consisted of "powdering her hair, and painting her face, going with Neck-laces, with Jewels in her ears, and Bracelets upon her hands," was designed to set her apart from other, lower-ranked members of the community.[113] Yet, the same actions Rowlandson cited to condemn Weetamoo were appropriate to a wealthy sachem of the Pocasset with dynastic ties to the Wampanoag and the Narragansett, revealing a woman aware of her important position in the region's politics.

Rather than depending on symbols of masculine power, Weetamoo presented herself as a culturally hybridized ruler. Indeed, Weetamoo incorporated both Native and European symbols of rank and power at a feast Rowlandson witnessed. According to Rowlandson, Weetamoo bedecked her English "Kersey Coat" with "Girdles of Wampom from the Loins upward: her armes from her elbows to her hands were covered with Bracelets." In addition to this display of wealth and status, Weetamoo wore "handfulls of Neck laces about her neck, and severall sorts of Jewels in her ears." Weetamoo also donned "fine red Stockins, and white shoos," powdering her hair and painting her face red for the occasion.[114] Both men and women of rank in the seventeenth-century Anglo-Atlantic world wore stockings and powdered their hair and, as one study notes, English coats, jewelry, and wampum displayed status and leadership in the region's Native societies.[115] By seizing these symbols, Weetamoo portrayed herself as a master of two worlds, her rank superseding yet coexisting with her gender.

A disastrous spring and early summer of 1676 turned the tide of the conflict in favor of the English. Starving and battered, the forces of the Native coalition dwindled. Some sachems with their followers even defected to the English, and Weetamoo's husband Quinnapin was captured in July 1676. Sources say very little about Weetamoo during the tumultuous period between Mary Rowlandson's departure and Weetamoo's death. As the coalition's defeat became increasingly likely, however, Weetamoo appears to have attempted to return to Pocasset. It was then that one of her men betrayed her position in late July or early August 1676, perhaps hoping to secure favorable treatment after hostilities ceased. Both Hubbard and Mather reported that Weetamoo escaped the attack but died of drowning, exposure, or exhaustion after crossing a river or "arm of the sea" on a makeshift raft.[116] Mather found it ironic—and providential—that "she her self could not meet with a Canoo" in the place where, one year before, she had assisted

Philip's men in escaping with the help of her own flotilla. He proclaimed that "God himself by his own hand, brought this enemy to destruction," and correctly speculated that with Weetamoo dead, "Surely Philips turn will be next."[117]

Upon finding her body, English soldiers cut off her head and placed it on a pole in Taunton where a number of prisoners were held. Increase Mather wrote that upon seeing her head, the prisoners "made a most horrid and diabolical Lamentation, crying out that it was their Queens head."[118] Weetamoo's head served not only as a trophy but also as a signal that an English victory was near. In the Native polities of southern New England, the mutilation and dismemberment of a leader may have also demonstrated a loss of "spiritual power," a factor that likely compounded the prisoners' grief as they recognized the multiple English and Native meanings behind the head's exhibition.[119] This calculated action and the outraged response it provoked from the nearby captives underscored how highly both Native and English participants regarded Weetamoo's power as a leader and the very real blow her death had dealt to the Native coalition.

Weetamoo's actions and the actions of her associates make a strong case for her importance and authority; however, the full magnitude of her influence only becomes apparent when we examine descriptions of her in the histories of contemporary chroniclers. Two prominent chroniclers of King Philip's War recorded their impressions of Weetamoo's role in these events. Increase Mather believed Weetamoo was a key player in the war—second only to Philip. In the early stages of the war, Mather described the coalition forces as "Philips and Squaw-Sachims [Weetamoo's] men."[120] Mather also recounted that she was "next unto Philip in respect of the mischief that hath been done, and the blood that hath been shed in this Warr."[121] Saltonstall went further, arguing that beyond being "as Potent a Prince as any round about her," she "willingly consented, and was much more forward in the Design, and had greater Success than King Philip himself."[122] Mather's and Saltonstall's words demonstrated that English leaders clearly understood Weetamoo's status and power in the region.

Scholars have shown that in the decades following the war, elite men in New England began a slow process of marginalizing Native female leaders, often through legal machinations, by questioning the lineages of potential leaders, and by appointing male puppet rulers.[123] Even the English ally Awashunkes of the Saconet found her leadership under attack when Plymouth authorities—with questionable jurisdiction—charged and acquitted Awashunkes and two of her children in the alleged infanticide of her daughter's baby, a highly gendered crime.[124] Historian Ann Plane explains that "growing English dominance" frustrated Native women's leadership ambitions as "sachems found their autonomy diminished and women found their opportunities for formal leadership reduced."[125] This colonial undertaking coincided with a greater ability to manipulate Native leadership more generally, although as Mary Beth Norton has argued, changes in English political culture resulted in attempts to restrict all women's access to positions of power in the late seventeenth and eighteenth centuries.[126] For the region's Indigenous societies that relied upon lineage and rank to determine leadership, these ideological developments threatened the right of Native women to rule their polities.

Europeans' deliberate disruption of Native gender systems was a significant tool in the project of colonization. But even these tactics, though often effective, did not spell the end of Native women's power in North America.[127] A reduced number of Native women in eighteenth-century New England continued to rule as sachems, and women's political participation within their communities persisted.[128] The act of following a female sachem might even serve as a rejection of colonialism. As scholar Amy Den Ouden has argued, when the sachem Mary Momoho referred to Eastern Pequot males as "her men" in a petition from the early eighteenth century, she was engaging in "an assertion of her political authority by her own community's standards, not those of colonial society." Despite signing the petition using her own title, the General Assembly of Connecticut emphasized Mary Momoho's status as widow of the deceased sachem Momoho, describing her as "Momoho's Squaw."[129] The Mohegan nation's choice of a female sachem such as Anne of the Mohegan in 1736 was, in Den Ouden's words, "a most blatant gesture of defiance to colonial authority," as Native and English attitudes toward gender and rank moved further apart.[130]

The careers of seventeenth-century female sachems such as the "Queene" of the Massachusett, Matantuck of the Narragansett, and Weetamoo of the Pocasset demonstrate both the space available for female sachems in Native polities and the widespread colonial recognition of their rank and right to rule—regardless of whether that rule supported colonial objectives. Their role as leaders in war making—and English recognition of this role—diminished following the deaths of Weetamoo and her contemporaries, a result of both a lack of sustained conflict in southern New England as well as English pressure to conform to their newer preferred gender hierarchy. In spite of these changes, Native women continued to engage in other forms of war making—including acting as spies and participating in ritual torture—

playing important military roles in the conflicts that extended beyond King Philip's War and into the eighteenth century.

"So-ho, Souse the Cowards": Female Armies in the Streets of New England

Despite lacking access to the formal roles in wartime leadership exercised by Native women, Englishwomen did take a significant interest in the leadership of New England's wars. One of the more effective ways women expressed this interest and desire to influence policy was through the pursuit of violent action within the informal public sphere under the cover of a mob. An informal army that challenged the decisions of members of the formal public sphere, the female mob attacked real and perceived combatants and even attempted to reshape colonial military policy through group action. These women were not prosecuted by authorities for their violent or disruptive behavior and, indeed, they often received support from men in their communities. That women faced no punishment for seemingly insubordinate acts is partially due to the extralegal nature of the informal public sphere. Outraged women, distrustful of colonial governments and their ability to protect their people or mete out justice, took matters into their own hands. Men in their communities often supported these interventions, which were expressions of a larger sense of frustration within the informal public. This does not mean that actors within the formal public approved of such female intervention. On the contrary, most reports described women challenging the policies of leaders who, though frustrated by their actions, were unable to prosecute the women due to the legal protection provided by coverture and the silence of witnesses.[131]

Examples of Englishwomen who participated in mob action in King Philip's War and Queen Anne's War demonstrate women's willingness to provide the formal public sphere with unsolicited advice and extralegal military action. Perhaps the most shocking incident of women's violence in colonial New England's history occurred in Marblehead, a fishing community north of Salem, Massachusetts. The testimony of thirty-year-old sailor Robert Roules in July 1677 reveals the fluidity of boundaries between terrestrial borderlands and the Atlantic world as well as the intensity of the violence women might perform as members of the informal public sphere. Early on the morning of July 8, approximately nine or ten Indians in a canoe approached and boarded Roules's employer's fishing vessel, the *William and Sarah*. Roules later testified that "they bound him & the other 4 English marriners . . . one after another stripping them of all their cloathes" with the exception of the "gresy" (greasy) clothing the sailors wore when fishing. Later that afternoon, the men were unbound and ordered to sail toward Penobscot. The prisoners and their captors later commandeered another vessel, and the men of the two ships were mixed together and divided to form two new crews. Roules remained on the *William and Sarah*, testifying that their captors left Roules as "Master" of the ship and in control of the helm. Hours later, according to Roules, "espying a Saile wee were Comande to saile for them which wee did till it grew dusky." When Roules refused to "bear up on the helme" as commanded, the other Englishmen on board took advantage of the ensuing confusion, throwing at least two of their captors overboard and binding another two. The mutiny accomplished, Roules and the crew "made all the Sayle they could . . . & so through mercy came safe to Marble head" with their two prisoners, one week after the initial encounter.[132]

Roules noted that the coastal town was already mourning the presumed loss of the mariners, and that "a Rumour being gon out that wee were killed, many people came to the water side" to greet the crew and ask about their prisoners. Residents had only just left Sunday services at the meetinghouse when the men arrived. Initially, the crowd that formed to welcome them was delighted by their unexpected return, but Roules reported that the crowd grew angry upon learning that the two prisoners had been left alive. Braving the crowd's anger, the sailors requested promises of help to "Carry them [the prisoners] on shoure to the Constable to secure them their so they might be carried to the Court at Boston." Roules and his crew pointed out that "they had lost all their cloaths & hoped by this meanes to Gett somewhat towards there losses" through judicial means.[133] The crowd was slightly mollified, and several men agreed to bring the Indians to Marblehead's constable.

When the prisoners were brought ashore, "bound with their hands behind them," the crowd, made up of the "whole Towne flocking about them," again grew unruly, and members of the crowd-turned-mob, "especially the women layd holt on the Indians hair at which the Indians laught." The women, whom Increase Mather described as "in a boisterous rage," began shoving and hurling rocks at the men escorting the prisoners.[134] Their aim was not to injure their fellow townspeople but to strip the Indians of their protection. Roules testified that the women "Gott the Indians into there hands & with stones & billets [sticks] & what else they know not they made an end of the Indians which they saw not till they saw them lye dead & all there heads bones & flesh pulled." Roules's testimony suggests that the men of Marblehead were willing to look the other way during this vigilante dismemberment. Suspiciously oblivious onlookers claimed "that the tumultation was such by the weomen that for their lives they Could not acertain or tell any particular woman."[135] Apparently, although the "whole Towne" was present, none of its residents were able to recognize any of its female inhabitants.

For their part, the women were defiant, "Crying out if they [the Indians] had bin Carried to Boston they would have lived but if there had bin forty of the best Indians in the Country they [the women] would kill them all though they [the women] were hanged for it." Whether from fear or— more likely—complicity, the women faced no consequences as "neither Constable Mr. Mavericke nor any suffered to come nere them."[136] Acting as part of the informal public—and with the tacit approval of Marblehead's men—the women expressed their skepticism of the colonial government's willingness to mete out suitable punishments at a time when the primary theater of the war had shifted to the northeast, toward their own community. One Abenaki raid had reportedly killed seven colonists in northeastern Massachusetts just days before the sailors returned to Marblehead. Writing in his diary, Increase Mather noted that a devastating English defeat along the coast north of Marblehead in the final days of June was the result of cowardice on the part of colonial troops.[137] It is possible that the stunning failure of colonial soldiers and leaders to prevent these attacks contributed to a loss of confidence in officials. When combined with violent anti-Indigenous sentiment, this loss of confidence may have led to the enraged women's mob action against the Abenaki combatants. The government did take the time to acquire a deposition from Robert Roules, suggesting some sort of inquiry, though Roules's deposition focused mainly on the naval drama that had played out off the coast, not the impromptu execution on land. Formal inquiries aside, the women's actions within the mob and the informal public sphere went unpunished, as ordinary people, and perhaps even Marblehead's constable, remained silent.

The women of Marblehead were not the only women willing to assert themselves in challenging New England's leadership from within the informal public sphere during King Philip's War. Daniel Gookin, best known for his attempts to convert New England's Native peoples to Christianity, wrote disapprovingly of an incident in Marlborough, Massachusetts, in March 1676. Gookin himself faced a backlash from his hometown of Cambridge during King Philip's War, losing a leadership position in his church for his defense of allied Christian Indians.[138] The repercussions Gookin experienced were representative of a larger anti-Indian sentiment that gripped New England during King Philip's War.[139] Many colonists distrusted their Indigenous allies, unable or unwilling to distinguish between the numerous polities fighting in complicated alliances on both sides in the war. Hundreds of Christian Indians were sent to live on Deer Island—ostensibly for their protection—in miserable conditions. Gookin reported that many of the "vulgar" among the colonists felt powerless to strike against the enemy, who had conducted a number of successful raids and who were widely viewed as "too crafty and subtle for the English." In this atmosphere of dread and distrust, many colonists would have "wreaked their rage upon the poor unarmed Indians our friends, (had not the authority of the country restrained them)."[140] Despite attempts by the "authority of the country" to protect Native allies, women in the town of Marlborough would challenge that same authority.

In March 1676, a party consisting of the Native minister Tuckapawillin, his family, and the friends and children of a Native ally named Job arrived at Marlborough on their way to Boston, where they had been promised protection. The group had already been robbed on the road when English soldiers "took from them all those few necessaries they had persevered," including "a pewter cup" that Tuckapawillin used "at the administration of the sacrament of the Lord's Supper." Although Marlborough's constable had promised to shelter them for "one night or two," the people of Marlborough resented their presence. The promises of officials were no match for the rage of the frightened members of the public. Gookin recounted that "there came some people of the town (especially women) to their quarter, some of whom did so abuse, threaten, and taunt at these poor Christians." Again, women assumed prominent places in the mob action, their threats prompting Tuckapawillin's wife, his twelve-year-old son, a woman who served as a nurse for Job's children, and that woman's daughter to "[escape] away into the woods." The threats were serious enough, the time they had to escape so brief, that Tuckapawillin's "wife left a nursing infant behind her, with her husband, of about three months old, which affliction was a very sore trial to the poor man, his wife and eldest son gone, and the poor infant no breast to nourish it." All but one member of the party eventually reached Deer Island. Tuckapawillin's son who fled Marlborough died of "famine" before he could be reunited with his family.[141] In this incident, a group of Marlborough's residents—led by women—doubted both the sincerity of New England's allies and the judgment of their own government in its ability to protect them. Their frustration boiled over in the presence of Job's friends and family, and their actions resulted in the death of a child.

Examples from King Philip's War featured women leading attacks on Indians as part of the informal public sphere, though an incident in 1707 demonstrates that acceptance of women in this role was not limited to violence against Indians or even enemies. In July 1707, following a failed attack on the fortified community of Port Royal in Acadia, a group of women met a boat with colonial officers bearing official news of the expedition at Scarlet's Wharf in Boston. The news had already reached Boston through less official channels. According to John Winthrop, the women mocked their own soldiers, greeting them, "'Welcome, souldiers!' & presented them a great wooden sword, & said withall 'Fie, for shame! pull off those iron spitts which hang by your sides; for wooden ones is all the fashion now.'" Angered by this insulting treatment, "one of the officers said, 'Peace, sille woman, &c,' which irritated the female tribe so much the more." In response, the greeting party of women accompanied the soldiers along their route and "cal'd out to one another as they past along the streets, 'Is your piss-pot charg'd, neighbor? Is your piss-pot charg'd, neighbor? So-ho, souse the cowards. Salute Port-Royal. Holloo, neighbor, holloo.'" Upending Boston's gendered, aged, and economic order, the women were joined by a group of children and servants who followed the officers through the town. This remarkable mob taunted the officers, carrying wooden swords and other children's war toys while shouting "Port-Royal! Port-Royal!"[142]

In an encounter reminiscent of traditional "shaming" processions such as charivari and its English counterpart, skimmington, this mob of women publicly shamed the returning men for failing to successfully perform the roles of man and soldier.[143] They had been planning the encounter, meeting the soldiers at the wharf with a large wooden sword. By presenting the soldiers with a wooden sword and demanding their iron equivalents, the women of Boston simultaneously challenged the soldiers' manhood and adulthood. Winthrop—speaking from the perspective of the formal public sphere—described the group of women as a "female tribe," a phrase that hints at a wild nature associated with Indigenous women. When an officer called one of the members of the group a "sille woman," the women increased the force of their gendered assault. Adopting a military cadence in their chant—"Is your piss-pot charg'd, neighbor? Is your piss-pot charg'd, neighbor?"—the women took on the role of soldiers themselves. They called upon the other women of the neighborhood to empty their chamber pots on the heads of the passing men. In doing so, they asked their neighbors "is your piss-pot charged?" mockingly linking the charged, masculine—even phallic—musket to the full receptacle of a chamber pot.[144]

In a second account of the incident at Scarlet's Wharf, Cotton Mather accused Governor Joseph Dudley's forces of being "afraid of having the Fort fall into their Hands" and of running home "as fast as their Canvas Sails cou'd carry them." In Mather's narrative, the women of Boston were the heroes of the day. He wrote, "The Good Women in Boston, could not forbear their Out-cries, when they met in the Streets, on this Occasion. Says one of them, *Why, our Cowards imagined the Fort at Port-Royal would fall before them, like the Walls of Jericho. Another Answers, Why did not the Block heads then stay out Seven Days to see? What ail'd the Traitors to come away in Five Days Time after they got there?*" This taunting reportedly had the desired effect. "The Cry of the People must be Satisfyed," Mather crowed. The governor attempted another attack with similar results. As it happened, Cotton Mather loathed Governor Dudley and, wasting no opportunity to undermine him, published this account in London. He clearly relished the idea that a group of women could shame Dudley into a second failed attempt at Port Royal. It is interesting to note that in Mather's account, he omitted the masses of children and servants so prominent in Winthrop's telling. Instead, Mather chose to highlight the women's role in channeling "The Cry of the People" and focused on their accusations of treason.[145]

This incident appears to have split the opinions of men working within the formal public sphere along political lines. As usual, the larger community appears to have supported (or at least sympathized with) the small uprising. Among prominent men involved in the business of secular leadership, Governor Dudley did not appreciate the women's martial activities, while John Winthrop seemed uncomfortable with the work of the "female tribe." Only Mather's report of the incident portrays the women as heroines, likely due to the trouble they caused Dudley. Cotton Mather—as well as many other men—had little problem turning positive accounts of women's participation in the border wars into political and religious propaganda.

New England's writers and policy makers viewed English and Native women's war making in the seventeenth and early eighteenth centuries within the context of early modern gender spheres. Modern historians—despite their awareness of later developments that began to more formally exclude women from war making—have forgotten or overlooked accounts of women's impressed and voluntary participation in the region's wars. Only now are we beginning to see clearly once more what Cotton Mather and others considered commonplace: women were necessary participants in

New England's wars of colonization. Whether marching as a mob through the streets of Boston to shame ineffective colonial soldiers or defending a fortified settlement that served as both vanguard and bulwark of the colonial strategy, English women assumed central and supporting roles in these conflicts. They were public actors whose violent war making protected existing territorial and economic gains and who sought, through further colonization, to increase those gains for themselves, their communities, and their polities. As their behavior was conservative rather than transgressive, English women who made war found support in government policies and preexisting gender ideologies that relied upon their wartime participation within the informal public sphere and as members of settler-soldiers' households. Native women found a more mixed reception, as New England's elite initially accepted female sachems' authority, casting them as actors within the formal public sphere through the late seventeenth century. But these same players rejected ordinary Indigenous women's formal roles in ritual torture and as combatants, seeing them as indicative of a disorderly and savage nature. By the middle decades of the eighteenth century, however, New Englanders would become engaged in a transatlantic conversation that sought to reimagine all women's martial roles within a changing relationship between gender and spheres of action.

CHAPTER TWO

Everyone Ran to Help
Rank and Gender in the Wars of New France

In fall 1699, Madeleine de Verchères, a young Canadian woman of rank, wrote a letter to the comtesse de Maurepas citing rumors that French noble-women had led peasants against France's enemies in the European theater of King William's War.[1] Verchères had heard stories of the daughter of the marquis de la Charce, Philis de la Tour-du-Pin de La Charce, who success-fully led her father's peasants against Savoy-allied armies in southeastern France with the help of her sister in 1692.[2] In her letter, Verchères requested a reward for her own military service, appealing to patriotism as she asserted that the women of New France were equally eager to take up arms in the name of their king. As she wrote, she may have kept in mind the reputation for fierceness that the women of New France had developed during several decades of war against the Iroquois and the English.

Eyewitness as well as anecdotal evidence suggests that both French and Native women of all ranks living in or near the colonies that the French called Canada and Acadia took part in the conflicts of the northeastern bor-derlands. This was particularly true in the highly contested upstream re-gion of Canada near Montreal. In her memoirs, Canadian-born Sister Marie Morin wrote that while living at Montreal's Hôtel-Dieu in the 1660s, she was able to look down from the bell tower onto fighting near the city. Mo-rin recorded the fear she felt when battles raged too close for comfort as well as the surging pride when watching battles farther away, as "everyone ran to help their brothers and risk their lives" to save the lives of others. Morin also recalled how, "many times" she saw ordinary women, "like Am-azons," armed and running to fight in the battles.[3]

Distinctions between ladies of rank and nonelite women in war were far more important under New France's seigneurial system than in New England, where wealthier Englishwomen tended to live in safer regions and lacked more formal military roles. New France's seigneurial system of he-reditary land grants held by lords and ladies ensured that rank—and the social hierarchy it imposed—would significantly influence women's par-ticipation in the border wars. The nature of the seigneurial system, with its stratified society and insufficiently protected settlements huddled along the

St. Lawrence River, helped define specific wartime roles for elite and non-elite women. Elite French women, exercising authority within the formal public sphere, took on leadership roles as wives and daughters of seigneurs, as well as in their own names, after inheriting a seigneury. Ordinary women, who often had to choose to join a battle or flee to the nearest fort, participated in these wars as actors within the informal public sphere. French authors also drew distinctions between Native women of rank and nonelite Indigenous women, often associating allied, nonelite Native women rhetorically with their nonelite French counterparts. In doing so, French writers framed both European and allied Indigenous women's military participation within European traditions regarding the proper roles of ladies of rank and their social inferiors in the formal and informal public spheres.[4]

Writing later in her life, in the 1690s, Sister Morin's memoirs of Montreal described a period in New France's history known as the Iroquois Wars or the Beaver Wars. A series of brutal regional conflicts that saw some of the most dramatic examples of women's participation in colonial conflicts, the Beaver Wars dominated the first major phase of French colonization in Canada during the mid-seventeenth century. Although French colonists and their Huron and Algonquin allies fought the Iroquois for control of the St. Lawrence region throughout the seventeenth century, fighting was fiercest in the middle decades of that century. Indeed, the nascent settlement at Montreal barely survived, and the once-powerful Huron Confederacy was destroyed in 1649. The royal takeover of the colonial government in 1663, along with assistance from the newly arrived French Carignan-Salières Regiment, ultimately led to the temporary defeat of the Iroquois in 1667 after decades of devastating conflict.[5]

It was during the Beaver Wars and King William's War of the seventeenth century that women in New France gained their reputations for jumping into the fray. As in the case of New England, an expansionist system based on families pushing outward in vanguard communities contributed to laws that placed these families on the front lines. Similar to their British counterparts, French leaders embraced a strategy based on the establishment of a "safe" city (such as Quebec) and the gradual expansion outward from that beachhead.[6] French settlement in the St. Lawrence Valley was anchored by two major towns, a highly fortified administrative center at Quebec, founded in 1608, and Montreal, founded in 1642 as a center for trade and missionary work. Both settlements had approximately four hundred people in 1667. Neither had more than ten thousand in 1759. Merchants, religious orders, colonial administrators, and military officials used these

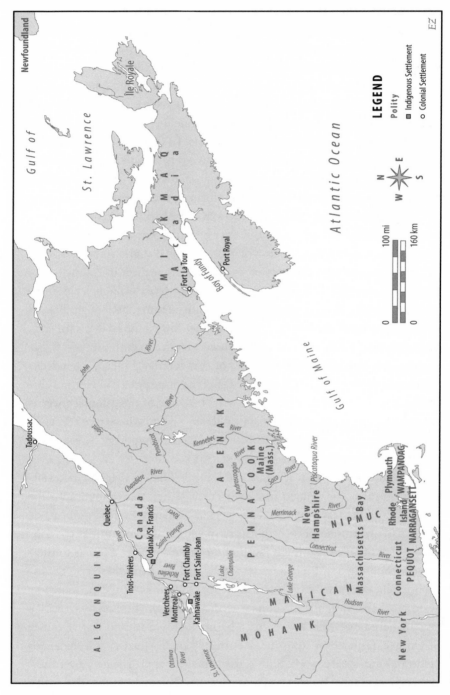

Northern extent of the northeastern borderlands, c. 1630–1700

LEGEND

Polity

■ Indigenous Settlement

○ Colonial Settlement

N

W E

S

100 mi

160 km

Newfoundland

Gulf of St. Lawrence

Atlantic Ocean

Gulf of Maine

Île Royale

MI'KMA'KI

Acadia

Port Royal

Bay of Fundy

Fort La Tour

St. John River

Saint River

Penobscot River

Kennebec River

Androscoggin River

Saco River

Piscataqua River

Merrimack River

Connecticut River

ABENAKI

PENNACOOK

Maine (Mass.)

New Hampshire

Massachusetts Bay

NIPMUC

Plymouth

WAMPANOAG

Rhode Island

Connecticut

PEQUOT NARRAGANSETT

MAHICAN

MOHAWK

New York

Hudson River

Lake George

Lake Champlain

Richelieu River

Fort Chambly

Fort Saint-Jean

Kahnawake

Montréal

Verchères

St. Lawrence River

Ottawa River

Trois-Rivières

Odanak/St. Francis

Saint-François River

Chaudière River

Québec

Canada

ALGONQUIN

Tadoussac

EZ

small towns as bases for their operations throughout New France. Despite strong official support, even in the early decades of the eighteenth century only about one-fifth of Canada's population lived in "urban" centers.[7] Rather than pushing outward in all directions from these centers as colonists did in New England, French colonists established seigneuries along the banks of the St. Lawrence River. By 1663, most of the colony's seigneuries— approximately 82.5 percent—were located downstream, near Quebec and Trois-Rivières, with more than half of those near Quebec. Although only nine seigneuries were established near Montreal by 1663, these lay closest to Indian-controlled territory to the west and were thus the most vulnerable to attack.[8] Indeed, most of the incidents of women's participation in war making from the seventeenth century took place near the seigneuries in and around Montreal.

As part of the colony's defensive strategy, French men from sixteen to sixty years of age were required to serve in a militia that protected the area near their homes. Another force, comprising Native allies and Canadian volunteers, responded to more distant military threats. Although lacking the better organization and fortifications of their counterparts in New England, both groups faced the greatest danger when caught off guard by raids that occurred while they worked near their homes. Canada's forts could only exercise control over a small area surrounding each installation, and settlers who chose to live closer to the fields they farmed lacked the protection of a palisade. Some homes near Montreal had reinforced shutters, while others downstream became increasingly less fortified, a response to the lower likelihood of attack. Colonists living near Trois-Rivières took shelter at the nearest fort when under attack, and those settled near Quebec faced incursions even less frequently, though they, too, experienced the pervasive sense of oppressive fear that characterized life in the northeastern borderlands.[9] In nearly all cases, Canadians lacked the benefit of the fortified villages and towns that, when properly staffed, protected New Englanders from devastating military campaigns.

"La Bonne Femme Primot":
French and Native Women as Obedient Warriors

Sister Marie Morin's enthralling description of French women as Amazons running to battle in the early decades of Montreal's history speaks to a larger pattern of women's war making in the region. Such women were likely not of elite social status and suffered from the dearth of fortifications in the region. Few accounts detailing their actions have survived, probably due to a general lack of sources from the period as well as to the hectic nature of the battles. Of the incidents that were recorded, many demonstrate similar characteristics in regard to language and narrative. Most noted a woman's courage and bravery, occasionally referring to her as an "Amazon" or even a "lioness," while also placing her actions within the context of early modern gender roles. Unlike their counterparts among New France's nobility, most of these women would not have been considered women of rank with their own roles to play in a formal public sphere. Their informal martial activities as public actors were—in theory—undertaken with the approval of husbands or priests. Indeed, women who participated in the colony's wars were described as upholding both European gender roles and Christian morality.

One of the best-documented incidents of the mid-century wars involving a nonelite French woman occurred when a small group of Iroquois soldiers attacked Martine Messier Primot. It was in Primot's story that French writers fully articulated the idea of the violent and virtuous peasant woman of French or Native origin. At least four separate accounts noted the incident at the time and in the immediate decades that followed. The earliest version appeared in the 1651–52 edition of the *Jesuit Relations*, the Jesuit order's annually published report of their missionary activities abroad. In this account, Father Paul Ragueneau wrote that a French woman had "received five or six wounds" but "did not die of them; her courage brought her out of the danger."[10] He also elaborated on the story in his journal. According to Ragueneau, on July 29, 1652, two Iroquois men, using a field of corn as cover, attacked "Martine, wife of Antoine Primot, who defended herself courageously" until help could arrive from the nearby fort at Montreal. The Ursuline Mother Superior Marie de l'Incarnation also wrote briefly of the incident to her son in September of that year, indicating the value religious leaders placed on Primot and her courageous defense.[11]

These earlier accounts did not, by themselves, explain the extraordinary cultural impact of this event. In Francois Dollier de Casson's *Histoire du Montréal*, new details fleshed out the story. As the Superior of the Sulpician Order in New France, Dollier de Casson had direct access to many of his subjects when he wrote his history in the early 1670s. By that time, Martine Primot had become something of a folk heroine, known in Montreal as "la bonne femme Primot" and "Parmanda." Dollier de Casson wrote that this "woman of virtue . . . was attacked within two gun-shots of the château. As soon as she was attacked she shouted loudly." Three Iroquois men emerged from hiding and "threw themselves upon her to kill her with their hatchets." Primot defended herself like a "lioness," but was knocked down and nearly scalped. As her attacker moved in for the kill, "our amazon . . . raised herself and, more fierce than ever, caught hold of this monster so forcibly by a place which modesty forbids us to mention that he could not free himself." Although hit with a hatchet several times, Primot fended off the attack until several French men arrived to help. In the aftermath of the melee, Primot became confused when one of the rescuers embraced her in relief. Using her remaining strength, she struck him forcefully. Primot received the curious nickname "Parmanda" when, asked why she hit the man, she replied, "Parmanda . . . I thought he wanted to kiss me." Dollier de Casson remarked that the word "Parmanda" was a garbled version of Primot's own words. According to the author, Primot spoke with a provincial accent, and it is likely that she said, "par mon dieu!" or "I swear to God, I thought he wanted to kiss me!" Her alternate pronunciation of the phrase stuck with the colony's favorite early heroine as a nickname into old age.[12]

This compelling incident reflects several major themes common to reports of both European and Native women in combat. Dollier de Casson carefully reminded readers of Primot's virtue at the beginning and the end of the story. Although Primot transformed into both a lioness and a fierce Amazon who grasped and injured an Iroquois man's genitals, the author lauded her "as a woman of virtue" and emphasized that she continued to defend that honor when she hit one of the French men who came to her rescue. These common elements, the virtuous woman compelled to perform graphically violent acts and subsequently praised by men who sanctioned her actions, were repeated in stories about French and Native women.

Due to the nature of New France's society, particularly the prominence of religious orders and the greater literacy of their members, more sources describing the wartime actions of nonelite Native women than nonelite French women have survived. Jesuit missionaries, as well as women such as the Ursuline leader Marie de l'Incarnation, took great interest in the actions of ordinary Native women. The founder of the Ursuline order in New France, Marie Guyart Martin, joined the order as Marie de l'Incarnation in 1633 at the age of thirty-four following the death of her husband. More than any other writer in New France, Marie de l'Incarnation reported numerous accounts of Indigenous women who fought against their attackers and would-be captors. Moreover, far greater numbers of Native women lived in the highly contested area around and west of Montreal, increasing the likelihood that they might be required to fight. Many of these women also appear to have been captured or attacked while traveling through the forest. Nearly all of these accounts of nonelite Native women's participation in the wars followed patterns similar to those of nonelite French women, praising their violence yet highlighting their virtuous obedience to God and to their husbands.

That colonial accounts of nonelite European and Indigenous women's violence deployed such similar tropes testifies to the importance of rank in French understandings of the relationship between women's war making, leadership, and status—regardless of national origin. French reports of Indigenous women's martial activities clearly demonstrate that French authors recognized distinctions in rank among these women. As with ideologies that favored rank over gender in determining access to power and the formal public sphere, studies suggest that European colonists at times also privileged rank over ethnic and racial identities in the sixteenth and seventeenth centuries. This phenomenon was particularly evident before European gender and racial ideologies became increasingly fixed in the eighteenth century. Tellingly, the privileging of rank and lineage over gender or ethnicity was especially apparent and most persistent in regions where Indigenous polities held greater power to shape these discourses.[13] Although French missionaries certainly never lacked for words to describe colonial encounters, the power to shape such encounters did not come so easily. Given that the tattered French colonial project barely limped its way through the wars of the mid-seventeenth century, it is perhaps unsurprising that French authors sometimes saw more similarities between women of the same rank than of the same race or ethnicity.

When Marie de l'Incarnation wrote to her son in September 1654, she related news of the recent peace treaty between the French and the Iroquois. Obviously intrigued by Iroquois women of rank among the visiting delegation, she mentioned that the Iroquois had promised to send five women to live among the French. These women were the daughters of "women of quality" who held a rank that de l'Incarnation translated as "*capitainesse*." The Ursuline leader reported that these female leaders "have voting powers in the councils" and advocate for political action "as the men do." In this case, the capitainesses apparently initiated the current peace efforts by sending the first ambassadors.[14] The following year, Marie de l'Incarnation seemed pleased to announce a new alliance that she had established with one of the women. This "*capitainesse* with her company" had visited the Ursuline mission and, apparently persuaded by the testimony of a young Huron girl, promised to send her own daughter to the French. Marie de l'Incarnation later received word that the Iroquois leader would be sending her sister instead of her very young daughter. To cement this potentially valuable friendship, de l'Incarnation sent the Iroquois leader a dress for her daughter and gifts for women who de l'Incarnation identified as retainers or courtiers of the capitainesse. Ultimately, the relationship forged between the two women resulted in the Iroquois leader's growing interest in Christianity and her willingness to use her influence to encourage other Iroquois to investigate the religion.[15]

Religious leaders in New France valued the conversion of Indigenous women of rank who might encourage further conversions and even lead other converts in their polities. For instance, in addition to proselytizing to her followers, the Iroquois capitainesse of de l'Incarnation's letters took under her wing a newly arrived Jesuit, Father Dablon, and began teaching him her language in 1655.[16] A beneficiary of the support of a Native woman of rank, Dablon eventually became the Jesuit Superior of New France. In 1674, he reported to the French Jesuit Superior that Marie Tsaouenté, "an Iroquois woman of rank," fled her people after her conversion to Christianity had "deprived [her] of her rank in the councils and assemblies." Dablon described Tsaouenté as "very intelligent" and praised her understanding of Christian doctrine. French missionaries likely appreciated the recreation of familiar hierarchies that even an exiled woman of rank offered Christian Indians. Despite a loss of stature within her own polity, Tsaouenté appears to have assumed a position of leadership within the Native Christian community, "instructing the Iroquois catechumens" and leading informal worship in the cabin she shared with three other families.[17]

In addition to the leadership positions French authorities recognized and even—to a certain extent—attempted to preserve among Indigenous women of rank, accounts of nonelite Native women's war making also reflected European ideas regarding the appropriate behavior of women based on rank. Marie de l'Incarnation was particularly interested in accounts of nonelite Native women killing to save themselves or their families. A close follower of the colony's military situation, she sent letters reporting these incidents to correspondents, most notably her son in France. In one 1655 letter, she wrote of an Algonquin woman who was kidnapped with her husband and children by the Iroquois. The Iroquois bound the woman's husband but left her free. The husband encouraged his wife to free the family, saying that "if she wanted, she could save them all." De l'Incarnation wrote that the woman "understood what that meant" and "took her time before seizing a hatchet." Then, "with an unparalleled courage" she "split the captain's head, cut the neck of another," and frightened off the rest with her "furious" fighting.

She then untied her husband and the group made their way to safety.[18] Marie de l'Incarnation portrayed the wife's performance of almost uncontrolled violence as a display of order and obedience—an act approved by her husband when he granted his wife permission to transform into a "furious" warrior. As a result, a potentially transgressive moment was reworked into a vignette illustrating Native couples adhering to European and Christian ideas about the proper relationship between a husband in charge and his dutiful wife.

Writing of an event with a similar moral, Marie de l'Incarnation recounted the story of a husband and wife team from the Algonquin Petite Nation. The couple embarked together in a canoe to warn their people of an impending attack in 1647 after a group of Iroquois killed their parents near Trois-Rivières. When the pair discovered another canoe with seven or eight Iroquois, the husband told his wife that he wanted to attack the Iroquois, "provided she was willing to assist him." The letter reported the woman's reply that "she would follow him willingly, and that she would live and die with him." Although perhaps romanticized, these words evoke the image of an officer and a soldier, a husband and wife, setting out on what seemed to be a suicide mission while maintaining a "proper" hierarchy. After making their decision, the husband and wife advanced on the Iroquois canoe. As they approached, they heard the Iroquois shouting triumphantly and saw four other canoes filled with men. Quickly changing their plan, the husband left his wife on the bank and, shooting his gun in the air, pretended to be an Iroquois rejoining the group. Returning his signal with their guns, the Iroquois signaled that they had taken forty prisoners from his own Petite Nation. He rejoined his wife and the two slipped away to gather a group of young men who helped the husband rescue the captives.[19]

While obedience and virtue in marriage was a favorite moral in stories of nonelite Native women's war making, submission to colonial power served just as well. In a 1658 letter to her son, Marie de l'Incarnation told of the capture of two Algonquin women and their children. She described one of these women as particularly "courageous," stabbing her captor in the stomach with his knife and driving off his companions—who had likely decided that subduing these particular captives was not worth the potential gain. Marie de l'Incarnation then noted that following their victory, the women gathered the weapons and baggage their captors had left behind and "brought their booty to the feet of Monsieur the Governor."[20] The Ursuline's approval of the women's purported decision to lay their spoils of war at the Governor's feet suggests a satisfying submission to European authority and a reassuring return to order at the end of the incident.

Jesuit missionaries used similar language to recount instances of Native women's war making, emphasizing virtue and obedience to both husband and to God. The *Jesuit Relation* of 1660–61 described an incident in which eighty Iroquois attacked a trade expedition made up of two French men and thirty Indians from the Poisson Blanc nation near Trois-Rivières. During the attack, the Poisson Blanc "fought with such ardor that they suffered themselves to be riddled with bullets rather than surrender" to the Iroquois. The author of the account went on to praise the women in the group, who "were no whit inferior to the men in courage, sparing no effort to secure their own death, rather than fall alive into hands that would surely have made them suffer as many deaths as they were given days to live."[21] Fighting alongside French and French-allied Algonquin men, these women attempted to preserve their lives as well as Franco-Algonquin control of the region. Equally important to the author, the women also fought to save themselves from torture and a disorderly paganism he believed they would face as captives of the Iroquois.

In 1667, Claude Jean Allouez related the story of a pair of converts, mother and daughter, who escaped Iroquois detention only to be recaptured. As captives, the women would have likely faced pressure to integrate into their new community and renounce Christianity. In his report, Allouez was careful to note their piety and submission to God, writing that they "had received from [God] unfailing and extraordinary succor, very recently learned by experience that God never forsakes those who put their trust in him." Allouez wrote that the two women, left alone with only one guard, "asked the Iroquois for a knife to use on a Beaver-skin" that the daughter "had been ordered to dress." The daughter stabbed the guard in the chest, "at the same time, imploring Heaven's aid," while the mother struck him on the head with a piece of wood. The two "left him for dead" and successfully escaped with some food. Allouez clearly equated what he described as "the fires and cruelties" of the unconverted Iroquois with the fires of Hell. He also saw the women's actions as proper and blessed by a patriarchal God, their father in heaven.[22]

Despite widespread French admiration of allied Native women who fought against the Iroquois, writers expressed their revulsion when witnessing these women as participants in ritual torture. This revulsion was, perhaps, one reason why French writers made a greater effort to place allied Native women's "proper" actions within accepted European gender conventions whenever possible. As in the case of New England, French observers either did not recognize or did not accept the formal role Indigenous women played in ritual torture, preferring to interpret their actions as disrupting gendered order rather than upholding it. In 1635, Father Paul Le Jeune recorded a visit to an unnamed polity at war with the Iroquois. Le Jeune wrote that on October 23 a group of men returned with an Iroquois prisoner. Clearly disapproving of the treatment the man had already received, Le Jeune watched as the man was led to a cabin, "children, girls, and women striking him, some with sticks, others with stones, as he entered." His hosts attempted to reassure him with the information that the captive had been involved in the death of three French men. As Le Jeune and his companions were considered fictive kinsmen of the Frenchmen who had died, Le Jeune's hosts even graciously offered to allow their French guests to participate in the ritual. In spite of the offer—or perhaps as a result of it—Le Jeune seemed particularly pleased when his hosts chose to spare the young Iroquois man's life in favor of negotiating a peace.[23]

In a 1636 report, Father Le Jeune described an incident involving another captive so as to contrast what he viewed as appropriate and inappropriate behavior for Native women in war. His subject was a young female captive who arrived marching on an empty stomach "at the head of the whole troop." The woman led the tired group, as she had noted that her captors killed prisoners who fell behind, "enduring the fatigue better than a man." Le Jeune observed that in addition to a "modest face," she had "so bold an eye that I took her for a man."[24] The Jesuit seemed fascinated by this woman who, in spite of her boldness verging on manliness, demonstrated resourcefulness and an ability to suffer quietly. After describing the captive woman's positive attributes, Le Jeune then went on to criticize the behavior of his own allies. The male prisoners in the same party as the modest yet bold woman faced death at the hands of their captors. Le Jeune observed that when one man reached the shore, "the women and children fell upon him, each one trying to see which could strike the hardest blows." Comparing his allies to animals, Le Jeune expressed his distaste when a woman bit a man's finger, "trying to tear it off, as a dog would do." She eventually cut the finger off and attempted to feed it to the prisoner. After her effort failed, "this Tigress" roasted the finger and gave it to a group of children.[25] When Le Jeune objected, a group of women approached him, saying that the Iroquois "did still worse things to their fathers, husbands, and children, asking me if I loved such a wicked nation."[26] Unmoved, Le Jeune continued to berate both the men and women participating in the ritual. The following day, a group of Algonquin criticized a lack of French participation in the war, but still presented the captive Iroquois woman as a gift to the French. They hoped she might serve to mollify the French, who they believed remained angry over the earlier death of the three French men. At Le Jeune's urging, the French then made plans to eventually send the woman to study with nuns across the Atlantic in France, perhaps a seemingly appropriate choice, given her reported physical and mental fortitude.[27]

Several similar accounts of women participating in torture appeared in the *Jesuit Relations* during the 1630s, although only a few surfaced in later decades.[28] It is possible that Native allies may have simply given up trying to share this aspect of their war making with their French friends. These accounts of nonelite Indigenous women participating in what appeared to be disorderly, senseless torture contrasted with positive stories of ordinary French and Native women. Reportedly fighting for Christian virtues under the approving gazes of European authority figures and even God, these other women appeared to act appropriately as nonelite women within the informal public sphere. Accounts using similar language to describe non-elite French and Native women's participation in the border wars largely disappeared by the mid-1670s. Documents written by government officials would replace the earlier reports and letters from missionaries who had a special interest in those women.

Changes in colonial authority also resulted in new military strategies and roles for nonelite women and their families. Between 1687 and 1697, the region to the south and west of Montreal underwent a period of increased fortification in response to devastating Iroquois attacks. Montreal built a formidable palisade in 1688 capable of harboring refugees, and in rural areas, farmers were required to fortify the area around a public building located in a centralized area such as a church, where families could retreat with their possessions. As in New England, life in these communities during times of danger was unpleasant; however, the organization of people within the fortified areas reflected differences between the two societies. In New England, where town-based militias were of greater importance and the British military had not yet taken on a substantial role, settler-soldiers hosted assigned families in their homes. The rural communities of New France were often forced to surrender crops, timber, and even their better buildings to officers, while soldiers and residents lived in "makeshift" homes with bark roofs and straw for beds. This arrangement, quite different from the household-forts of New England, represented a growing stratification within the military institutions of New France as well as greater imperial control over matters of defense.[29]

Despite a new reliance upon metropolitan France, Canadian officials continued to acknowledge the strategic potential of ordinary families. The Conseil Supérieur took preventive action in January 1686, when the war that would later be called King William's War seemed imminent.[30] Acting on concerns that the population of New France was insufficiently armed, the Conseil passed a law regulating the transfer of firearms, in which members agreed that the safety of the colony depended on each household possessing sufficient weapons. Reports had reached the Conseil that creditors had been seizing guns in lieu of payment and that inhabitants had been selling their weapons to make ends meet. The new law applied to all people "of whatever quality and condition" and specified that inhabitants might sell any excess weapons beyond the number needed to "arm each father of the family, his [presumably male] children and servants who had reached fourteen years of age." Those who failed to comply faced a fine of 50 livres.[31]

Although the 1686 order only mandated the arming of male members of households, accounts of nonelite French women's participation in these conflicts suggest that women remained potential combatants and defenders of New France and its Native allies throughout the seventeenth century. Madeleine de Verchères's letter to the comtesse de Maurepas announcing the willingness of French women to fight in the king's wars suggests this practice continued. Her words were corroborated by a report in Sulpician Superior Francois Vachon de Belmont's history of Canada, written in the first decades of the eighteenth century. Vachon de Belmont reported that on May 7, 1691, "Guillon's wife; Grégoire, his wife; Goulet, the farmer from Lachenaye, and some others defended a breach of forty feet against 300 Iroquois."[32] Regardless of the veracity of the claim that a handful of settlers—with the help of "some others"—succeeded in their defense against such improbable odds, Vachon de Belmont's account suggests that ordinary women still had a role to play as public actors in warfare.

In one later case, a widow attempted to defend her home from an Iroquois attack on the seigneury of Chesnaye, near Montreal, with the help of a neighbor. According to a chronicle written shortly after the end of Queen Anne's War, the Iroquois approached the seigneury in the autumn of 1693. The residents of the seigneury were settled in for the winter, and the widow had been entertaining an unmarried male friend that night. When he attempted to leave, the widow, purportedly afraid, asked him to stay. The man complied and remained at her house with his gun and his small dog. In the middle of the night, the man awakened to the sound of the dog barking. When he saw that the seigneury was on fire, he woke the woman, who had her own gun, and put her to work as a sentinel at the corner of the house. As the Iroquois closed in, the French man and woman went inside and began their defense. Alternating between guns, the man shot at the Iroquois while the woman charged the used gun and handed it back to him. After holding out the entire night, the man and woman were able to escape to a French fort in a canoe.[33] Much as they did in the Beaver Wars that Marie Morin watched from her bell tower, nonelite women received praise as they continued to defend against attacks alongside their husbands and neighbors until the Great Peace of 1701 shifted the theater of war to the Atlantic coast.

La Commandante: Women of Rank in New France

The earliest account of a French woman of rank taking part in a battle in New France comes from 1640s Acadia, a time and a place marked by a bloody struggle between two local seigneurs, Charles de Saint-Étienne de la Tour and Charles de Menou d'Aulnay. Both sought greater control over Acadia and favor with the King of France, frequently resorting to armed conflict and vicious diplomatic maneuvering. Living in the heart of this contested region, La Tour in particular was not above seeking help from Boston when backed into a corner. His wife, Françoise-Marie Jacquelin de la Tour, played a large role in her husband's Acadian empire, traveling twice across the Atlantic to France to formally seek aid from the vice admiral. Following the second, disastrous visit in 1643 or 1644, after her husband had been branded a traitor for his dealings with Boston, Madame La Tour returned to Acadia with the help of the English. This assistance was necessary because the king had forbidden her return to Acadia.[34]

When Sieur La Tour left the fort to seek help in Boston in early 1645, d'Aulnay seized the opportunity and attacked the La Tour seigneury near present-day Saint John, New Brunswick.[35] Madame La Tour and the remaining soldiers at the fort held off the attack for three days and nights before d'Aulnay was forced to withdraw outside the range of the fort's guns. On the fourth day, Madame La Tour and her men were betrayed by a Swiss man in their company who had formed an alliance with d'Aulnay. Madame La Tour finally surrendered to d'Aulnay under the condition that he spare their lives. In his 1672 account (written after Sieur La Tour's death), Nicolas Denys used language that placed Madame La Tour in command, referring to "her guns" and "her men" and giving her the title "*la Commandante*."[36] He noted that as a woman of rank, Madame La Tour was not hanged with her men when d'Aulnay broke his word. Instead, d'Aulnay forced her to watch with a noose around her neck as her men died. Madame La Tour would die approximately three weeks later, reportedly by poisoning.[37]

D'Aulnay mounted a vigorous and successful defense of his actions against La Tour and his wife, producing documents from inhabitants and missionaries that convinced the king that d'Aulnay had acted to protect Acadia while smashing a nascent rebellion. In a deposition taken in May 1645, La Tour's own men painted a picture of a Protestant wife who mistreated representatives of the Catholic faith in Acadia. They also testified that she had hoped to convert the fort and draw her husband into a betrayal she had planned with the British. According to his witnesses, d'Aulnay attacked the stronghold of a rebellion against the king and Catholicism. After her capture, they claimed, Madame La Tour was well cared for but died three weeks later of emotional distress.[38] D'Aulnay and his deponents sidestepped Madame La Tour's role in the defense of the fort, preferring to emphasize her part in stirring up a rebellion against God and king, noting simply that these attacks were met with return fire. Neither d'Aulnay nor Denys contested Madame La Tour's position as head of the fort; they chose merely to present either unflattering or heroic portrayals of her leadership, depending upon their perspective and agenda.

Madame La Tour's military leadership and sporadically skillful diplomacy was not out of place in the Atlantic world of the mid-seventeenth century. French women of rank at that time took on highly visible roles as public actors in the country's conflicts, leading troops in battle and defending their estates. During the English Civil War, the Royalist Charlotte, Countess of Derby, negotiated and sustained a three-month defense of her husband's castle in Lancashire in 1644.[39] Such incidents represent the waning of an older tradition that included Emma, Countess of Norfolk (c. 1075), Blanche of Castile, Queen of France (d. 1252), Isabella, Duchess of Lorraine (d. 1453), and Margaret of Anjou (1430–82). These women of rank—along with dozens of others stretching back hundreds if not thousands of years— defended their castles and led troops on the battlefield as wives, regents, and landholders in their own right. At play was a complex melding of ideas regarding the concept of a deputy husband, a widow or regent in control of an estate, and pre-eighteenth-century noblewomen's roles within the formal public sphere. A woman of rank could and did represent a keep or fort and reserved the right to direct troops under her own or her husband's command. In New France, where—unlike New England—a system of nobility persisted throughout the colonial period, women continued this tradition during the seventeenth century.

Participation in military activities and colonization was not restricted to women in charge of forts and seigneuries. Female leaders of religious orders and institutions in New France also took a keen interest in wars that they viewed as both secular and sacred struggles.[40] Well-educated, informed, and unmarried, some of these women—as Sister Marie Morin noted—watched as melees raged uncomfortably close to the institutions where they lived and worked. Of the few surviving sources written by women in seventeenth-century New France, most were composed by nuns and their lay associates. Unsurprisingly, these women also received the most substantial biographical treatments of the early female colonists.[41] Their actions, letters, and memoirs reveal a remarkable understanding of the colony's military strategy and offer more intimate insights into the ways in which a well-connected woman might understand and participate in New France's earlier wars. In the case of Jeanne Mance of Montreal, their stories also demonstrate that, despite early attempts to establish separate roles for men and women in the new settlements along the St. Lawrence, these boundaries sometimes broke down quickly. In such cases, a suitable woman might rush in to fill voids in leadership.

Jeanne Mance was perhaps the most active female leader in the early wars, a laywoman closely connected to the major religious orders in New France. Recruited in France by the Société de Notre-Dame de Montréal, Mance cofounded Montreal with Paul de Chomedey de Maisonneuve in May 1642 and established its hospital, the Hôtel-Dieu, soon after. As a laywoman unconfined by a nun's vows, Mance seemed to embody the secular and sacred parties that comprised New France itself. One of Mance's contemporaries, Dollier de Casson, contended that her participation in the founding of Montreal was essential to its success. Dollier de Casson described her cofounders' search for a "girl or woman of character sufficiently heroic and of determination sufficiently masculine to come to this country and take charge of all the supplies and merchandise while at the same time acting as nurse to the sick and wounded." This quasi-martial language celebrated a woman who chose a vocation Dollier de Casson referred to as "almost unheard of" and who became a minor celebrity before she left home, even meeting with the Queen of France.[42]

The description of Mance as "heroic" and of a "masculine" determination may have also referred to her role in saving the town she founded. Originally chosen to "take charge within" the town while another was to take "charge of the colony as a whole and lead in war," the arrangement fell apart as Mance became increasingly involved with these other aspects of governing. In the late 1640s, devastating military attacks and financial catastrophe severely weakened Montreal. Iroquois military successes had left "this whole country ... terror-stricken, especially by the sufferings and wholesale destruction of the Hurons." Dollier de Casson wrote that Mance feared for the continued existence of her town as well as "all of Canada," which she realized depended on the security Montreal provided as a "bulwark" against attacks further downstream. Deciding to seek help in France, Mance left the colony in 1649. She returned the next year, having recruited a new French director for the company and in possession of an official contract establishing Montreal that she hoped would bind the colonists closer together.[43]

Despite Mance's efforts, conditions continued to deteriorate and, in 1651, Mance dispatched her cofounder, Paul de Chomedey de Maisonneuve, to France. Aware that Montreal desperately needed military reinforcement, Mance offered to exchange 22,000 livres she had received from the hospital's benefactress, the widowed Angélique Faure de Bullion, for "one hundred arpents of the seigneury's domain, with half of the buildings." The deal was lopsided in Maisonneuve's favor and designed to protect the town. Maisonneuve left for France in possession of a letter Mance wrote to Bullion that he used to secure the 22,000 livres. Madame de Bullion donated an additional 20,000 livres, which helped fund reinforcements for the city and prevented the destruction of Montreal.[44]

Living in the relative safety of Quebec (downstream from Mance's Montreal), Marie de l'Incarnation wrote hundreds of letters to correspondents, including her son Claude Martin. Although she did not experience the frequent attacks that Jeanne Mance faced upstream in Montreal, she maintained a high level of interest in the colony's military affairs, politics, and diplomacy. Responding to her son's request for information regarding a major French invasion of Iroquois territory, the Ursuline leader described how the French detachment had forded rivers and traveled on narrow roads littered with "stumps, roots, and dangerous holes."[45] Her vivid accounts of battles, troop movements, and strategy suggest that women of rank—whether through birth, marriage, or office—held strong, informed opinions regarding New France's military situation.[46]

Following the actions of Madame La Tour and Jeanne Mance in the 1640s and 1650s, authors in New France did not record further instances of women of rank defending seigneuries or towns until the final decade of the seventeenth century. Although Madame La Tour defended her husband's fort in 1640s Acadia, fortifying seigneuries in mainland Canada was not common practice until the 1680s. Rather, colonists under attack ran for shelter to the nearest town or fort or attempted to stand and fight in skirmishes similar to those Marie Morin saw from her bell tower. Furthermore, a period of relative peace between the Iroquois and the French from 1666 to 1686 reduced the need for women to defend seigneuries.

An account of one woman of rank who assisted in the defense of Montreal in 1661 sheds some light on this period prior to the fortification of the seigneuries along the St. Lawrence. That year was particularly successful for the Iroquois who, according to Marie de l'Incarnation, attacked areas near Quebec and captured or killed more than one hundred people near Montreal. Although the Ursuline leader described 1661 as one of their most difficult years, the *Relation* of that year was even more dramatic in its description. According to the *Relation*, an earthquake and a comet portended a disastrous year, the comet's "tail . . . pointed toward us and seemed to threaten us with a flagellation."[47] Supernatural language aside, the *Relation* did report two surprise attacks on Montreal in late winter and early spring of 1661, resulting in the capture of more than twenty men.

It was against this backdrop that one woman helped save a number of French men defending Montreal against an Iroquois attack in February 1661. Dollier de Casson reported that even as the French were outnumbered and thirteen were captured, the outcome would have been far worse were it not for "the courage displayed by the wife of . . . M. Du Clos." The woman in question was Barbe Poisson, married to judge and Montreal seigneur Gabriel LeSel Du Clos. The French were unprepared for an attack during the winter and only one man, Charles Le Moyne—a soldier, interpreter, and future seigneur of Longueuil—had a gun. Seeing that the defense was failing and knowing "that there was no man in her house to go to their aid, she herself took a load of muskets on her shoulders." Poisson, "fearless of a swarm of Iroquois whom she saw rush from every direction towards her house . . . ran to our Frenchmen who were being pursued." Recognizing Le Moyne as leader of this seemingly doomed group, Poisson "handed over her arms to him, thereby marvellously strengthening all our Frenchmen, and holding back the enemy." Although Dollier de Casson noted that not all of the weapons were in working condition, the guns "this amazon" delivered allowed the defenders to resist "until stronger assistance reached them."[48]

The case of Barbe Poisson suggests that both physical location and a certain amount of variation between degrees of rank among the elite played a role in how women's actions were perceived. As the wife of a prominent public figure in Montreal, she had access to a significant stash of weapons, which she was able to deliver to a man of similar rank, Charles Le Moyne. Although described as the wife of a "Monsieur," Poisson's actions were not those of a lady of rank defending a keep, but of a highly respectable woman acting as a member of the informal public sphere. Indeed, Dollier de Casson was particularly careful to note that she took this action because "there was no man in her house to go to their aid."[49] Poisson's narrative more closely follows those of respectable, nonelite wives helping to defend a group of houses and represents a period before the development of fortified seigneuries along the St. Lawrence River. As a resident of a town, rather than a mistress of a fortified seigneury, Poisson was cast as a woman of a slightly lesser rank.

The fortification of seigneuries in the 1680s increased opportunities for women of rank to lead troops in defense of their seigneuries. Unfortunately, fewer relevant sources are available from the final decades of the seventeenth century, and at least one instance of a woman of rank defending her seigneury was not recorded for another thirty years. That story, regarding Madame de Verchères, mother of Madeleine de Verchères, illustrates the difficulties in obtaining all accounts of such incidents. Madame de Verchères's own experience as a commander may have been even more successful than her daughter's later, more famous defense of their seigneury. However, her defense of the Verchères seigneury would not have been recorded were it not for her daughter's persistence and the family's dire financial straits following the death of her husband.

Madame de Verchères's war making only came to light in a 1722 history of New France written by an acquaintance of the family, Claude-Charles Bacqueville de la Potherie. In his history, La Potherie focused on Madeleine's efforts but asserted that Madame de Verchères's martial activities also deserved recognition. In 1690, two years before Madeleine's own defense, the Iroquois, "who had caused much disorder" along the St. Lawrence near Montreal that year, approached the Verchères seigneury. Seeing the Iroquois, Madame de Verchères ran to the redoubt, a separate, square fortified tower approximately fifty paces away. After watching one of her three or four men die from an Iroquois bullet, Madame de Verchères seized her gun, powder, and shot and returned to the redoubt through a covered walkway. According to La Potherie, she fought with the "courage of a seasoned soldier" and held out until help arrived from the marquis de Crisafy.[50] The belated recognition of Madame de Verchères's actions, which would have otherwise gone unnoticed, hints at the possibility of other, unrecorded incidents.

The heroism of Madame de Verchères's daughter, Madeleine, is one of the foundational narratives of Canadian nationalism.[51] Accounts from the late seventeenth and early eighteenth centuries agree that in October 1692, Madeleine de Verchères took command of her father's seigneury in the absence of both her parents. After seeing that a group of Iroquois had captured approximately twenty prisoners, Verchères ran inside, secured her family's fort, and climbed the watchtower. Putting on a soldier's hat and ensuring that Verchères possessed the appearance of a well-armed fort, Madeleine de Verchères fired a canon that alerted nearby seigneuries and allegedly forced an Iroquois retreat. Scholars believe that Verchères either wrote or approved two accounts of the incident. She wrote her first letter, a request for a pension for herself or a commission for her brother in 1699, seven years after the October 1692 incident. She also composed a much more elaborate—and less believable—version in the late 1720s that appears to have significantly influenced the later Canadian appropriation of Madeleine de Verchères as a national figure.[52]

Despite the fact that most accounts of Verchères's exploits were penned long after the event, Madeleine de Verchères did compose one letter describing the attack within a decade of the incident. Written with the hope of securing military compensation following her father's death, Verchères's letter to the comtesse de Maurepas made its way to France attached to a longer letter from the Intendant of New France, Jean Bochart de Champigny. Champigny sent the letters to the Minister of the Marine, Louis Phélypeaux, comte de Pontchartrain, who oversaw France's colonies along with its navy. The intendant's letter vouched for Verchères as well as for the contents of her letter to the comtesse de Maurepas—who was also the minister's wife. Madeleine de Verchères's early letter, unlike later accounts, told a much more credible story. The letter described how, after seeing twenty of the seigneury's people captured, she escaped to the fort and "mounted the bastion where the sentry was posted." There, she "donn[ed] the soldier's helmet, and went through a variety of movements intended to create the impression that we had quite a number of men in the fort."

Madeleine de Verchères also claimed that she set off the cannon to alert nearby garrisons that an attack was underway.[53]

When placed within the context of other attacks on forts in the north-eastern borderlands and corroborated by the letter Champigny sent to France not long after the battle, Verchères's experience falls into a familiar pattern. Perhaps, after successfully capturing people from the surrounding fields, the Iroquois approached the fortified portion of the seigneury. Believing it to be undefended, the raiders may have hoped to take more captives or set it on fire. Madeleine de Verchères's decision to use the tactic of inflating a fort's numbers to intimidate the enemy had been used successfully by men and women throughout the northeastern borderlands. When she shut the door and demonstrated with a cannon that the Verchères seigneury was capable of mounting a defense and calling for reinforcements, the Iroquois—who knew that taking a defended fort was difficult and time-consuming—simply turned and left Verchères, bringing their captives with them. Curiously, Madeleine de Verchères's triumph may have also been an Iroquois success.

Even if Verchères's account was exaggerated, those very embellishments and attempts at self-promotion offer insight into the relationship between rank and women's martial activities. In her letter, Verchères walked a fine line between expectations of femininity, patronage, and appealing to the ancient image of the woman of the keep exercising authority within the formal public sphere. The letter opened with false modesty as she demurred, "while my sex does not permit me to have other inclinations than those it requires of me, nevertheless, allow me, madam to tell you that I entertain sentiments which urge me on to aspire to fame quite as eagerly as many men." At the same time, Madeleine de Verchères put herself forward as a representative of the tradition of the lady-as-defender, setting herself apart from the other, lower-ranked women present at the attack, and noting that she paid "no heed to the lamentations of the women, whose husbands had been carried off" as she mounted her defense. Capping off her assertion of rank, she placed herself in the shoes of "women in France during the late war who went forth at the head of their peasants to repel the attacks of enemies invading their provinces."[54] For all its provincial reputation, the New France that Madeleine de Verchères presented replicated the social hierarchies and gendered martial ideologies of the French metropole.

Madeleine de Verchères located her actions and rank within an increasingly important network of transatlantic imperial relationships, claiming a Canadian identity as a female combatant in a war that demanded loyalty and bravery from all subjects of the French Crown. In seeking compensation for her military service, she first placed Canadians under the protection of Madame de Maurepas's husband, the French Minister of the Marine, "whom [Canadians] look upon as their protector." Following this display of deference to the royal minister and his wife, Verchères celebrated Canadians' devotion to the king, stating that the wars against the Iroquois "have enabled many of our people to furnish proof of their great zeal for the service of the Prince." Emphasizing similarities between French subjects on both sides of the Atlantic, she compared her leadership to that of "women in France during the late war" who led armies of peasants in defending against "attacks of enemies invading their provinces." She then extended this willingness to make war to women of all ranks, declaring that "the women of Canada would be no whit less eager [than the fighting women of France] to manifest their zeal for the king's glory should the occasion arise." At first glance, Verchères's letter might appear to be a sycophantic attempt to capitalize on her military success. Perhaps it was, at that. Yet, her letter also recognized New France's greater integration into French imperial systems and the growing importance of a transatlantic martial bureaucracy while offering a valuable glimpse into colonial women's martial roles at the turn of the eighteenth century.[55]

Despite Madeleine de Verchères's belief that the women of New France would take up arms for the king, the incident that prompted her letter was one of the last and best promoted examples of women taking up arms to defend their homes, their families, and their communities along the St. Lawrence River and in Acadia. New France's peace with the Iroquois in 1701—combined with increased English naval attacks—redirected French military focus toward coastal areas. As a result, reports of both elite and non-elite women's physical participation in these conflicts would disappear. At the same time, women's roles in trade and finance increasingly supported the development of an imperial military society in New France. Officials welcomed women's support of French war efforts through their construction of fortifications and naval vessels. Of course, the transition was not entirely smooth. As French military strategy placed greater importance on fortified towns at the edge of the Atlantic world, officials in both France and New France expressed growing concern over affairs between soldiers and women living in liminal or vulnerable towns near the sea. These liaisons seemingly threatened both the security and morality of New France's military society, and they would result in transatlantic scandals that combined elements of sex, treason, and commerce.

CHAPTER THREE

Deploying Amazons
Women and Wartime Propaganda

In 1632, the Jesuit Superior of New France, Paul Le Jeune, began sending reports back to the Jesuit Superior in France. These reports detailed events in the New World, with a special emphasis on interactions between the French and Native peoples. After some editing, the Jesuits in France published the accounts, known as the *Jesuit Relations*, for the masses. These stories played a particularly important role in Jesuit fundraising, providing entertaining and engaging narratives that credited the church while emphasizing the civilizing mission that it represented. Excerpted in newspapers and republished as anthologies in addition to the official Jesuit publications, the *Relations* captivated French readers.[1]

The accounts included in the *Jesuit Relations* represent some of the first examples of propaganda that deployed stories of women's participation in the border wars. Authors of these, as well as other, similar accounts disseminated their work throughout Europe and the northeastern borderlands of North America. Stories of women wielding hatchets, muskets, and boiling soap, and drawing upon a militarized Christian strength to convert or subdue Indian populations furthered secular and sacred agendas of officials in both colonies. Producers of this propaganda attempted to reach a wide range of people—from commoners to royalty. In doing so, they sought to solicit support for projects such as missionary work, endeavored to boost morale, worked to elicit political and financial support from European readers for colonial ventures, and meddled in imperial politics.[2]

Using the *Jesuit Relations* as their primary medium, Jesuit priests in New France sent home exciting stories of French and Native women's wartime actions that played on popular French literary themes of Amazons and "strong" or "heroic" women—*femmes fortes*. In these accounts, French-allied Indigenous women who killed their Iroquois captors fought as sisters-in-arms with French Ursuline nuns in a war with secular and spiritual dimensions. In addition to entertaining French audiences and drumming up support for the Jesuit mission in the New World, these accounts also paired their praise of courageous French and Native women with pleas for funds from "brave" French women.

In New England, political officials, authors, and ministers used similar stories to bolster morale and claim divine favor in the face of devastating losses. The Reverend Cotton Mather even sent accounts of women's participation back to England in attempts to interfere with imperial affairs and destroy the political careers of his foes. One such report praised a mob of women who assaulted troops returning from a botched mission led by Mather's enemy, Governor Joseph Dudley. Although New England's use of women's war making as propaganda was far less centralized than the Jesuits' edited, official, published reports, both groups exploited cultural and literary conventions in combination with accounts of violent women for political ends in North America and Europe.

French and English authors of propaganda who made use of stories of women's war making deployed familiar language from early modern European literature. Chief among these literary terms were terms such as "Amazon," "femme forte," and, to a lesser extent, "virago." In particular, the combination of the image of the Amazon with New World conflicts tapped into a broader early modern fascination with Amazons.[3] European encounters with the New World and its unfamiliar, non-Christian women encouraged an even greater interest in Amazons.[4] It is not surprising that one of the most popular contexts for the figure of the Amazon was a New World that had never been exposed to the teachings of Christianity and early modern gender hierarchies. European colonizers perceived rampant disorder in Native societies that assigned to women "male" tasks such as farming and the torture of captives. Native men, whom many Europeans believed shirked their masculine duties, seemingly submitted to overly powerful women in an exotic world turned upside down.[5] Indeed, many missionaries and explorers of the apparently unstably gendered New World actually expected to find the legendary Amazons of Greek myth just over the next ridge.[6]

Early modern writers in Europe and the Americas did not transfer the figure of the Amazon unaltered from classical literature. During the Middle Ages, authors of the French *roman* genre penned poems and prose stories of epic adventure and romance that modified the classical tradition of the Amazon, incorporating chivalric qualities such as beauty and heterosexual love into the more traditional warlike image of the Amazon. Transformed into a feisty love interest, the early modern Amazon often used her considerable fighting prowess in the service or the defense of her male partner, a literary addition that reinforced the existing patriarchal order. It was also in this early modern context of the Amazon's weakened independence that a new literary trend emerged featuring the Amazon as a woman of politics, letters, and, above all, Christian piety and fortitude.[7]

Both France and England experienced political turmoil, uprisings, and civil wars in the early to mid-seventeenth century that produced portrayals of "hybrid" fighting women. These new literary figures blended the shift toward pious, less independent Amazons with contemporary accounts of women engaged in war making. This hybridization created or encouraged the popularity of the figures of the devout, courageous, and often widowed French femme forte and the defender of household and realm—the usually married—English virago. The Latin noun *virago* borrowed from the word *vir* (man), which was associated etymologically with masculine virtue and strength in combat and virago was, even then, applied to valiant fighting women during the classical era. In a seventeenth-century English context, writers predominately used the term to evoke positive images of heroic women, and virago lacked the connotation of shrewishness it later acquired. Collectively, these representations appeared alongside the Amazon in European accounts of women's war making in the early-to-mid seventeenth century.[8] These archetypes were particularly useful in describing women's martial activities in expansionist wars that blurred the sacred and the secular and that featured combined military and domestic spaces as well as Indigenous women who appeared to be classical Amazons come to life. For writers in New England and New France, the Amazon, femme forte, and virago provided ideal figures to both explain and exploit women's participation in the border wars through propaganda.

Amazons, Femmes Fortes, and Fundraising in New France

In 1648, the Jesuit Superior of New France, Jerôme Lallemant, composed a particularly memorable narrative about an Algonquin woman. Although Lallemant did not provide a name for the protagonist of the story, he described the woman as an "Amazon" who "bravely escaped" from her captors.[9] A captive of an Iroquois war party, she had spent ten days on the move when the Iroquois stopped for the night, binding her by "both feet and both hands to four stakes—fastened in the earth, and arranged like a St. Andrew's cross." Upon discovering that she was not properly bound, she freed herself. As she left the cabin, the woman saw a hatchet nearby, "seize[d] it, and, impelled by a strange warlike fury, she deal[t] a blow from it, with all her might, upon the head of a Hiroquois lying at the entrance of the cabin."[10] After this dramatic moment of redemptive violence, the account is laced with Biblical allusions that hint at possible liberties taken with the narrative by its Jesuit presenters. For example, the Algonquin woman spent nearly forty days in the wilderness, a likely reference to Christ's similar experience. Insects plagued our protagonist, confounding her attempts to reach the place along the river where she had heard that her people traded with the French.[11]

The former captive was naked and traveled by night. According to the Jesuit account, she chose this method in order to preserve her modesty—although she might have been exercising simple common sense. French readers of that year's *Relation* may have been surprised to note that, although an Indian, she reportedly was fully aware of her nudity despite her status as a non-Christian, perhaps even living an existence similar to that of Adam and Eve before the Fall. This seeming contradiction placed her in an interesting liminal space between "native" and "civilized." Nearing the French settlement, she encountered a group of Hurons, who she warned to stay away out of respect for her state of undress. One of the Huron men threw a mantle to her and escorted her to the Jesuits at Trois-Rivières, where she arrived on July 26, the feast day of St. Anne, the mother of Mary and a figure historically associated with Canada and Quebec. The Jesuit fathers questioned her about her ordeal and lamented that she had not been able to suffer "these crosses" for "her god" because she had never been introduced to him.[12]

It is unclear what happened to the Algonquin woman after arriving at Trois-Rivières, although Lallemant reported that she was very impressed by the charity of the French. The narrative hinted that she became a Christian through the use of biblical imagery in Lallemant's retelling, which styled itself after biblical stories of Moses, Christ, and the French patron saint, John the Baptist. Although the story alluded to biblical events, it was more a pastiche than an allegory. The wilderness as a liminal space of spiritual struggle and transformation as well as the vivid image of a plague of insects hinted at a spiritual journey using language chosen to evoke a response from the educated Christian reader. At the end of the Algonquin woman's ordeal, she received clothing, a first step on the path to civilization and one that was followed in short order by an introduction to the Jesuit mission and Christianity. The reader is left to speculate that she eventually converted, the inevitable culminating stage of a voyage that demonstrated the efficacy of the Jesuit mission in New France and the potential of missionization as an instrument of the larger project of colonization.

The story of the escaped Algonquin woman deftly incorporated the inverted form of a trope popular in the hagiographies of nuns who traveled to New France to minister to the region's Indian population. In the traditional narrative, pious Frenchwomen undertook a perilous journey from civilization to a New World filled with evil, assuming the role of Jesus in the desert with piety and fortitude as their only protection.[13] In this story, the courageous Algonquin Amazon (and potential convert) traveled from the wilderness to the relative civilization of Trois-Rivières, enduring a thirty-five day trial on her way, as the author hinted, to salvation and the protection of French missionaries. In light of this reversed trope—and a long-standing European tradition of referring to active religious women as Amazons—it should not be surprising that the Jesuit missionaries in New France also referred to the subjects of the original trope, nuns, as Amazons.

It was in the foggy, mosquito-filled country of seventeenth-century Quebec that the figure of the Indian Amazon and her mirror image, the Ursuline Amazon, collided in the minds of the Jesuit missionaries. The events described in these publications took place against the backdrop of what historians call the "Beaver Wars," which erupted intermittently between 1609 and the end of the seventeenth century. These wars, particularly the conflicts near the middle of the seventeenth century, were exceptionally brutal. During this period, members of the powerful Iroquois Confederacy, particularly the Mohawk, fought from their base in what is now upstate New York to defend and expand their territory and to increase their role in the burgeoning fur trade. In these conflicts, boundaries between the secular and sacred as well as the cloister, the salon, and the battlefield became blurred. Marie de l'Incarnation, who established the Ursuline order in New France, described the Beaver Wars to her son as a "war against the enemies of God and of public peace," a telling sentence that reveals the lack of distinction between civic and spiritual order.[14]

Nuns in Montreal, who lived in one of the most dangerous areas of Canada, saw themselves as proselytizing in the wilderness, seeking "savages" who might be converted in a contest for souls. Despite the spiritual focus of the nuns' activities and their supposedly safe haven within the Hôtel-Dieu, secular warfare was a constant presence in the lives of these women. Sister Marie Morin wrote in her memoirs that she witnessed battles from the bell tower of the Hôtel-Dieu in which women, "like Amazons," armed themselves and ran to fight alongside men.[15] During these difficult years, authors of the *Jesuit Relations* worked to drum up support for their cause in France, seeking brave Amazon-nuns willing to traverse the Atlantic, as well as Amazon-donors to finance the missionizing arm of the colonial project.

The nuns of New France were exemplary models of a new, more active female saintliness, establishing schools and hospitals along the banks of the St. Lawrence River, ministering to French and Indians alike. This new form of active female spirituality gained popularity quickly, and the male-dominated early modern Catholic Church scrambled to come to terms with it, often attempting to restrict the activity of these pious women. Still, female missionaries in New France tended to enjoy a somewhat greater measure of freedom than their European counterparts, a condition likely attributable to life in a borderland. In this complex, dangerous environment, recruiting Amazons and femmes fortes capable of participating in—or financing—a colonial war with such high spiritual and secular stakes was essential. Despite cultural contradictions inherent in the new female spirituality embraced by female missionaries in New France, Jesuits ultimately exploited and encouraged the image these women projected.[16]

In encouraging women to aid their mission, Jesuit authors drew on established language used in seventeenth-century French religious conflicts to appeal to readers of the *Relations*. The images of the Amazon and femme forte had long provided a common language for use in European religious conflicts of the early modern period. In early modern France, particularly in biconfessional areas, observers engaged in a *querelle des femmes*, a dispute over the nature of powerful women within Catholic and Protestant churches. In keeping with early modern literary notions of Amazons and femmes fortes, French women in positions of power came close but did not overturn or subvert traditional gender roles.[17] Savvy Jesuit propaganda materials aimed at winning funding and support for their missions in New France deployed this familiar language in accounts that resonated with eager audiences across the Atlantic.

Women, particularly widows with financial control over their late husbands' wealth, were prime targets for Jesuit fundraising, particularly in the order's early years. Their efforts often caused tension within the widow's family as large amounts of wealth were diverted away from the kinship group. Salacious rumors of women's—especially widows'—close relationships with their Jesuit confessors spread throughout Europe, and families became uneasy about the influence these young, enthusiastic, and reportedly virile men had over their older female relatives.[18] Despite the controversies such methods produced, similar fundraising practices extended into the seventeenth century, favored by Jesuits and nuns in New France. Many of the fundraising pleas in the *Jesuit Relations* were directed toward women and

Une Dame Chrétienne et Française (A French Christian
Woman), by Gilles Rousselet and Abraham Bosse, appeared
in Jesuit Pierre Le Moyne's book *La gallerie des femmes
fortes* (Paris, 1647). This woman of rank represents the
spiritual and secular strength embodied in the *femme forte*,
holding lilies, which symbolize chastity, and a sword. She
stands before an image from the story of the widowed
heroine, Judith, who saved Israel by beheading the enemy
general Holofernes. The text reads: "A French Christian
lady fights to the death for her chastity; and by a victory
like that of Judith, France equals Judea." (*Source:* The
Metropolitan Museum of Art, New York, Harris Brisbane
Dick Fund, 1953.)

clearly employed the language of the femme forte movement, often even using the word "Amazon." Given the pressure placed upon widows to avoid
Jesuit entanglements and preserve their inheritances, perhaps the act of financing the mission in New France truly did require the courage of an
Amazon or a femme forte.[19]

Even before the founding of the Ursuline mission in New France, Jesuit
supporters infused their fundraising propaganda with references to Amazons and femmes fortes. In a 1635 plea for capital, Jesuit Superior Paul Le
Jeune lamented that there were many "tender and delicate Virgins all ready
to hazard their lives upon the waves of the Ocean, to come seeking little
souls in the rigors of an air much colder than that of France, to endure hardships at which even men would be appalled." These "tender and delicate
virgins" needed only a monetary "Passport," which would be used to build
a new dwelling to house "these Amazons of the great God." In appealing to
the qualities of the femme forte frequently present in the new female spiritual ideal, Le Jeune described the nuns as at once, "tender and delicate virgins" and "Amazons of the great God." In this *Relation*, he asked, "will not
some brave Lady be found who will give a Passport to these Amazons of
the great God, endowing them with a House in which to praise and serve
his divine Majesty in this other world?"[20] As such, Father Le Jeune associated the more obvious spiritual and physical bravery of the Amazon-nuns
with the bravery of those wealthy women who, although risking the disapproval of their families, might donate their fortunes to the Jesuit and Ursuline missions in the New World.

Propaganda linking French missions and missionaries with the femme
forte movement frequently invoked the widowed Marie-Madeleine de
Chauvigny de la Peltrie, who responded to Le Jeune's 1635 plea seeking a
"brave lady" of means. After concocting a false marriage to a male friend to
secure her fortune, La Peltrie financed the Ursulines in New France, traveling to Quebec to help build the mission and support the work of the cloistered sisters. A hagiography of the recently deceased Mother Marie de Saint
Joseph recounted how "Madame de la Pelterie—having read in the same
Relations that it was desired in new France that some Amazon should un-
dertake a voyage, longer than that of Æneas," the Trojan hero who sailed
across the Mediterranean to Italy bringing with him civilization and an excellent pedigree. Through his marriage to a Latin woman, Æneas would
produce offspring who went on to found Rome. In this literary parallel,
Madame de la Peltrie chose to attempt a harrowing, lengthy journey to the
New World "in order to provide for the instruction of the little Savage

girls."[21] Considering the active role La Peltrie assumed in the mission, it is not surprising that she was so often called an Amazon. As was the case with many literary Amazons, Madame de la Peltrie was the ultimate example of a liminal figure. She served as a go-between who was neither secular nor a member of a religious order, an independent woman acting as an intermediary between groups in New France and setting an example to other laywomen who might support the mission financially.

Reporting on the arrival of Madame de la Peltrie and the group of nuns who founded the Ursuline convent and the hospital in Quebec in 1639, Jesuit Superior Paul Le Jeune praised the pious, hands-on La Peltrie. Employing a biblical cadence, Le Jeune wrote of La Peltrie: "And there was found an Amazon, who has led the Ursulines, and established them on these outer confines of the world." In doing so, he drew upon Amazon lore while casting her as an Amazon queen—heralded by his scriptural tone—leading an army of holy women to a mysterious Othered land. Father Le Jeune was quick to point out that Peltrie was a "modest and virtuous Lady," traits befitting a model femme forte.[22] Although Le Jeune praised the arrival of a new crop of nuns the following year, "young Amazons, who, in spite of the Ocean, came to seek the salvation of these barbarians in these farthest confines of the earth," he knew that their success in New France depended upon the generosity of additional Amazon-financiers.[23] In a *Relation* detailing the years 1640 and 1641, Father Le Jeune appealed for additional funds, noting that there were many eager nuns willing to travel across the Atlantic to New France but that the mission needed "secular sisters who would consent to bring their fortunes and spend their lives in this New World." He harshly chastised the rich women of France, comparing them unfavorably to Madame de la Peltrie, and asking: "Indeed! is it possible that all the generous sisters that were in old France have come over into the New? and that there are no longer found hearts brave enough to follow the footprints of these first Amazons?"[24] Again Le Jeune's propaganda linked the philanthropy of wealthy French women to the bravery of spiritual Amazons and the survival of France's missionizing program.

Jesuit authors, eager to depict their mission as a successful venture, also employed the language of the Amazon and the femme forte in accounts that portrayed their encounters with converted and unconverted Indigenous women in a positive light. The Jesuits did not use the terms "Amazon" and "femme forte" indiscriminately to describe a warlike or violent woman; the Amazon and the femme forte were more or less respectable figures. Missionaries instead appropriated another classical figure for the repulsive violent woman. In the *Jesuit Relations*, women who committed violent acts against Christians and children, women whose acts were exceptionally gory, and women who attempted to prevent others from converting were described as "Megaeras." The term "Megaera," which (as *mégère*) serves as the French word for "shrew," is a reference to the Greek Fury of that name who was associated with jealousy and marital violence. In other words, these were women who were likely untamable by men or even Christianity, and whose actions were determined to be entirely dishonorable and often, but not always, associated with their gender.

The opposition of the Amazon and Megaera is evident in the same edition of the *Jesuit Relations* that described the experience of the captive Algonquin woman who split her captor's head with a hatchet. Within weeks of her arrival at Trois-Rivières, another woman who escaped from the Iroquois approached the Jesuits. This woman was a Christian who had been taken captive along with her daughter, another woman, and that woman's daughter. The protagonist of this story patiently waited to escape from captivity for several years until she could successfully arrange to bring her daughter with her. By contrast, the non-Christian woman, a "very Megera, and hostile to the Faith," was apparently mad with fear, and "laying hands on her child, she murdered it, and threw it at the feet of the Hiroquois." She then "slipped her head into a halter, she pulled with one hand to strangle herself, and with the other she cut her throat with a knife." The escaped Christian woman reportedly lamented that the other woman "soon found a more devouring fire than that of the Hiroquois."[25]

The figure of the Megaera appears several other times in the *Jesuit Relations*, including a reference to an Iroquois "woman, or rather a Megera" who sloppily cut off the thumb of the captive Father Isaac Jogues in 1642. After his ransom from captivity in 1643, Jogues returned briefly to France before making a second voyage to the northeastern borderlands, where he was killed by the Iroquois in 1646. Jesuits also used the word "Megaera," along with the unflattering "tigress," to describe a woman who beat her brother to death and forced her nephew to strangle his sister so that she would take him with her to safety in a canoe.[26] Father Le Jeune included an account from another Jesuit who witnessed the torture of an Iroquois man, which used language from Greek mythology to describe women participating in ritual abuse. In this incident, a woman he referred to as a Megaera "appeared, armed with a whip of knotted cords, with which she rained blows upon him around his arms, with as much rage as she had strength." Appropriately, this single "Fury" was joined by two other women who attacked him with stones and a knife. After a confrontation with French observers, the Algonquins brought the prisoner to the other side of the river, where they discreetly killed him in an attempt to appease French sensibilities.[27] The men who wrote the *Jesuit Relations* clearly reserved "Megaera" for women whose behavior seemed beyond their ability to correct as Christian men. Unlike the Megaera, our Algonquin Amazon—for all of her "savage fury" and hatchet-wielding ways—had possibilities. In her story, she fulfilled the male fantasy of the Amazon who entrusted herself to the care of a worthy man.

Imagery associated with the femme forte could occasionally be applied to Native female converts under Jesuit and Ursuline tutelage. In 1647, Jerome Lallemant approvingly described a session in which the Father in charge of Native students' instruction offered the very active St. Catherine of Siena as a model of Christian womanhood, praising "the Faith and constancy of that Christian Amazon." The Father concluded, "that is what it is to be a Christian."[28] Occasionally, Jesuits were able to reach a delicate balance in their depiction of spiritually courageous qualities of an Indian Amazon. It was in these stories that the Jesuits best demonstrated the efficacy of their conversion methods to supporters. According to a letter written by Father Paul Ragueneau, on August 3, 1657, a group of Huron women Ragueneau described as femmes fortes was attacked by the Onondaga, a nation-member of the Iroquois Confederacy.[29] The Huron Christians, along with Father Ragueneau, were traveling with a different group of Onondaga on their way to help found a mission on the shores of Onondaga Lake near present-day Syracuse, New York. Ragueneau wrote that an Onondaga captain, frustrated by the continual rebuff of his sexual advances toward a young, converted Huron girl, allegedly split her head open with his tomahawk. The ensuing violence from this episode resulted in the deaths of seven Christian Huron men.

Upon reaching Onondaga, several men, now captors of the Huron women, began attacking women in the party, stabbing and burning the women and their children alive. It was at this point in Ragueneau's narrative that he referred to the captive women as femmes fortes, women who, unbowed by fear of violence and death and solemnly embracing their new position in the European patriarchal hierarchy, asked that God might "'mingle my blood with my husband's, and let them take my life to-day; never will they be able to take away the faith which I have in my heart.'" Father Ragueneau wrote that during the assault at the entrance to Onondaga, another Christian Huron woman, Dorothée, "was being butchered with hatchets and knives" and "seeing the tears of a little girl eight years old who had been at the Ursuline seminary, she said to her: 'My daughter, weep not for my death, or for thy own; we shall to-day go to Heaven together, where God will have pity on us for all eternity. The Iroquois cannot rob us of this great blessing.'" As they died, the account claimed, both woman and child cried "Jesus, take pity on me!" remaining exemplary models, faithful and submissive to the male Christian deity even at the moment of death.[30] Accounts such as this reminded readers that, despite military setbacks, the Jesuit mission produced devout Christians, femmes fortes, brave and un-afraid of facing death at the hands of the enemy if it assisted their attainment of eternal life.

In another example of the Indian Amazon as femme forte, Father Paul Le Jeune wrote of "one of our old Christians," an Indigenous woman, who "displayed the courage of an Amazon" during two separate rape attempts by an Iroquois and a Frenchman. Here, Le Jeune equated an Indian's Amazon nature with the spiritual strength similar to that of a femme forte. Accord-ing to the woman's Jesuit confessor, she had been pursued by a group of Iroquois, fleeing almost naked into the woods after leaving her possessions behind in her escape attempt. Exhausted and feeling that all was lost, she grasped her crucifix, prayed, and was filled with a renewed physical strength that allowed her to continue running.[31] The incident is reminiscent of the story of the Algonquin Amazon who killed her captors while "impelled by a strange warlike fury" and fled naked through the woods. This converted "Amazon" instead drew upon strength provided by Christianity to protect her virtue and received even greater praise than the woman in the earlier story.

Later, the Christian woman claimed the same crucifix helped repel a vi-olent Frenchman who had dragged her into a cabin and thrown her on a bed in another attempted rape. According to her confessor, the woman re-counted that after she brandished a crucifix at her attacker, reprimanded him, and appealed to his fear of God, the man fled, leaving her bewildered and alone but grateful. Father Le Jeune added that "this same Amazon also performed another action as godly as it was generous." Involved in a bitter dispute with a female relative, the Christian Indian approached the woman who had "grievously offended" her and "begged her to forget the past, and to live with her as if they were sisters."[32] In this example, we see a potential female ideal in the figure of a converted Indigenous woman, a spiritual Am-azon relying entirely on God and her male confessor, forgoing violence, and preserving her feminine virtue through faith, prayer, and forgiveness.

The cessation of the publication of the *Jesuit Relations* with the *Relation* of 1673 was the result of Pope Clement X's ban on the release of accounts from missions abroad. By then, the catastrophic series of mid-century wars had ended. Stories of danger and adventure along the St. Lawrence in Quebec had lost their punch, and the Jesuits turned their attention to missions in the west and south. In the four decades of their publication, however, the *Jesuit Relations* revealed unique strategies of gender-role negotiation as Jesuit missionaries catered to the tastes of their wealthy female donors while grappling with changing concepts of female saintliness, both in European and Native women.

The end of the Jesuit mission in New France coincided with a decline in the popularity of stories of fighting women in France as well as in England. Scholars have noted a shift near the close of the seventeenth century, arguing that the end of mid-century conflicts and relative peace at home in England and France removed the cultural impetus that made literary figures such as Amazons, femmes fortes, and viragos popular with men and women alike. Both nations moved toward a new appreciation of an increasingly passive female figure. In France, the femme forte transformed into the figure of the secular *précieuse*, an often ridiculed figure who embraced the idea of the Amazon from the comfort of her *salon*.[33]

"A Tribe of Female Hands, but Manly Hearts": Propaganda in New England

Although the most compelling examples of French propaganda that drew on themes of fighting women disappeared after the Jesuits ended publication of their *Relations* in 1673, New England did not begin producing such propaganda of its own until the very end of the early modern European fascination with Amazons, femmes fortes, and viragos. Unlike post-civil war Britain, New England did experience violent wars in the late seventeenth and early eighteenth centuries that required the participation of women. But because New England did not experience its first major regional war until 1675, we do not have accounts of women's war making from before that time. Instead, propaganda from New England displays fascinating shifts in the use of the literary terms discussed earlier during the late seventeenth and early eighteenth centuries.

The use of the word "virago" to describe women in the context of battle largely disappeared in New England after King Philip's War ended in 1676. In fact, the only example appears in William Hubbard's description of the young woman—discussed in an earlier chapter—who held the door against an Indian raid at Tozer's garrison in Maine while her fellow inhabitants escaped. Hubbard referred to her as a "Virago" who was "endued with more Courage then ordinarily the rest of her Sex use to be."[34] Instead, a discourse of "borrowing" appeared in later writings. When described as Amazons in accounts penned after 1676, New England's women, unlike their earlier English and French counterparts, were depicted as borrowing the mantle of the Amazon. In Cotton Mather's account of an attack on Wells, Maine, in 1692, women firing alongside men "took up the Amazonian Stroke."[35] The women of Oyster River, New Hampshire, "assum'd an Amazonian Courage" in Samuel Penhallow's narrative.[36] More common than the use of either the words "virago" or "Amazon" to describe such women was the use of masculine compliments. Male commentators bestowing their highest praise on fighting women honored them with adjectives associated more often with men. Penhallow borrowed the complimentary—and masculine—word "briskly" to describe the shooting prowess of the women of Oyster River. In addition to "t[aking] up the Amazonian Stroke," the women of Wells fired "with a Manly Resolution." In a 1708 work published in London, John Oldmixon praised violent captive Hannah Dustan as "a Woman of masculine Spirit."[37] In much the same way women in New England borrowed their husbands' guns and took on their roles as settler-soldiers, their courage and prowess were described in terms of gender borrowing.

Popular balladry from this period celebrated the exploits of fighting women in Europe and America, featuring gender borrowing as a staple of the genre.[38] Rather than serving as cautionary tales or condemned as transgressive, warrior women in ballads demonstrate the flexibility of relationships between sex and gender. Gender might be borrowed in early modern cultures, and women could find praise in performing traditional, manly roles. Women celebrated in ballads for their courage and skill earned that praise as "exemplary" figures. The celebrated woman was merely the most successful performer of this role. If we extend the concept to reports of women fighting in New England's fortified communities, all women could potentially take on the male role of settler-soldier. The notion of the fighting woman as "exemplary" surfaced in New England as women vied for compensation based on "exceptional" and "extraordinary" service. The language of "borrowing" seen in descriptors such as "brisk," "manly," and "Amazon" derives from this tradition. Although popular ballads referred to a more literal transvestism, the borrowing inherent in that action resembles the borrowed adjectives of real-life tales from New England.

One account that did involve cross-dressing, Samuel Penhallow's exciting yet brief description of the Oyster River incident, presents unique analytical opportunities but should be read cautiously. Scholars who have noted in those lines the evocative combination of gendered adjectives and cross-dressing see the author's language as suggesting that dressing as men bestowed eligibility or capability with regard to the garrison's defense.[39] Although these readings make valid points, particularly in light of the discourse of borrowing, it is important to understand the passage within a larger context of female participation in the wars of the northeastern borderlands. The cross-dressing itself was almost negligible in comparison to descriptions in popular ballads. The women of Oyster River merely took their hair down and shoved hats onto their heads. The extent of the women's disguise likely was limited by the time the women had to prepare and—depending on the garrison's fortifications—the amount of a person's body visible behind the fortifications. If the camouflage did play a critical role in the garrison's defense, it was for another reason entirely.

Defenders and Indians alike recognized the low likelihood of taking a fully staffed, alert garrison. In 1712, Esther Jones called out to a nonexistent force from her garrison's watch box. Penhallow described how, despite the lack of men at home, "Jones supplied the place of several." In Penhallow's account, Jones "couragiously advanced the Watch-box, crying aloud, *Here they are, come on, come on.*" Believing that the garrison had a full complement, the attackers retreated, "terrified . . . without doing any further Mischief."[40] Madeleine de Verchères used a similar tactic in her defense of her father's seigneury in New France. Although in a number of instances women found success with this tactic, its use was not limited to women. Thomas Bickford single-handedly defended his garrison in 1694 by "Chang[ing] his Livery as frequently as he could; appearing Sometimes in one Coat, Sometimes in another, Sometimes in an Hat, and Sometimes in a Cap." Cotton Mather, who recorded the incident, wrote that the attackers left after Bickford's plan "caused his Beseigers, to mistake this One for Many Defendents."[41] When seen in this context, Penhallow's narrative may have simultaneously hinted at popular tropes while describing a familiar military tactic.

The discourse of borrowing is also visible, though in a less clear-cut fashion, in a poem from the 1670s. Included at the end of Benjamin Tompson's 1676 history-in-verse of King Philip's War, *New Englands Crisis*, the poem reflects this shift in language and describes a fascinating but unsubstantiated incident.[42] It tells of a group of Bostonian women who, upon seeing that the thin "Neck" or strip of land connecting Boston to the mainland was vulnerable, rushed to erect fortifications. Tompson begins his poem with the Latin line "Dux Fœmina Facti," an allusion to both Virgil's powerful but tragic queen, Dido, and a medallion that celebrated Elizabeth I's Armada victory in 1588.[43] The short poem, "On A Fortification At Boston begun by Women," recalls the effort as "A Grand attempt" by "Amazonian Dames." These "Dames"

> . . . Contrive whereby to glorify their names,
> A Ruff for Boston Neck of mud and turfe,
> Reaching from side to side from surfe to surfe,
> Their nimble hands spin up like Christmas pyes,
> Their pastry by degrees on high doth rise.
> The wheel at home counts it an holiday,
> Since while the Mistris worketh it may play.
> A tribe of female hands, but manly hearts
> Forsake at home their pasty-crust and tarts
> To knead the dirt, the samplers down they hurle,
> Their undulating silks they closely furle.
> The pick-axe one as a Commandress holds,
> While t'other at her awkness gently scolds.
> One puffs and sweats, the other mutters why
> Cant you promove your work so fast as I?
> Some dig, some delve, and others hands do feel
> The little waggons weight with single wheel.
> And least some fainting fits the weak surprize,
> They want no sack nor cakes, they are more wise.
> These brave essayes draw forth Male stronger hands
> More like to Dawbers then to Martial bands:
> These do the work, and sturdy bulwarks raise,
> But the beginners well deserve the praise.[44]

Composed at the close of the first major war in which New England's women figured in wartime policy and played martial roles, the poem may reflect an early ambivalence regarding these policies as well as a change in language regarding viragos.[45] Although still Amazons in their own right, the women took on a role similar to that of the deputy husband. Using household imagery, the author playfully described them sewing a collar for Boston's neck, setting aside their embroidery in favor of pick-axes. As a "tribe of female hands, but manly hearts," Tompson's women represented the blurring of the household and the military, the Amazons, Jaels, and viragos of the mid-seventeenth century as well as the "borrowers" of the end of that century. Even as the language used to describe fighting women in New England shifted toward the discourse of borrowing, events in New England rein-forced the need for the continuous presence of women and children in fortified communities. The development of this gendered martial language to praise and even encourage women's war making through propaganda was part of a larger effort to bolster morale as the wars of the late seventeenth and early eighteenth centuries ground on.

The protracted natures of King William's War and Queen Anne's War, combined with northern New England's dedication to its expansionist program and a well-defined Catholic enemy, resulted in an even greater emphasis placed on the presence of families in garrison houses. As Cot-ton Mather's tract and John Houghton's petition demonstrated earlier, life in fortified communities—especially when several families crammed into a single garrison house—was brutal. Mather's acknowledgment of their "uneasy condition, when you are Thrust and Heap'd up together in Garri-sons, where the Common Comforts of your Lives must needs have an Ex-treme Abridgment brought upon them" and Houghton's complaint that "neither men nor women can doe but very litle towards the supply of theire familyes: theire being so mutch time spent in watching warding & many allarrums" significantly affected morale.[46] Writers in New England turned to propaganda as well as to legal remedies to discourage desertion.

Indeed, Mather's words are part of a longer work of propaganda meant to offer advice and bolster the spirits of garrison families. Purportedly the response to requests from desperate frontier families, *Frontiers Well-Defended* used the idea of order as a unifying theme. Much as the home was indistinguishable from the front, the well-ordered frontier became bound up with the well-ordered community and family. At the same time, the pres-ence of whole families—not merely men—on the frontier boosted morale throughout New England society. In this tract, Mather recommended pi-ety as a solution to the problems of frontier families, noting that "Well-Ordered Families" might set positive examples for any "Wild, and Vain, and Lewd" soldiers sent to live within their communities. Mather observed sym-pathetically that "such continual Watching and Warding, as you are put upon, must needs tire out an Ordinary Strength, and it cannot be wondred at, if some Remissness do grow upon your tired Vigilance." Thus, he equated piety and a community that kept watch for internal weaknesses with a com-munity successful in avoiding surprise attacks by the enemy.[47]

Recommending chastity and sobriety as appropriate virtues in frontier towns, Mather concluded his tract with a longer discussion of the impor-tance of the well-ordered family's role in the defense of the frontier.[48] To prevent the catastrophic failure of a garrison community that often followed incursions, Mather prescribed family prayer, noting that even "the very Salvages, by whom you are annoy'd, of whom you are afraid; These do maintain a Family Worship among them." Of course, this "Family Worship" was not well-ordered and Protestant but disorderly and Catholic. For Mather, only the prayers of a New England Protestant family could neutralize the family prayers of Catholic French-allied Indians. He argued that families that prayed together would also be less tempted by Catholicism if captured and separated. Employing language associated with more martial aspects of the frontier, Mather urged settler-soldiers to "Fortify them with strong Preservation . . . that you may have a People of Well-Instructed Protestants." In emphasizing an association between manhood, Protestantism, family governance, and national loyalty, Mather's words demonstrated why the well-ordered family was critical to the well-ordered frontier during wartime.[49]

From her vulnerable position in the frontier town of Salisbury, Joanna Rossiter Cotton, who we met in an earlier chapter, articulated many of the themes of *Frontiers Well-Defended* eleven years before its publication. In a letter to her brother-in-law, Increase Mather (Cotton Mather's father), Joanna Cotton reassured the elder Mather that Salisbury "hath bin and is yet very willing to uphold religion and the ministry." Salisbury's piety persisted, according to Joanna Cotton, despite the fact that the town's families struggled to survive as the military impressed their men, sending them to areas in greater peril. Frightened for her family and her weakened—but still righteous—neighbors, she explained that her "intent in writing these dolefull lines to yourself is to stir up your prayers." Insisting that Salisbury remained a godly town, worthy of the prayers she sought, her description of the town was of a community facing imminent collapse. Wartime disruption and a lack of order had driven inhabitants of Salisbury and the surrounding region to despair, leaving her to wonder "what shall thay doe if the lord dont help immediately." She reported hearing that many were "very neare famishing" and that "never did I heare such a cry for bread," admitting that "some begin to steale at exseter [Exeter] from the mils merely to save ther lives." In the absence of Protestant fathers' good governance and the resulting lack of social and moral order, perhaps the prayers of Mather and other "choys christia[ns]" might save the morally and materially threatened town of Salisbury.[50]

Essential as the presence of this pious, patriarchal order was in fortified communities at war, it is nonetheless unsurprising that Cotton Mather and other authors did not consider stories of women maiming or killing the enemy signs of disorder. The loss of English women to the French was a great blow to the patriarchy and Protestantism that were the foundations of New England society.[51] If the return of a woman from Canada was a political, social, and spiritual victory for New England, women who took up arms to defend the New England way of life might serve as inspirational figures—and sources for propaganda—in these lengthy military struggles. Indeed, along with other writers, Mather held up these women as examples to follow. The Amazons of Wells and Oyster River were such role models, as were the women in Tompson's poem and the infamous Hannah Dustan.

Captivity narratives traditionally have provided scholars' primary evidence of women's wartime experiences while also hinting at behaviors considered proper for women in colonial New England.[52] The captivity narrative's popularity—then and now—has contributed to perceptions that acceptable women's behavior was limited to actions modeled in such narratives. However, captivity was not the only wartime situation in which women's behavior was modeled, nor were passivity and contemplativeness the only behaviors available to women. The ubiquitous Hannah Dustan gained fame for killing and scalping ten sleeping Indians—men, women, and children—in 1697 with the help of her nurse, Mary Neff, and a boy, Samuel Lennarson. Dustan had been recovering from childbirth when she was taken from her bed. Her celebrity was the result of an extraordinary early modern propaganda campaign organized by Hannah, her husband, and the Massachusetts elite.[53] Scholars have focused largely on Cotton Mather's accounts of Dustan's exploits, a reliance that has produced a sometimes convoluted and tormented understanding of an incident that many colonial officials appear to have taken in stride.[54] Her story had a role to play outside of Mather's machinations, and the propaganda value of Dustan's actions at home and abroad are best understood when examining Mather's text alongside other colonial reactions.[55]

Official reactions to Dustan's captivity and escape suggest immediate and unquestioned acceptance and promotion of her deeds. As Thomas Hutchinson later wrote, "the fame of so uncommon an action . . . soon spread through the continent."[56] Members of the male New England elite ran to their diaries to record their meetings with Hannah Dustan. The powerful judge Samuel Sewall mentioned Dustan twice in his diary. Sewall's April 29 entry was dedicated to Dustan, the day "signalised by the Atchievment of Hannah Dustin, Mary Neff, and Samuel Lennerson." He wasted little time in arranging to meet with the trio. Sewall wrote that less than two weeks later, "Hannah Dustan came to see us." Dustan was accompanied by Neff and Lennarson but was the sole recipient of a gift of a "part of Connecticut Flax."[57] Her greatest reward, according to Mather, came from Governor Nicholson of Maryland who "sent 'em a ver generous Token of his Favour."[58] This token, a pewter tankard, reportedly held "a little more than a beer quart" and featured a portrait of William III on the side.[59]

Positive opinions of Dustan were not confined to powerful politicians and ministers. The Braintree mason John Marshall noted in an April 1697 entry of his diary that Hannah and her companions had returned with a gun and "some other things." The timing of Dustan's success, he believed, was not random. As Marshall wrote, "this was done Just about the time the councell of this province had concluded on a day of fasting and prayer."[60] Rather than removing Hannah's agency by attributing her deeds to God, John Marshall's entry seems to suggest that God might work through either a man or a woman to achieve Zion's military success.

Perhaps the most fascinating aspect of the entire affair is Hannah and Thomas Dustan's successful publicity campaign, as the pair carefully exploited the overwhelmingly positive public and political response to Hannah's actions. That Hannah Dustan returned with the scalps of her victims could only mean that she hoped to collect a financial reward. Unfortunately for Hannah and her husband—who lost most of his assets in the attack—the bounty on scalps had expired mere months before her return. Determined to collect a reward, Thomas Dustan prepared a petition to the General Court pleading for an exception for his wife. Thomas Dustan framed the exploits of Hannah Dustan and Mary Neff (whom he mentioned in parentheses) in dramatic terms. According to Dustan, both women had "been disposed and assisted by heaven to doe an extraordinary Action." He acknowledged that the law had expired but argued that "the merrit of the Action still remains the Same." Playing politics, he noted that "it seemes a matter of universall desire thro the whole Province that it should not pass unrecompensed." Finally, Dustan appealed to his own pitiful circumstances, "Los[ing] his Estate in that Calamity . . . render[ing] him the fitter object for what consideracion the publick Bounty shall judge proper." He closed with a reminder that the issue at hand stretched beyond the Dustans and Neffs to the "the Generall Interest" of the colony, suggesting that Hannah Dustan's actions were intertwined with New England's collective well-being and its success in the war.[61]

On June 16, 1697, the General Court approved a reward of 25 pounds for Dustan and 12 pounds, 10 shillings each for Neff and Lennarson. The council agreed that the money was a "reward for their service in slaying divers of those barbarous salvages."[62] Just as the term "extraordinary" became a common word in such petitions, so too did the word "service." The word "service" implies a kind of social belonging, suggesting that both Dustan and Neff were part of a larger wartime effort. In the decades to come, other women—and men—would petition for land grants based on "service." Hannah and Thomas Dustan would continue to milk the fame Hannah gained from her captivity and escape for over thirty years.

Stories of women's participation in the border wars provided female role models and boosted morale in New England, yet this propaganda also had value at the imperial level. On several occasions, Cotton Mather sent reports of women's war making back to England for his own political purposes. As noted earlier, Mather held a long-standing grudge against Massachusetts's crown-appointed governor, Joseph Dudley. Dudley, appointed to the governorship in 1702, initially had the support of many prominent New Englanders, including Increase and Cotton Mather. Dudley's supporters had hoped that as a native New Englander, Dudley would eschew the imperial tendencies of other recent crown-appointed governors. Although Dudley was born in New England, his time in London and in other British colonies shaped his approach to his new position. Dudley tended to think imperially, and his rejection of Puritanism disappointed many of his colonial supporters. Horrified by Dudley's worldliness, Cotton Mather spent the rest of Dudley's tenure attempting to destroy his career and reputation.[63]

Determined to remove Dudley from office, Mather published a series of attacks in London that included accounts of women's participation in the border wars. One such tract recounted an incident involving Hannah Bradley of Haverhill, who tried to avoid a second captivity by throwing boiling soap on her attacker.[64] In this colorful document, Mather appended his account of Hannah Bradley's experience to a longer tract that accused Governor Dudley of conspiring with the French and their Indigenous allies and included affidavits as proof of Dudley's wrongdoing. The second portion of the treatise tied Dudley's supposed perfidy to attacks he purportedly allowed on New England's vanguard communities. In his transition from the first to the second part of the treatise, Mather argued that "for a Governour to furnish the Enemy with Powder and Shot, &c. to destroy his own Country-men is a Wretch not only fit to be Discarded, but to be for ever forgotten among Mankind."[65]

In the parade of tear-jerking accounts of captivity that followed Mather's political accusations, Hannah Bradley's story occupied a place of honor.

Opening his narrative, Mather noted that Bradley had previously lived as a captive and, before revealing to the reader that she had been captured a second time, hinted ominously "But the Clouds return after the Rain." Following this foreboding introduction, Mather recounted how Bradley killed an armed Indian by "tak[ing] the opportunity to pour a good quantity of scalding Soap, (which was then boyling over the Fire) upon him" while an unidentified man—who was quickly killed—held him down. Mather was eager to share that after scalding a second Indian with her remaining soap, Bradley, who was only six weeks from giving birth, offered to take her sister's place in captivity. After describing Bradley's unpleasant winter journey across New England without the benefit of snowshoes, Mather emphasized her bravery in giving birth, her piety, and her rescue.[66] Mather concluded the lengthy account of Bradley's experiences with a letter from a captive in Port Royal, a bookend to a treatise aimed at destroying Governor Dudley. His portrayal of Bradley as a "Vertuous Woman" who killed and maimed two men allegedly in league with Dudley before suffering a second, lengthy captivity underscored his belief that publishing such stories might have significant political effects abroad.

In yet another treatise aimed at undermining Governor Dudley and published in 1708, Mather recounted the previously discussed July 1707 incident involving a mob of women who met a group of officers returning to Boston after an ill-conceived attack on Port Royal in Acadia. Mather praised "The Good Women in Boston" for confronting Dudley's forces and described Dudley's officers as cowards and traitors. By emphasizing the female mob's humiliation of Dudley's men and suggesting that their actions represented "The Cry of the People" that "must be Satisfyed," Mather at once attempted to politically emasculate Dudley while arguing that the entire city of Boston supported his removal.[67]

Whether employed to boost morale or meddle in transatlantic politics, New Englanders saw considerable propaganda value in accounts of martial women. In stories meant to lift New Englanders' spirits, such as incidents involving women fortifying Boston's harbor, defending the garrison at Wells, and the publicity surrounding Hannah Dustan's exploits, authors praised these women and reinforced traditional gender and military systems that relied upon women's war making. Although Cotton Mather's attempts to use similar stories to destroy his archrival appear less interested in boosting morale or encouraging women's martial activities than in the politics of personal destruction, Mather never called the propriety of the women's actions into question, and their value as role models remained intact.

A wide range of authors from New France and New England recognized the value in deploying these stories for financial, military, and political gain on a transatlantic scale. Jesuit missionaries in New France employed Reformation-era language that cast strong, pious women as Amazons and femmes fortes, encouraging wealthy French women to finance the mission. At the same time, the Jesuits portrayed converted Native women as spiritual Amazons—evidence of a successful colonial mission worthy of financial support. In New England, women willing to take up arms to defend the colonies' Protestant, male-dominated hierarchy served as role models in conflicts fought against dangerous, Othered enemies. During periods of intracolonial political conflict, authors such as Cotton Mather used positive depictions of women's war making as propaganda in attempts to influence imperial politics. Most of the authors of this propaganda—as well as its subjects—did not live to see the outcome of the series of conflicts in which they participated, though their stories survived. These accounts continued to hold great cultural meaning as new authors retold the same tales with slight but significant differences. The alterations would reflect changes in attitudes regarding religion, empire, domesticity, and gender that developed during the eighteenth century.

PART II | Redrafting Martial Women

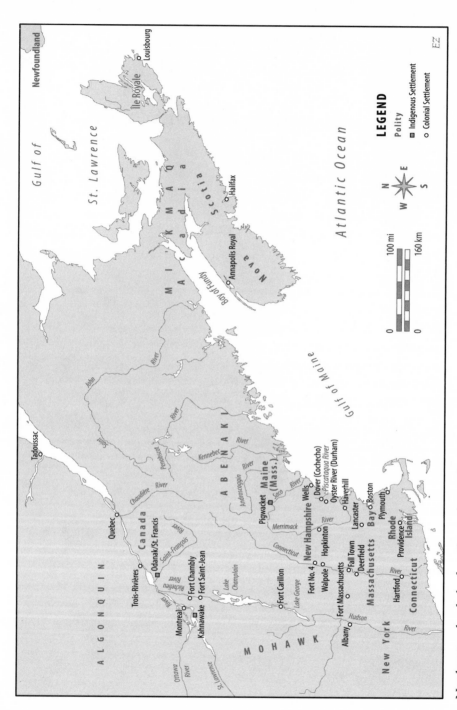

Northeastern borderlands region, c. 1713–1760

CHAPTER FOUR

Appropriate Combatants

Women in the New Imperial Military Societies of the Northeastern Borderlands

New England and New France engaged in devastating regional and imperial wars that ultimately bound those colonies more tightly to their European counterparts in the late seventeenth and early eighteenth centuries. New France's disastrous Beaver Wars against the Iroquois led the French Crown to seize the colony in the 1660s. In addition to heavy losses sustained during King Philip's War, New England faced decreasing independence as a result of upheavals during the Glorious Revolution of 1688–89. Massachusetts lost its remarkably permissive original charter in 1684 during a period of imperial consolidation, only to see it replaced in 1691 with a more restrictive document. This new relationship to the crown also included appointed royal governors such as Joseph Dudley, who worked to create closer ties to Britain and further contributed to a loss of colonial autonomy. Beginning in 1688–89 with King William's War, the first of four major transatlantic conflicts, both nations would take an increased interest in the military and economic affairs of their colonies in the northeastern borderlands of North America. These stronger imperial connections would have significant consequences for military strategy, economic policy, and gender roles during wartime.

Following the royal takeover of its colony in 1663, Paris forged ever-closer ties to New France. Although France's imperial wars with Britain beginning in the 1680s would substantially influence military strategy, it was only after the peace with the Iroquois in 1701 that metropole and colony turned their attention away from the forts and seigneuries of the St. Lawrence River Valley. No longer threatened by Iroquois raids, Canada looked toward the sea, where coastal fortifications in Quebec and Acadia could protect it from the English naval attacks that became the primary threat to New France's security.[1] This shift in strategy and policy had important ramifications regarding women's participation in war making. As Iroquois attacks on settlers and seigneuries in the St. Lawrence River Valley ceased, accounts of women joining battles and defending their family forts likewise disappeared. Women who lived in fortified coastal towns took shelter within their walls, while France's increased imperial presence and sociomilitary hierarchies eliminated the need for women to assume command of these fortresses. Through the end of the Seven Years' War, women in New France continued to play unchallenged roles in public spheres, their martial activities performed against a more maritime backdrop in the wake of the larger turn toward the French Atlantic world. Whether bankrolling French efforts to expand its navy, supervising the construction of new Atlantic strongholds, or crossing the ocean bearing military intelligence, women's less violent, more bureaucratic and economic roles reflected larger colonial and imperial transformations.[2]

In New England, Indigenous and French raids on colonists' homes continued throughout the period. Over the course of the early to mid-eighteenth century, colonists experienced a strengthened British imperial presence, as well as changes in ideas regarding the role of the monarchy, the identities of civilians and soldiers, and a growing distinction between home and front. Both men and women in the northeastern borderlands found themselves transformed from settler-soldiers to suffering subjects of a father-king. Although the task of fighting fell increasingly to provincial and British soldiers, women continued to defend their homes, themselves, and their families. Despite the emergence of a separation between home and front, women's physical participation in these conflicts was never formally prohibited. Rather, it was seen as an unfortunate consequence of a lack of British military support. These changes would alter women's roles in war making, often slowly, carving meandering paths through colonial societies seeking by turns to resist and to embrace empire.

Commerce Scandaleux: Trade, Treason, and Sex in the French Atlantic

The French word "*commerce*" is a particularly rich term that describes intimate human interaction as well as trade. An imperfect but useful English substitute is the word "intercourse," which can describe social and economic relationships in addition to its more modern association with sex. French writers used the term "commerce" to describe a variety of instances of women's participation in New France's wars, ranging from sexual affairs tinged with illicit trade and treason to female shopkeepers required to contribute to the defense of the colony. This portion of the chapter examines closer imperial ties between France and New France, a growing French military presence, and the shift to Quebec and Acadia as the primary targets of

English attacks. It explores two trends that began in the late seventeenth century but became more conspicuous in the early to mid-eighteenth century. Both trends reflect changes in women's roles in war making in New France, and both are related to increased connections to empire, to the Atlantic world, and to commerce. The first section traces how concerns in France and New France over affairs between military men and Canadian and French women seemingly threatened security and morality, combining elements of sex, treason, and trade. The second section examines women's financial roles in protecting New France, from the increasing demands on women to support the construction of fortifications to the bankrolling by wealthy women of the construction of naval ships that fought for New France throughout the Atlantic world.

In 1711, Captain Paul Mascarene, a French Huguenot serving in the British occupying force at Port Royal in Acadia, reported a remarkable encounter with an Acadian woman who called herself "Madame Freneuse." According to Captain Mascarene, she arrived by sea, "from the other side of the Bay of Fundy in a Birch Canoo" in the company of "an Indian and a young Lad, her son." Mascarene wrote that Madame Freneuse described how "want of all manner of necessary's had put her to the Extremity of venturing all," embarking in a canoe to traverse the bay "at that unseasonable time of the year." She concluded her tale with a request for assistance, explaining that "she was forc'd to come to try whether she could be admitted to live under the new Government." Her plea struck a chord with Sir Charles Hobby, commander of the occupying forces, who saw in Freneuse a woman of higher social status in need of his help. Mascarene reported that she was "received Very Kindly by Sir Chas. Hobby—and had the Liberty she desired granted to her."[3] Only later would Mascarene realize that Madame Freneuse was, in fact, a French spy and saboteur.

Following this warm welcome, Madame Freneuse took up residence in a town under siege. A French-Mi'kmaq coalition waged a punishing asymmetric military campaign to recapture the town that the British had rechristened Annapolis Royal. Occupying British forces—with the questionable help of the region's unenthusiastic inhabitants—struggled to repair breaches in the town's badly damaged fortifications throughout the winter.[4] Despite their efforts, Mascarene reported that by late spring, the garrison remained vulnerable to French and Native raids. The night following one such attack, Madame Freneuse entered Port Royal's lower town to wait for her sons, who spirited their mother back to Canada. Mascarene opined that there was "a great deal of Reason to believe" that Madame Freneuse's orders were to "keep the French in a Ferment and make them backward in supplying the Garrison with any necessary's, and pry into and give an Account of our Secrets, till occasion should offer of endeavouring to drive us out of the Country."[5] Mascarene does not say whether the British questioned Freneuse's story, though an inquiry would have revealed that the French removed her from Port Royal several times during the war amid a sex scandal and accusations of treason. Given her notoriety, it is almost certain that the French inhabitants knew her identity. The information may have even lent credibility to her plea for British protection.

Madame Freneuse's adventures as a possible double agent working for a joint French and Indigenous guerrilla force capped off a remarkable life. Her life was dominated by a nearly decade-long controversy surrounding a torrid affair with a naval officer that drew the attention of King Louis XIV and resulted in banishment from Acadia. Whether double agent or traitor, Madame Freneuse's decision to join the English at Port Royal undoubtedly stemmed from the scandal, which erupted in 1702. The disgrace that spread from Acadia to Canada as well as to France, was merely one of the more dramatic examples of how Canadian, Acadian, and French women's sexual encounters with military personnel—particularly officers and government officials—sparked fears of immorality, disorder, and even treason.

By the first decade of the eighteenth century, sex in New France had been a matter of official interest for over forty years. The French Crown became increasingly concerned with the small size of the colony's population following the royal takeover in 1663, and as such attempted to stimulate population growth by supplying the colony with marriageable women—"*les filles du roi*"—and enticing French soldiers and officers to stay in New France after they completed their service. As a result of this preoccupation with creating conditions favorable for reproduction, the colony faced an ever-present tension regarding who was having sex with whom. The intersection of the military with settlement, sexual relations, and security resulted in increasing anxiety over inappropriate or disorderly relationships between Canadian women and French soldiers and officers. By the late seventeenth and early eighteenth centuries, concerns regarding such liaisons erupted into scandals that combined elements of sex and treason and ensnared women and officers across the social spectrum.[6]

Officials in both New England and New France connected religious and sexual morality to military security and national and confessional loyalties. Unlike in New England, where Cotton Mather fretted over the moral effects of the presence of homegrown militiamen posted in frontier garrison houses, French leaders feared sexual encounters in the fortified cities that became increasingly vital components of French defense. In Montreal, where fur traders returned from a wilderness seemingly teeming with temptation, rumors of liaisons between Montreal's women and these men—as well as Indigenous men—were cause for official concern.[7] As important French military and trading centers facing English attacks, Quebec and Port Royal became focal points for anxiety over inappropriate sexual liaisons as well as other forms of commerce.

As early as 1688, the Provost of Quebec heard a case regarding Jacquette Moreau, a woman charged with the social-sexual crime of living a "*mauvaise vie*," an "evil life," and creating a "public scandal." Court documents describe how Moreau, the wife of Adrien Lecomte, created a public scandal that extended beyond her own home. These accusations appeared to stem from an affair Moreau had with a garrison soldier named Dupré. The trial documents claim that the effects of Moreau's "evil life" and her sexual liaison with a military officer had tainted both her neighborhood and the entire city of Quebec. Moreau's affair surfaced at a particularly unfortunate time. Her trial was held in August 1688 and France went to war the next month when King Louis XIV invaded several polities within the Holy Roman Empire along France's border. Tensions between New England and New France were also rising, accompanied by smaller skirmishes. The American front of that war erupted in full several months later. Quebec's provost had no mercy for Moreau, whom he feared would create a "new scandal," and sentenced her to banishment. The idea that a sexual affair with a member of the military could threaten both the morality of a city and the security of the colony would be echoed in later scandals during the devastating wars of the following two decades.[8]

By 1699, the king—through his minister—expressed concern to the recently installed Governor General of New France, Louis-Hector de Callières, that "places of debauchery" had been "established in Quebec." He wrote also that the city was rife with "public scandals" caused by officers in the military consorting with Canadian women. Louis XIV became increasingly concerned with morality in his realm during this period, influenced at least in part by members of the clergy and by his mistress and future wife, Madame de Maintenon. The king was likely responding to complaints from the Bishop of Quebec, who wrote in a letter of "public places of debauchery" responsible for "a very great scandal." The bishop also reported that the wife of an officer who had returned to France had established a new household with a different officer. In his instructions to Callières, Louis ordered the new governor to consult the bishop and the intendant—the officials responsible for the spiritual and secular well-being of the population—and "wholly apply himself to stopping these disorders by all means that he judges feasible."[9]

Ridding Canada's towns of this supposed debauchery was part of Louis's larger vision for the colony and its new governor. The king instructed Callières to fight drunkenness, disorder, and military unreadiness while promoting morality, piety, and discipline. He believed that strengthening Montreal's religious establishment would "significantly fortify the colony" and "firmly establish the Christian religion among the Indians" in the town closest to Iroquois territory. Louis also hoped that a more Christian Canada might "call all the Iroquois to the faith," with the ultimate goal of "submitting them to the obedience of His Majesty."[10] These instructions reflected Louis's increasingly moralistic belief that a combination of sacred and secular order with morality and military strength would bring prosperity and security to France's American colonies.[11]

Concern over affairs with soldiers was not limited to the colony of Canada, with its supposed places of debauchery, nor was it restricted to women of lower social status. In fact, the higher the rank of the participants, the greater the resulting scandal and scope of the perceived danger. This was particularly true when the women lived in Acadia, always a place in between. Although Acadians, for the most part, were culturally French, for much of its early history the colony was dependent upon a strong, if ambivalent, trade relationship with Massachusetts to the south. Acadia began to feel the pressure from that position more consistently after King Philip's War in 1675–76. That same war largely secured southern New England for the English while reorienting New England's frontier almost exclusively toward French and French-allied territories, a change that would have profound implications for Acadia. Indeed, one historian argues that this shift helped to convince New Englanders that Acadia's French and Catholic inhabitants planned to ally themselves with the region's dispossessed Native peoples. These Native allies would then restate their claim to the lands north of Massachusetts. Suspicion and the tightening of borders between English and French centers of colonial power increased in the late seventeenth and early eighteenth centuries. In the years leading up to the outbreak of King William's War in 1688, Acadia would be drawn more firmly into France's purview while becoming a prize New England greatly desired.[12]

Acadia became increasingly French in the late seventeenth century, yet French officials, too, worried that the colony's population was particularly susceptible to enemy influence. It was in Acadia that the intersection of sexuality, military security, and national loyalties would produce chaos throughout the French Atlantic. The wartime affair between Madame Freneuse and Lieutenant Governor Bonaventure that rocked Port Royal emerged amid growing fears of the related evils of debauchery and shaky political and military allegiances. For the first few years of Freneuse and Bonaventure's scandal, it was paralleled by a "twin" scandal involving the wife of a French notary and the Governor of Acadia, Jacques-François de Monbeton de Brouillan. Both scandals teemed with salacious details and featured high-ranking Acadian officials known to have commercial connections to Boston. The fallout of the scandals would bring down the most powerful men in Acadia and see the exile of their lovers.

Madame Freneuse was born Louise Guyon and married Mathieu Damours as a young widow on October 1, 1686. Damours, the seigneur of Freneuse in Acadia, was the son of Mathieu Damours, the seigneur of Chauffours and a member of New France's Conseil Souverain. Although a second son, the younger Mathieu soon secured a place on the Conseil following the death of his father. After the couple moved to the Freneuse seigneury in Acadia, Madame Freneuse's husband died in 1696 following an English attack on Acadia that devastated their seigneury.[13] Madame Freneuse settled in Port Royal a few years later, where she began her affair with Simon-Pierre Denys de Bonaventure.

Her liaison with Bonaventure, a naval officer who also served as the lieutenant governor of the colony, first appears in the historical record in 1703. In a letter largely concerned with Acadia's fortifications and military operations, Mathieu de Goutin, a high-ranking royal official, dedicated a surprisingly sizable section of the letter to discussing an extramarital affair.[14] He noted that Port Royal was in an uproar over the birth of a son to Madame Freneuse and Bonaventure. The scandal had created "great disorder," causing parents to fear that their children's souls would be damaged by its example. The couple's son, Antoine, was born in September 1703 and baptized two months later as the "natural son" of "Louise Dion de Freneuse."[15] The Bishop of Quebec also weighed in on the matter, proposing the banishment of Madame Freneuse, "who had been the cause of much scandal." He referred to her "*mauvais commerce*," a phrase that conveyed the immoral nature of the sexual relationship. In his letter, the bishop suggested sending Madame Freneuse and her children to Canada or to her late husband's land in

Acadia.[16] The guardians of Port Royal's moral and military integrity likely sighed in relief when Madame Freneuse passed through the settlement's fortifications as she went into exile in 1705.[17]

Meanwhile, in June 1705, Louis maintained his order for Madame Freneuse's exile despite a letter from Governor Brouillan explaining that her late husband's estate could not support Freneuse and her several children.[18] Governor Brouillan's justification for his lack of action on the Freneuse matter came from a position of weakness as he, too, was embroiled in a scandal resulting from his own extramarital affair. His lover was Jeanne Quisence, the wife of a French-born Newfoundlander, the notary-turned-embezzler Claude Barrat. In the wake of her husband's crime, Madame Barrat fled by sea, settling in Port Royal where she opened a tavern and supposedly lived with Brouillan as his mistress.[19] The ever-vigilant Bishop of Quebec, who was spearheading efforts to banish Madame Freneuse, asked authorities to return Barrat to her husband in Plaisance, Newfoundland. He was particularly concerned that her liaison with Brouillan had created a "*mauvais esprit*," an evil pall that had settled over Acadia, throwing the colony into a state of confusion.[20]

When during the previous year an expeditionary force led by New England's Benjamin Church had attacked Acadia in July 1704, Brouillan's affair with Barrat became tinged with accusations of military negligence and treason that reverberated throughout the region. Pierre-Paul de Labat, an officer and engineer of the fort at Port Royal, wrote that officials in the town hurried to prepare for the raid, having received little warning of the enemy's approach. Labat described officials as "surprised" that they had not been given adequate notice by the soldiers on watch, though "their surprise ceased" when they learned that "Brouillan, at the request of Dame Barrât" had reduced the guard to a mere two soldiers who were unable to provide the needed alarm.[21] It is unclear why Barrat would make such a request or why Brouillan might agree to it. Labat had clashed with Brouillan in the past over matters relating to the fort and it is therefore possible that this information was merely a rumor. Even so, the idea that a governor engaged in an extramarital affair might risk the safety of his colony based on the whims of his mistress displays clear cultural connections between moral disorder and military unpreparedness.[22]

Governor Brouillan died in September 1705, and Bonaventure, his likely successor, came under renewed scrutiny. Bonaventure justified his lenience toward Freneuse, noting that her late husband's land was deserted, that she could not travel to Canada (possibly due to the war), and that she had taken two of her sister's children into her household while her brother-in-law languished in a Boston prison. According to Bonaventure, rather than remaining in Acadia, Madame Freneuse boarded a ship traveling across the Atlantic to France that year, purportedly to seek justice from the crown.[23] Fearing Freneuse's influence in the colony, Recollet priest Justinien Durand argued in a letter that she be prevented from returning to Acadia from France.[24] Port Royal's chaplain, Félix Pein, added his voice to this transatlantic debate, arguing that the allegations against Freneuse and Bonaventure were true. Writing of Freneuse, Pein claimed that "this woman has led a scandalous life" and that she had a child with Bonaventure.[25] Efforts to regulate Madame Freneuse's movements and tarnish Bonaventure's reputation continued unabated into 1706, when word arrived in New France that Madame Freneuse would again traverse the Atlantic—though to Canada, not Acadia.[26] By 1707, however, it was clear that Madame Freneuse would never go quietly into exile, as a royal order to leave Acadia showed.[27] Reports continued to reference her *"commerce scandaleux,"* while Bonaventure received a letter from the king's minister in June 1707 clearly stating that his "public scandal" had cost him his chance to become Acadia's governor.[28] It also noted that rumors had reached the king that Bonaventure had sold a ship filled with coal to a group of Boston men. The minister's letter warned that if Bonaventure engaged in illicit trade with Boston, his conduct would have dire consequences.

When Acadia's new governor, Daniel d'Auger de Subercase, received a letter from the king's minister regarding English threats to the colony in 1708, he learned that the crown still counted the "scandalous commerce" of Bonaventure and Freneuse among the dangers facing Acadia. According to his minister, the king had received "new complaints" that the affair had continued and had even produced several children, though no one seemed to know where they were. The letter also reflected fears that the affair would push Bonaventure—a man with suspected trade connections to New England—to betray France. The king again ordered Madame Freneuse out of Acadia and commanded that Bonaventure be watched carefully.[29] Between 1707 and 1710, government officials and clergymen composed at least twenty documents discussing the location and activities of Madame Freneuse.[30] Officials in Acadia continued to fret over her whereabouts until May 1710, when word arrived that she had settled in Canada.[31]

The two lovers ultimately met very different fates. Bonaventure remained part of Acadia's military, participating in battles relating to the fall of Port Royal before dying at a naval base on the French coast in 1711. Madame Freneuse made her way back to Canada after spending time with the

English in Port Royal. She last appears in the historical record in 1714, creating a formal plan for the guardianship of her children, an unremarkable act.[32] In this document, she is described as "Louise Guyon, widow of the late Monsieur Mathieu Damours ... Sieur de Freneuse" and "Councilor on the Conseil Supérieur."[33] This title hints that she had been restored to at least some degree of respectability. No longer the scandalous "Madame Freneuse" in official documents, the court recognized her as Louise Guyon, a woman of rank, and the widow of a seigneur and former member of the Conseil. This reputational rehabilitation suggests that there was some truth to Mascarene's account; either Madame Freneuse had proven her loyalty to France as a spy and saboteur or her sons succeeded in convincing others that she had.

A number of public figures became caught up in sexual scandals throughout the final decades of the French regime in Canada. None of these, however, matched the sensationalism—or the volume of correspondence—of the cases of the late seventeenth and early eighteenth centuries. Reports of scandals that did come to the attention of French officials received replies instructing officials in New France to make the problem disappear.[34] It is unclear why sexual scandals involving military officers diminished in importance after Queen Anne's War. Perhaps the death of Louis XIV or the relative peace New France enjoyed following the conflict played a part. The decades following the contest for Port Royal would see the growth of the French military bureaucracy in New France and the development of women's roles within that system.

Women's Roles in the New French Military Society

In the aftermath of the royal takeover of 1663, New France began a project of extensive militarization. Over subsequent decades, French martial institutions were woven into the fabric of Canadian society and politics. At the same time, the colonial elite became intertwined with the French military as social status and military rank merged.[35] The military and government of New France also began demanding more in the way of mandatory labor to repair fortifications (corvée) and military service while increasingly requisitioning goods and quartering soldiers. In its final decades, Canada, in the words of historian Louise Dechêne, "resembled more and more a large garrison, commanded rather than governed" in an attempt to maintain military security and public order.[36]

Unsurprisingly, the primary participants within this new system were men, though women also took on roles within a militarized New France.

One way the government incorporated women into the new order was by requiring their participation in a new welfare system for veterans. In 1709, the French government issued an order establishing a tax to fund pensions and half-pay for wounded and aging soldiers.[37] This safety net for veterans was funded by a tax on the pay of a wide variety of people who benefited from the French military and affiliated institutions, including officers, sailors, and even workers in the armory. As the crown refined its policies regarding pensions and half-pay for former soldiers over the subsequent decade, it included space for women within this system.

A 1720 order clarified and further established the role of the military and the crown in providing for former soldiers, while also defining the duties of the wives and widows of these men.[38] Although disabled veterans were exempted from providing *services personnels* that would have obligated them to work in strengthening their city's defenses, this exemption did not always apply to their wives. For example, the order specified that wives of disabled veterans who "keep shop and trade will contribute to the civic guard of the city gates and châteaux, as in the case of widowhood, according to and in proportion to their commerce."[39] That these women contributed to the civic guard for the protection of châteaux is particularly intriguing, as Château St. Louis served as the governor's residence in Quebec. This imposing building fulfilled political and military functions as a prominent symbol of imperial power and as the anchor of that heavily fortified city's military apparatus. In contrast, Château Ramezay, home of Montreal's Governor Claude de Ramezay, was the private seat of a public figure in the more commercially oriented Montreal. Perhaps it is appropriate, then, that government orders requiring women to contribute to this public project of fortification determined the extent of these women's obligations through the degree of their commercial presence in the colony. Yet, in that earnest attempt to delineate the gendered and civic boundaries of the growing military establishment, officials revealed just how conspicuously political, commercial, and military functions had fused in the frenzied fortification of New France.

The demands placed on women in trade in the 1720 order only hint at how gender, commerce, national loyalties, and war making would become intertwined in New France's increasingly militarized society. One consequence of the thirty-year peace between Britain and France that followed Queen Anne's War was greater competition in the fur trade. Iroquois demands for English goods pushed Montreal's merchants to violate the law and carry foreign merchandise. In response to these demands, a significant portion of French furs were sent to Albany, not Montreal. Despite the loss of revenue and attendant economic disorder, the most worrisome aspect of this development was, in the words of one scholar, "the way it unhinged national loyalties and allegiances."[40] But this treacherous, disturbingly porous physical and political landscape also presented possibilities to women, particularly women of rank, who possessed commercial acumen and an ability to navigate intricate transatlantic networks.

The opportunities and hazards for women operating within this complex military society through commercial and political connections are particularly apparent in the case of Madame Thiersant, the Canadian-born wife of a French officer. Born into a family of social climbers, Marie-Joseph Fézeret secured a highly advantageous marriage to François-Gabriel Thiersant, the son of a French nobleman. The new Madame Thiersant was active in promoting her husband's career, requesting a lieutenancy for him in 1717.[41] She astutely grounded this request in transatlantic family connections, namely the service of her father and brothers in the war against the Iroquois and the English while also citing her father-in-law's position as president of the Parlement of Metz. Throughout much of their marriage, she acted as her husband's agent, administering their financial and legal affairs.[42] Undoubtedly, the experience she gained while participating in New France's ongoing militarization would prove essential when she waded into larger imperial conflicts over trade and loyalty.

While visiting Paris in 1725, Madame Thiersant became involved in a complicated transatlantic commercial and political relationship with the chartered trading company, the Compagnie des Indes. It was an opportune moment to be a Canadian woman of rank in Paris—especially when one held critical knowledge regarding the state of the fur trade. The newly appointed Governor of Canada, the marquis de Beauharnois, and the new Intendant of New France, Claude-Thomas Dupuis, were also in Paris and planned to address the issue of the imperiled fur trade before returning to Canada. With impeccable timing, Madame Thiersant composed an account describing rampant fraud, treasonous commerce with New England, and an English beaver hat factory operating openly in Montreal. Convinced of the veracity of her statement and impressed by the solutions she proposed, the high-ranking colonial officials and Compagnie leaders reacted quickly, dispatching new orders across the Atlantic.[43]

Canada's governor, its intendant, and the director of the Compagnie all wrote letters testifying to the efficacy of the new policies that drove English traders from Montreal, reduced smuggling, and revitalized the fur trade in the first year of implementation. The intendant even hinted that Madame Thiersant had been involved in the decision to build Fort Niagara. This controversial but successful project established a French presence at the portage between Lake Ontario and Lake Erie and blocked British access to the primary fur trade corridor in 1726.[44] In what was likely the high-water mark of Madame Thiersant's career, the General Assembly of the Compagnie des Indes granted her 500 livres as a reward for "the essential service which the said Dame Thiersant rendered to the Company."[45] In the years following this triumph, however, Madame Thiersant struggled to attract colonists to work her land, and her fortunes took a downward turn.[46] She would spend the remaining years of an increasingly impoverished life petitioning the crown for further compensation.

Trade, treason, and military security were bound tightly in the borderlands of the early American northeast, and Madame Thiersant's colorful correspondence with representatives of the crown reveals much about the ideologies of a militarized, imperial New France. Born in a remote, rustic province, Thiersant perceptively emphasized her identity as a loyal subject of France, framing her service to the Compagnie des Indes as service to the larger French Empire. Portraying herself in a 1731 letter to the Minister of the Marine as a heroic actor who rescued both a powerful company and an empire, Madame Thiersant declared that "in serving my country of birth I have served the state." She wrote that she had been instrumental in "removing the English from the colony" and in boosting France's ability to compete in the fur trade, obtaining commercial and military security.[47] In return for such significant acts, Thiersant asked that the crown convert a curious new award from the Compagnie des Indes, one hundred pistols, into a pension or other monetary reward befitting her service.[48] It is unclear whether Thiersant ever received this or other additional compensation, though if she did, she was unable to salvage her financial situation. Madame Thiersant took to the sea a final time, traveling to France from Canada in 1735, all the while maintaining her efforts to receive a reward from the crown.[49] Despite her poverty, she wielded enough influence as a woman of rank, as a formerly influential public actor, or, perhaps, as both, to retain the support of well-placed representatives of the crown in Canada.[50]

As the French Empire sought to shore up existing strongholds and construct new ones in North America, authorities often depended upon women's participation in financing warships and physical fortifications intended to protect New France. Although women frequently sought financial support from the French military bureaucracy in the form of pensions and commissions for their male relatives in the French armed forces, women's contributions to the French military buildup represented more active martial roles for women. It was not until the 1720s and 1730s, however, that significant reports of women's participation in the fortification of New France surfaced. In September 1731, Madame de Ramezay requested a position for her son as well as reimbursement for land that had been lost due to the expansion of fortifications.[51] Records also show that the widowed Madame Planton, née Antoinette Isabeau, took over her brother's work as a fortifications contractor at the island fortress of Louisbourg in the late 1720s.[52]

By the mid-1720s, the Treasurer General of the Marine began regularly issuing both annual and supplemental reports, *"lettres de change,"* regarding payments for supplies and services provided by residents of New France in support of the colony's military operations. A majority of the surviving reports include payments made to women, married and unmarried. The bulk of the recipients of these payments were men; however, most reports include payments to at least several different women.[53] *Lettres* drawn up in the 1720s and 1730s were often vague regarding the nature of these services and supplies. By the 1740s, some reports were dedicated to the construction of specific ships and included the names of payees and amounts owed. Shipbuilding projects were particularly important in the mid-eighteenth century, as France hoped to develop Canada's maritime industry into a vital part of a French Atlantic empire that relied heavily upon its navy.[54] A report from 1743 shows that three women provided assistance in the construction of a ship called the *Caribou*.[55] One woman, Madame Berthier, received 2,200 livres, while another woman, Mademoiselle Pommereau, received two separate payments of 1,000 livres each. The third payment was for 150 livres to Madame Laporte. The next year, two other women involved in the construction of the frigate *Castor* received payments of 300 and 618 livres.[56]

In addition to payments made to women who provided supplies and services that supported the construction of warships, women also received compensation for aiding in the preparation for war. In 1744, the first year of King George's War, the Treasurer of the Marine paid Madame Duburon 1,577 livres, while Mademoiselle Lestage received 2,879 livres according to a report regarding "expenditures made in preparation of war."[57] The following year, Madame Duburon received another disbursement of 3,000 livres. Four other women received payments ranging from 500 to 1,500 livres in the same report, which covered expenditures regarding "preparations of war" and "the construction and armament of royal vessels," among other related categories.[58] These reports are unavailable for the period following the end of King George's War in 1748, with the exception of 1749–50. The reason for the absence of these reports is unclear. Surviving reports further indicate that women's martial activities in later conflicts had largely shifted to financial involvement as New France became more fully integrated into the empire's war machine.

Peace with the Iroquois and English reliance on naval attacks largely eliminated the need for women's physical participation in the wars of the eighteenth century. This was particularly true along the St. Lawrence River. The English continued their attacks on Acadia, culminating in the expulsion of much of Acadia's French population beginning in 1755 and lasting until the end of the Seven Years' War in America.[59] It seems likely that ordinary Acadian women resisted and even fought the English invaders, though hard evidence for this is lacking. In New England, where raids on settlements persisted through the first six decades of the eighteenth century, women continued to take on physical roles in these conflicts. Changes in the political and cultural climate reduced the need for their participation, and by the end of the Seven Years' War, both male and female colonists lived in a society where the distinction between settlers and soldiers had become more defined and the idea of a gendered home front began to take shape.

From Settler-Soldier to Suffering Subject: Political Identity in New England

In October 1757, the *Boston Gazette and Country Journal*, which advertised itself as "Containing the freshest Advices Foreign and Domestick," reported a story from eastern New York. According to the *Gazette*, an Indian "seized a young Woman that was washing at the Door" but was delayed by the appearance of another woman who "ran to her Assistance, rescued her, beat off the Indian, and shut the Door." The man had not come alone, and his friends "fired into the House, and killed 2 Women." Although they were eventually driven off, the author—or perhaps an editor—added a note to the story. The addendum argued that "'Tis Matter of very great Concern, that notwithstanding the Number of Soldiers we have now in this Province, his Majesty's Subjects shou'd be thus savagely butcher'd on the Frontiers, and no Provision made for their Protection!"[60] Despite the fact that the attackers "were repulsed by two Men who fired out on them," the article curiously portrayed the inhabitants of the house as lacking the protection of real soldiers sent by the king to his subjects.

Published in the second year of the Seven Years' War, the article in the *Boston Gazette* reflects larger changes in New Englanders' attitudes toward gender, the crown, and the identity of the proper defenders of the frontier. Between 1713 and 1760, New Englanders described a growing distance between home and front, spaces that had been often indistinguishable in previous decades. Sources ranging from legislative records, petitions, and newspapers to sermons, personal correspondence, and published accounts of these wars depict slow but significant changes in military strategy and in gender ideologies. By the Seven Years' War, the line between home and front, which had been blurred throughout the seventeenth and early-eighteenth centuries, became more fixed. No longer settler-soldiers in their own right, men and their families in the northeastern borderlands would become helpless civilians, subjects under the tender—if inconsistent—care of a Protestant father-king.

Scholars have identified the first half of the eighteenth century as a period of profound transformation in New England. Colonial identities became increasingly intertwined with larger imperial ideologies and agendas that typically emphasized anti-Catholic and anti-French sentiment. During this period, as one study has found, Anglo-Americans began to embrace the monarch as a loving, paternal figure who guarded his subjects from popery and attacks from Catholic countries.[61] At the same time, ideologies of masculinity began to change, likely reflecting the needs of this developing imperialism. Indeed, historian Ann Little has discovered a cultural shift away from "a masculinity based on household headship, Christian piety, and the duty to protect both family and faith by force of arms" to an Anglo-American nationalist manhood grounded in "anti-Catholicism" and "soldiering for the empire."[62]

But if a man could choose to exchange the identity of a defenseless civilian at home for that of a soldier away at the front, the same could not be said of New England's women who made war in the northeastern borderlands in the mid-eighteenth century. It was during these critical decades, as historian Mary Beth Norton has argued, that the formal public, informal public, and private—that is, personal or secret—spheres of the early modern era were slowly replaced by an emerging masculine public sphere and a domestic, feminine private sphere.[63] At the same time, women's physical participation became less necessary due to changes in military strategy that favored offensive attacks and dedicated military forts. Despite these strategic and ideological changes, women continued to live in remote areas, making war in defense of their communities. Yet they did not do so as members of fortified vanguard communities or as fully public actors. By the wars of the 1740s and 1750s, most women in more remote areas of the northeastern borderlands would remain at half-formed home fronts, their war making laudable yet lamentable examples of the failure of soldiers and kings to protect civilians at home.

The first decades of the eighteenth century marked the beginning of a new Anglo-American military alliance. It was also during this period that policies and practices regarding military strategy and personnel that would dominate the wars of subsequent decades first developed.[64] Central to these changes was Governor Joseph Dudley of Massachusetts, who was instrumental in securing the support of the British military in the conflict known as Queen Anne's War. The greater professionalism, manpower, and strategy British military leaders brought to New England slowly began to transform the nature of war in the northeastern borderlands.[65] Most of this assistance came in the form of British troops, strategists, and supplies in the support of offensive expeditions against Canada in conjunction with provincial troops. By the 1720s, New Englanders would also begin investing greater resources in the construction of larger, dedicated forts in more remote areas, manned by provincial soldiers on active duty rather than by settler-soldiers serving as members of defensive militias. The goal was to redirect attacks away from fortified towns and establish a new first line of defense that would replace the older settler-soldier/garrison house model.[66] The change would not be an easy one.

The often slow and painful strategic transition that began with Queen Anne's War lingered through the first half of the eighteenth century. Even the 1723–26 Anglo-Abenaki conflict known as Dummer's War relied heavily on the settler-soldier/garrison house model. Lacking British support for a local conflict fought between Massachusetts and New Hampshire versus an impressive Abenaki coalition over colonial encroachment on Abenaki lands in present-day Maine, colonial leaders turned to garrison houses and "scalp-hunting rangers" as solutions in the war.[67] As the crisis between colonists and the Abenaki escalated in 1721, the *Boston Gazette* printed Governor Samuel Shute's August 1721 proclamation responding to reports that settlers on the western frontiers had joined their eastern counterparts in deserting their towns. Blamed for incompetent leadership that led to this crisis, the embattled governor noted that "very considerable Sums of Money have been lately expended in the Defence and for the Preservation of the Settlements in the Frontiers." Outraged, he chastised the "many Persons and even whole Families" who "have quitted their Habitations in those Frontiers and removed into other Towns." Arguing that this "Desertion" weakened "the Strength of those Settlements" and gave "great Encouragement" to their adversaries, the governor commanded that "all Persons by Law fit to bear Arms who have deserted the Frontiers, immediately and without Delay return to their Habitations." Shute's words were not particularly unusual, given the legislation passed in the previous two wars. He did add a remarkably hostile warning, however, declaring that "no Person whatsoever upon any Rumour of Danger from the Indians do presume to leave their Settlements upon Peril of what may ensue upon their Desertion, and as they expect the Protection of this Government."[68] Speaking as if to children, Shute's angry message signaled that settler-soldiers who did not fulfill their defensive obligations should not expect the protection of the province.

Concern over the fate of colonists grew as war appeared inevitable, and families ignored warnings to remain in place even as the official government position insistently maintained the tradition of frontier families as the first line of defense. A September 1721 committee report prepared in response to the governor's August proclamation noted that families in "our Eastern parts" along the coast of Maine were beginning to suffer greatly from the effects of increasing skirmishes. The sympathetic committee worried that without "relief and succour" provided by the government, these families might be forced "to quit their Habitations." The authors noted that they were "very sensible their feeble condition and posture to defend themselves, required a number of men for their safe-guard."[69] Recently returned from Maine, Isaac Taylor and Robert Temple reported to the Massachusetts House of Representatives in March 1722. Their testimony described how families in the Eastern settlements continued to struggle, and they warned that "some Families have gone down, and others that were ready to fly off, have been Induced to stay in Obedence to his Excellencies Proclamation, forbidding the Remove of any from the Eastern Frontiers."[70] When war was finally declared in August 1722, Massachusetts passed a familiar law ordering the fortification of frontier towns and setting out penalties for men who left the town or who refused to assist in building fortifications.[71] Remarkably similar to the laws of earlier conflicts, its passage indicates that colonial policy relating to the defense of the frontiers during Dummer's War remained unchanged. In the absence of imperial assistance, colonial leaders would retreat to the familiarity of the garrison house model of war.

Just as Dummer's War demonstrated how imperial military strategies took hold only slowly in the absence of imperial influence and assistance, so, too, did more traditional ideologies of women's wartime participation as public actors persist throughout the 1720s and 1730s. Women had far fewer opportunities to act as combatants during this period, though their petitions to the Massachusetts government demonstrate the variety of public roles available to women—as well as a continued acceptance of women's martial activities. The petitioners included women serving as emissaries and as would-be rescuers of captive men. Petitions also show women receiving compensation for war making in conflicts dating back to King William's War at the end of the seventeenth century.

Dominating the first half of the 1720s, Dummer's War featured the petitions of several women who offered to partner with the Massachusetts government to secure the return of captives. Although women had petitioned for the return of impressed husbands and sons in earlier wars, petitioning for captives was less common. It is likely that the higher number of female petitioners reflects the specific tactics and strategies of Dummer's War, particularly the central role that hostage-taking played on both sides. In an attack on Merrymeeting Bay in 1722, Indians captured nine families, kept only five adult men as hostages, and released the other sixty inhabitants.[72] In three of the cases, Indians captured husbands and children at sea, a decided departure from more traditional accounts of captivity, in which the women and children of garrison houses were the primary targets. Appropriately, with roles reversed, women would attempt to redeem the missing men.

Christian Newton and Margaret Blin filed the first of the Dummer's War petitions after fitting out a sloop with the intention of retrieving Newton's son and Blin's husband. Christian Newton was the widow of Thomas Newton, a Massachusetts judge and attorney general who had died the year before. Her son Hibbert, one of the captives, was a customs collector in Nova Scotia. Margaret Blin's husband, James, had been captain of the ship ferrying the group when they were captured.[73] Newton and Blin submitted a petition to the General Court requesting the use of "some of the Province Arms for their Defence."[74] Although unclear whether Newton and Blin hoped to accompany the sloop or if they planned to send a search party, it is likely that the women's ability to finance part of the mission, Christian Newton's status in Massachusetts society, and the prominence of the captives attracted the attention of the House of Representatives, which agreed to their proposal. Ultimately, the upper house failed to support the decision, possibly due to the brief amount of time that had passed since the men were taken captive.[75] The politics and timing of hostage negotiations may have also influenced the upper house's decision, though the gender of the petitioners does not appear to have been a factor.

In 1723, two pairs of women approached the Massachusetts General Court in an attempt to recover relatives who had been captured. Abigail Cabbott and Miriam Johnson submitted a petition "praying this Court would engage to Restore them."[76] The court rejected this petition, as well as another entreaty from Jane Edgar and Margaret Watt, each of whom had lost their husbands, as well as a combined seven children, to captivity.[77] They hoped that the court would agree to a prisoner exchange: their families for a Native woman named Elizabeth and her children who were prisoners of Massachusetts. Again, the court refused, and while unclear, the decision may have been influenced by the lower social status of the petitioners, their inability to outfit an expedition, or the added complications of a prisoner exchange.

The Dummer's War petitions may have been inspired by the actions of a woman named Christian Baker, who first approached the General Court in 1721. Baker was born Margaret Otis, daughter of Richard and Grizel Otis of Cochecho, New Hampshire. Only three months old when her father was killed in the famous 1689 attack on the town, Margaret was taken captive along with her mother. After taking the Catholic name Marie Madeleine, the widowed Grizel married a Frenchman, Philipe Robitaille, in 1693. Previously, her infant daughter Margaret had been rebaptized Christine and separated from her mother to be raised as a French Catholic child. Despite this separation, Christine and her mother maintained a close relationship in Canada, perhaps because her mother adapted so well to life in the French colony, even as an adult. Christine would later marry Louis Le Beau, a carpenter, in 1707 at the age of eighteen, and two of their children—Marie-Anne and Marie-Madeleine—survived infancy. After the death of her husband, Christine Le Beau fell in love with Captain Thomas Baker, an interpreter traveling with Deerfield's Rev. John Williams (father of the famous captive Eunice Williams) and John Stoddard on their 1714 journey to recover captives in Canada. Before leaving for New England, the colonial government of Canada invoked Christine Le Beau's status as a prisoner of war taken during a previous conflict to limit her legal rights. As a result, Le Beau was compelled to leave the property she had inherited from her husband to her two young, culturally French daughters, who remained with her mother in Canada by order of the colony's governor.[78]

Sporting a newly anglicized name, Christian Baker and her husband approached the Massachusetts government in 1721 with the hope of securing backing for an expedition to recover her children. Perhaps to sweeten the deal, the Bakers offered to try to persuade other captives to return home with them. Christian Baker's connections to both the French and Anglo-French population of Canada and Thomas Baker's experience as an interpreter who had participated in a similar expedition must have seemed like an ideal combination. In March 1722, the House of Representatives presented Christian Baker with twenty pounds from the public treasury in support of her mission to recover her children and "to perswade many others, in the Hands of the French & Indians to return to their Countrey, & Religion."[79] New England was not at war with New France, and Christian and Thomas Baker traveled with Joseph Kellogg, who carried a letter from the Governor of Massachusetts addressed to Governor Vaudreuil of Canada. Baker proved a remarkably successful emissary, persuading several captives to return. In what was likely a bitter disappointment, her own children remained behind in Canada.[80]

By the 1730s, Thomas Baker had fallen ill, requiring Christian Baker to seek new sources of income. In 1735, the House of Representatives of New Hampshire granted her permission to run a public house.[81] Baker also successfully petitioned the House of Representatives of Massachusetts, receiving a land grant of five hundred acres in York County that she could sell for monetary support. The decision to grant the petition was based on "the particular Circumstances of the petitioner," and the fact that "she has been Instrumental in Regaining Divers persons who were formerly Carried Captive to Canada."[82] In granting Christian Baker the initial twenty pound allowance in her own name and in basing the land grant on her "instrumental" participation in persuading captives to return home, the House of Representatives made a critical distinction between Christian Baker's efforts as a public actor and those of her husband Thomas. The government would draw the same distinction several more times over the course of the following decade when approving land grants that recognized the military significance of women's participation in the border wars.

Between 1727 and 1739, Massachusetts began awarding land grants in Maine, New Hampshire, and northeastern Massachusetts to veterans of earlier wars and their descendants.[83] For the most part, these grants were not presented to men for service as settler-soldiers in garrison houses. Rather, recipients tended to be colonists who had shown exceptional merit during expeditions and other offensive campaigns outside of fortified communities. Among their number were women and their descendants, all of whom successfully petitioned the government for land specifically on the basis of the women's individual service to the colony. In every case, these women left their fortified communities and ventured into the wilderness of the northeastern borderlands, seemingly taking on more formal public roles similar to those of the offensive, expeditionary troops the grants were designed to reward.

Haverhill's Hannah Dustan, who killed nearly a dozen Indians during her captivity in 1697, was a veteran of both an impromptu military campaign and an extensive publicity campaign. Unsurprisingly, she became the first of these women to request a land grant for military service. Dustan clearly realized that these grants rewarded a different form of war making than the award of twenty-five pounds that stood in for an expired scalp bounty in 1697. In contrast, Dustan's 1731 petition sought compensation for her active military service, not for the physical presentation of scalps. The joint petition with her husband asked that the government award them land "or otherwise extend their Bounty, beyond the Twenty Five Pounds formerly allowed them, for the Services within-mentioned." The House responded to the petition by forwarding the missive to the Committee for Petitions in December 1731. Two weeks later, the House granted Hannah Dustan and her husband two hundred acres of land.[84]

Joseph Neff, the son of Mary Neff, Hannah's partner in the killings and scalpings, submitted his own remarkable petition in 1739 for land based on his mother's service. In his entreaty, Joseph Neff described how his mother was "Carried into Captivity and kept a prisoner for a Considerable time and in Endeavouring her Escape was assistant with Mrs. Duston in Killing and Scalping Divers Indians and whereby they obtained their Relief." Joseph Neff augmented his account of Mary Neff's experience as combatant and captive with a description of the party's determined struggle to return to patriarchy and order, writing that the group "in their Return home past through the utmost hazard of their lives and Suffered distressing want being almost starved before they could Return to their dwellings." Perhaps taking advantage of Massachusetts's preference for compensating effective veterans of offensive campaigns, Neff argued that despite his mother's "Great Service to this Province in the destruction of a number of Indians," she had not "Received any Reward for her said Especial Service." Adding that his advanced age of seventy years had reduced his ability to support himself, Neff echoed the successful petitions of other combatants and their heirs.[85] After several months of consideration, Joseph Neff received two hundred acres of land for his mother's actions in King William's War. According to the award, "Mary never had a reward from this Government," a finding that rendered her son eligible to receive the grant.[86] It is unclear whether the House was aware that Mary Neff had received a portion of the bounty in 1697.[87] Regardless, that Massachusetts rewarded a woman's son for his mother's "killing and scalping" of "divers Indians" in King William's War—in the same way that the dependents of male veterans received land—demonstrates that space still remained for the celebration of women who made war as public actors in early America.

In seeking the land grant for his mother's service, Joseph Neff enlisted the help of another petitioner, Hannah Bradley, the twice-captive resident of Haverhill, who was taken along with Dustan.[88] Bradley was known for having killed attackers with boiling soap in an attempt to avoid her second captivity. According to local tradition, Bradley also shot and killed an Indian when defending her home alongside her husband in a third attack in 1706.[89] In addition to supplying a deposition in support of Joseph Neff's petition, Bradley petitioned the House of Representatives in 1737, requesting a land grant as a reward for "extraordinary Sufferings and Services in the late Indian Wars." The House agreed, awarding her 250 acres "in Consideration of the very great Sufferings as well as Service of the Petitioner" and to "her Heirs and Assigns for ever."[90]

Petitions for compensation in the wars of the late seventeenth and early eighteenth centuries frequently employed the terms "suffering" and "service" in their pleas for land. The use of the word "service" generally referred to acts taken in the service of the government or the "publick," such as Daniel Tucker's 1715 petition for relief while recovering from "a Gun-shot Wound he received in the Service against the Indian Enemy, in the late War." The term "suffering" described hardships, such as injury and captivity. The use of the word "suffering" alone and in combination with "service" was not confined to women's petitions. For instance, in 1716, John Arms of Deerfield argued that he deserved compensation from the Massachusetts House of Representatives for his "forward Service in the late War against the Indian Enemy, and his Sufferings by them, having been Wounded, and carried Captive to Canada."[91] These women's petitions, though few in number and confined to women who participated in more noteworthy incidents, suggest that public spheres and public roles were not entirely closed to women, even by the mid-eighteenth century.

Massachusetts's decision to expand its frontier through these new land grants was accompanied by an unprecedented fort-building initiative. Previously, New England had only a handful of forts at any one time. Built even further out into the northeastern borderlands than the new land grant communities, these forts acted as quarters for provincial forces and as symbols of Massachusetts's presence in the region. The forts also acted as "magnets," diverting attacks away from towns and toward these new installations. Although some soldiers stationed at these forts did bring along their families, the gender ratio was very different from those of garrison communities. Women who lived in the new forts appeared more akin to camp followers than to those inhabitants of earlier fortified communities that blurred lines between home and front.[92]

"We That Tarry at Home": A Home Front Emerges

The growing professionalization of the military and the related transformation of martial gender roles in Britain and New England sparked a raging debate that appeared in humorous fashion in an October 1739 edition of the *Boston Evening Post*. At stake was British masculinity and the potentially dangerous consequences of establishing a standing army.[93] A reprinted opinion piece that had appeared in the British newspaper *Craftsman*, the critical yet witty article examined gender and martial behavior over time. The author pondered whether the young ladies of his time were especially frivolous, pointing back to ill-defined "past Ages" when women "were not only good Wives, but useful Subjects." He noted that in Britain's history, "Female Patriots . . . sacrific'd their Money, Plate, Jewels, to the Good of their Country." In England of old, martial queens "conquer'd with their Arms abroad, as much as with their Eyes at home." He seemed to lament that "such Military Virtues" would not appeal to "our modern polite Ladies."[94]

The article's author attributed the lack of military-minded females to the presence of standing armies that extinguished Britain's need "to call in the Female Powers to our Aid." Questioning the masculinity of the nation's standing army, the author suggested that its members "look as smug, and make as pretty a Figure at a Review, when their Hair is nicely ruck'd up and well powder'd, as if They were to make their Appearance in Petticoats, (for which I am told there is actually a Project in Agitation)."[95] For this author, the might of the British military's past and future depended on an idealized, wholesome army of ready, devoted volunteers. Certainly, he argued, it should not rest on the costumed shoulders of a man wielding little more than a fussily dressed coiffure and an inflated sense of self. The writer concluded that although women were currently not needed as warriors, they might act as sensible wives and daughters, making their own clothes and reading good books. Despite his transatlantic audience and cutting sarcasm, the author alone could not reverse an imperial trend that separated the men who fought from the men who stayed at home.

Rhetoric associating the home front with the suffering subject in the northeastern borderlands emerged during the 1720s and 1730s—even as military strategy and a willingness to award land grants to female veterans suggested continuity existed in practice. As early as May 1725, the growing separation between soldiers and civilians appeared in a sermon given in Bradford, Massachusetts, by Thomas Symmes. Bradford, a community adjacent to the hapless, repeatedly sacked town of Haverhill, was still firmly within the designated frontier area during this conflict. In his sermon, Symmes responded to the death of Captain John Lovewell in Dummer's War. He reminded his listeners that prayer was the most powerful weapon in New England's arsenal. Declaring that "our Soldiers . . . must be a Praying Legion," Symmes reminded his listeners and readers that "we that tarry at home" must also pray, recommending that civilian men lingering in the frontier region near Haverhill might do their duty through prayer. Ignoring decades of women's wartime participation, Symmes suggested that "a good Woman in her Closet, (tho' she's afraid to take a Gun in her Hand) may serve her Country to very good purpose, even in respect of the War."[96] His use of the word "closet" is particularly telling, as it referred to a smaller, private room often set aside for prayer and contemplation. In one stroke, he reduced women to frightened creatures, relegating their martial activity to prayers offered in a cloistered, domestic space. Symmes's sermon also reflects the growing divergence between home and front while embracing a newer model of a feminine private sphere that would grow in popularity in the decades that followed.

In a sermon delivered in June 1737 to an artillery company in Boston, Rev. William Williams expressed concern with Massachusetts's preparedness and strategy in previous wars that had placed a large defensive burden on settler-soldiers. Williams cautioned that although the colony had deliberately settled "a Line of Towns on our Frontiers, in as defensible a manner as may be," the defense of the colony should "not be left only to the Care and feeble Attempts of the Grantees" of these towns precariously straddling the line between battlefront and home front. Instead, he argued, defense must "be directed and very much encouraged and assisted by the Government . . . [that] these may prove a Barrier and Defence to the scatter'd Plantations and Villages which lie expos'd to be an easy Prey to little Bands of merciless Robbers and Plunderers." Williams's solution included "repairing and strengthening the Forts and Garrisons of this Province," and he appealed to the governor's "natural and paternal Concern" for New England, noting that his authority derived from "our rightful Sovereign King George." In doing so, Williams emphasized the growing connection between paternal concern, royal authority, and the intervention of a more professional military in conflicts that had earlier been fought by settler-soldiers and often unenthusiastic provincial soldiers ordered to assist town militias.[97]

Joining rhetoric with action, Lieutenant Governor Spencer Phips of Massachusetts declared war in the name of those suffering settlers in August 1745. Although the colony was already at war with France, Phips composed his declaration against Native nations such as the Penobscot, Norridgewock, their confederates, and French-allied Indians. Phips wrote of "his Majesty's good Subjects dwelling on the Frontiers of this Province [who] have many Months past endured most of the Inconveniencies and Disasters of War." He also noted that many of these inconvenienced colonists struggled to make a living. Some had even been "driven off from their Estates," a previously illegal response to raids in the earlier wars of settler-soldiers and fortified communities. Rather than fleeing their duties as settler-soldiers, colonists instead found themselves in the curious position of being subjects "for whose Protection and Defence this Government apprehend themselves obliged" to shield from harm. In this "just and necessary War," the crown and its colonial government would remedy earlier failures to watch over and defend "his Majesty's good Subjects."[98]

Massachusetts remained committed to this more sympathetic approach to vulnerable colonists living in remote communities during the conflict known as King George's War, passing a law raising money and men "for the defence of the Frontier." The government argued that this step was necessary because "the inhabitants as are so exposed to the Enemy as to be unable to support themselves by their Labour."[99] Bounties on scalps would be paid to a civilian who killed in "his own Defence, or in the Defence of any of his Majesty's Subjects."[100] Another act ordered that stockades, garrisons, and forts be placed in "the most prudent manner . . . for the Security & Defence of the whole Inhabitants of each place."[101] The order rewarded the military actions of settlers, though without the angry demands of the declarations of Dummer's War. Indeed, the government took a comparatively gentle approach in Governor Shirley's April 1746 direction to militia officers, ordering them to require "Inhabitants" to carry firearms "from Time to Time . . . as they shall judge needful, to prevent a Surprize" attack.[102] A law passed a month later required that all men in frontier towns possess a gun, that these settlements boast an adequate supply of firearms, and that military companies stationed in such vulnerable areas be "in constant Readiness for the Relief of any neighbouring Frontier-Town."[103]

Initially, New Englanders seemed pleased with the government's newly expressed commitment to the safety of frontier inhabitants of the emerging home front. In a dedication to his published military sermon delivered at the opening of King George's War in June 1744, Rev. Joseph Parsons praised Governor Shirley for his "unwearied Application" in which "we see our Fortifications in a Condition to free us from perplexing Cares about the Enemy; and such speedy and vigorous Measures taken to guard our exposed Frontiers as calm our Minds under the sad Apprehensions we had entertained of a War." Parsons went on to thank Shirley for his paternal "Concern."[104] But despite the smattering of gratitude for the parental concern expressed by Massachusetts's leaders, King George's War and the Seven Years' War were marked more by dissatisfied articles in newspapers and other publications demanding British protection. A piece in the June 5, 1746, issue of the *Boston News-Letter* reported that "the poor People on the Frontiers are in great Distress, the Indians being very numerous, and divided into many Parties."[105] One anonymous author who appended his observations to the publication of the Reverend Benjamin Doolittle's *A Short Narrative Of Mischief done by the French and Indian Enemy* sought to encourage divisions between settlers and soldiers.[106] The author complained that "great Injustice is done the Inhabitants in the Frontiers in pressing them out of their Business" to pursue the enemy without compensation. He also noted that these men were "sent out Day after Day with their Horses, and have not half so much per Day as they must give a Man to labour for them in the mean Time."[107] Such remarks reflected the tension between the demands of life as a farmer and as a potential combatant. In the seventeenth and early eighteenth centuries, the author's primary concern would have been adding more provincial soldiers to assist overworked settler-soldiers and their families, not whether settlers should be asked to serve in that capacity in the first place.

Relating an incident that reflected the transfer of masculinity from settler to soldier and from vanguard community to home front, Benjamin Doolittle wrote that during King George's War, a group of Indians in Massachusetts "Way-laid the Road; and as one Matthew Clark with his Wife and Daughter, and three Soldiers, were going from the Garrison to Clark's House, they fir'd upon them." Here, Clark was not the primary protector of his wife and daughter; rather, that position fell to the three soldiers acting as bodyguards. During the chaos, the Indians "kill'd and scalp'd said Clark, and wounded his Wife and Daughter." With Clark proven ineffectual as a protector and dead as a result, Doolittle reported that "one Soldier play'd the Man, fir'd several Times—defended and bro't off the Woman and her Daughter to the Fort, who are recovered of their Wounds." Curiously, with three soldiers as protection, the attackers still had an opportunity to reach and scalp Clark, and only one soldier appeared to have had any real role in their defense. While the incident seemed to represent a failure of the three soldiers' abilities, in this emerging gender hierarchy, it was the surviving soldier who retained the title of "man."[108]

Despite changing attitudes regarding the responsibilities of families on the frontier and the widening of the space between home and front, women's attempts to defend their homes, themselves, or their families did not elicit disapproving responses. Courage and a focused determination to defend the increasingly domestic home front were in fact qualities particularly prized in mid-century accounts of women's martial activity. Benjamin Doolittle reported that in May 1746, a soldier alerted the inhabitants of a fortified building in Fall Town that an attack was imminent. Although there were "but three Men in the fort," the women "assist[ed] in charging the Guns," helping to foil the attack.[109] In an August 1755 incident in Walpole, New Hampshire, John Kilburn and three companions returned to Kilburn's house ahead of an impending attack. After securing the door, Kilburn and the other men in the house prepared to defend the home, helped by "Kilburn's wife and his daughter Hitty, who contributed not a little to encourage and assist their companions, as well as to keep a watch upon the movements of the enemy." The account's author then noted approvingly that "the women, with true Grecian firmness, assisted in loading the guns, and when their stock of lead grew short, they had the forethought to suspend blankets in the roof of the house to catch the enemies' balls," which had lost much of their force when they hit or passed through the roof.[110]

Women's martial activities were not restricted to gathering ammunition and maintaining weapons; direct engagement in physical combat, too, remained an acceptable option for women. In April 1746, six Indians surprised the sleeping inhabitants of David Woodwell's garrison in Hopkinton, New Hampshire. His wife, Mary, who was "being closely embraced by a sturdy Indian, wrested from his side a long knife." According to the account of Mary Woodwell's daughter, Mary Woodwell Fowler, her mother "was in the act of running him through, when her husband prevailed with her to desist, fearing the fatal consequences." Aware that she would not be allowed to keep the weapon, she threw it into a well before they began their trek north. Tellingly, Mary Woodwell's first instinct was to arm herself and attack, not to meekly submit. Although David Woodwell persuaded his wife to spare her captor's life, his objection was practical, and neither moral nor based on a sense of proper female behavior. He knew that if she stabbed the man, his companions would kill her and, perhaps, the rest of the family.[111]

In the absence of weapons, two women resisted separate raids using their instincts, fists, and in one case, a clothes iron, during the Seven Years' War. The *Boston Evening Post* reported in July 1755 that three Indians approached a home near the border between Massachusetts and New York, where "they found a Woman who was at Work, ironing Clothes." According to the *Evening Post*, one of the Indians grabbed the woman and informed her that she had been taken captive. She responded by hitting him on the head with her "Box-iron . . . which made him sally [silly]." When another man from the group trained his gun on her, she was able to use her arm to hit the gun so that the shot "went off over her Head." Finally, the third man "wounded her in the Side" with his gun and took her from the house. After they attacked another home, a male colonist shot one of the Indians, dispersing the party and rescuing the injured woman.[112] In an account emphasizing the development of wartime roles that cast women as determined guardians of domestic spaces, the *New Hampshire Gazette* reported that a woman in Maine had been caring for her ill son in June 1757 when a small group of Indians attacked and killed her husband. One of the men forced his way into the house and aimed his gun at the young man in his sickbed. After his shot missed, he brandished a knife, but the mother "resolutely took hold of the Indian and turn'd him out of the House, and fastned the Door against them." The mother, reportedly acting to protect her son (now hidden in the cellar), was later killed by a stray bullet and her son was not expected to recover from his illness.[113]

Accounts of English women's participation in the wars of the 1740s and 1750s suggest that a woman's courage and her willingness to defend herself and others remained admirable qualities. Still, as the gap expanded between settler and soldier, home and front, so, too, did the distance between men's and women's public wartime roles. In New England, greater integration into the British Empire placed settler-soldiers under the protection of a benevolent father-king and a masculinized, increasingly professional military. The shift in strategy that demoted the settler-soldier and the garrison house in favor of manned forts slowly changed the nature of warfare and reduced the need for women to participate in those conflicts. This transition took time, progressing slowly even as women continued to receive praise and rewards for their actions in earlier struggles. In the end, the public roles associated with vanguard communities were subsumed by military companies and more distant forts that made soldiers out of helpless civilian men who "tarried" at home. For the women who remained on the home front, dwelling in increasingly domesticated, vulnerable spaces, their roles as public actors in war making began to vanish. Women's participation in armed conflict would thus become private, the act of a brave, resolute, individual woman making a final stand in defense of the home when, lamentably, "real" combatants were unavailable or simply not up to the task.

Meanwhile, changes in women's roles in New France depended more upon shifts in military strategy and geography than transformations of ideology. Although a new strategic reliance on fortified towns along the coasts initially produced anxiety over relations between female inhabitants and the soldiers stationed in those cities, reports of sexual scandals diminished greatly following the end of Queen Anne's War in 1713. Canada and Acadia would become increasingly militarized—fortress colonies and the linchpin of a transatlantic empire in the decades leading up to King George's War and the Seven Years' War. As in the raids and melees of the seventeenth century, the new military society of the eighteenth century still relied on the willingness of women to join the battle, albeit in a different fashion. The brave Canadian Amazons that Sister Marie Morin spied from her bell tower in Montreal in the mid-seventeenth century and the women of rank who defended their provincial keeps had become imperial Amazons wielding the weapons of commerce, information, and investment.

Accounts of women's participation in the wars of the northeastern borderlands became the stuff of memory after the Seven Years' War. In British-colonized Canada, the martial women of New France's colonial past awaited later rediscovery and repurposing by Canadians. New Englanders, reveling in colonial victories and, later, a successful revolution, would enthusiastically embrace memories of earlier martial women. Authors retelling these stories in New England during the late eighteenth and early nineteenth centuries portrayed the actions of these women as suitable for women of the past, though perhaps not appropriate for the civilized women of a newly formed United States. The cultural persistence of colonial stories—and how authors employed them—would help to shape new political identities and gender ideologies while advancing new expansionist projects.

CHAPTER FIVE

Resolute Motherhood

Memories of Women's War Making in New England

Benjamin Mirick published *The History of Haverhill, Massachusetts* in 1832, one of many local histories of New England towns written in the nineteenth century.[1] A former officially designated frontier town of strategic importance, Haverhill was the site of some of the most famous raids in the history of the northeastern border wars. It was also the home of several well-known female combatants from those conflicts, such as Hannah Dustan, Mary Neff, Hannah Bradley, and Susannah Swan. Mirick's work drew on a wide range of firsthand accounts, as well as oral and written histories from the seventeenth and eighteenth centuries. His sources reveal chains of transmission between generations of New Englanders and attest to the cultural persistence of stories of women's participation in the border wars. But however familiar or enduring these stories may have been, they were never static. Even as Mirick sought to interpret and retell earlier accounts of women's war making from the colonial period, he would add yet another cultural layer to those stories. His *History of Haverhill* hints at how Americans remembered and reconstructed colonial histories, appropriating accounts of women's war making to reflect and encourage the development of gender ideologies that delineated a masculine public sphere and a feminine private sphere in a republic engaged in its own colonialist project. The martial women of the colonial past would be deployed again.

While penning his manuscript, Benjamin Mirick became perplexed by reports of a 1704 raid on the town in which Hannah Bradley used boiling soap to gruesome effect in a futile attempt to fend off her attackers. Piecing together details of the raid, Mirick puzzled over a passage from the journal of Rev. John Pike of Dover, New Hampshire. Pike's entry recorded that six Indians had killed thirteen colonists and captured five more.[2] Dissatisfied with this ratio (which favored the Indians by a two-to-one count), Mirick pondered whether most of the victims had been children. Certainly, they could not all have been men. He also dismissed the idea that Haverhill's women had fallen to a mere six Indians. After all, women from the colonial period, Mirick noted, performed "some of the most heroic deeds accomplished by the inhabitants of this town." Mirick further opined that "it hardly seems probable to us, for women at that period, seem to possess, at times, as much courage and fortitude as the men."[3] His comment, suggesting that nineteenth-century women were more fragile than their colonial counterparts, was part of a larger local, state, and even national project of gendered identity building and memory making undertaken in the United States during the late eighteenth and early nineteenth centuries.

Across the new polity, men and women scoured texts, collected local traditions, and crafted imagery, histories, and memorials from the colonial past. Their goal was to lay a foundation upon which to place an upstart country in need of a usable history. Acting at levels from the local to the national and possessing diverse ideological objectives, citizens proclaimed themselves inheritors of the legacies of the ancient world, colonial America, and, somewhat precociously, the American Revolution.[4] But for all the enthusiasm with which these memory-makers approached their task, it would not be an easy undertaking. After all, the new past of the United States could only be constructed upon historically contested terrain, ground that would need clearing and careful cultivation.

One feature of this larger project of memory making was the identification and celebration of martial female heroines from the seventeenth and eighteenth centuries found in local accounts. As historian Jean O'Brien has pointed out, "including Indian hostilities in local histories underscored the heroic nature of colonial histories," crafting a narrative of brave forerunners who replaced savagery with civilization. These local histories became increasingly popular in New England beginning in the 1820s and 1830s with publications peaking in the decades around the Civil War.[5] Often combining oral accounts with primary and secondary sources, local histories employed both well-known and obscure descriptions of women's participation in the border wars, painting colonial women as frontier heroines who held the line against Native and French forces alike. These women belonged to an earlier time, however, and their public, martial activities did not necessarily conform to changes in gender roles that increasingly cast women as exclusively domestic creatures.[6]

In making sense of martial colonial women who "seem to possess, at times, as much courage and fortitude as the men," Mirick turned to a discourse of *resolute motherhood*.[7] Emerging in late eighteenth-century accounts of colonial women's martial activities in New England, the language of resolute motherhood became increasingly prominent in the early nineteenth century. Retrofitting martial women of the past with tender but fiercely protective natures, resolute motherhood combined the colonial language of "gender borrowing"—women's temporary assumption of masculine traits—with ideologies of domesticity and a separate, feminine private sphere. In this conceptualization, martial women's fighting prowess drew from borrowed masculine qualities associated with resoluteness, such as bravery, firmness, and rational thought. Even Mirick, who asserted that delicate women's "limbs were not made to wield the weapons of war" and that their "hearts could never exult in a profusion of blood," recognized that "there are times when these characteristics are laid aside, and she clothes herself with a steadiness, a thoughtfulness, and courage, which equals, and oftentimes surpasses, the same qualities in a man."[8] For historians writing in New England during the early republic, deploying the image of the resolute wife and mother as defender of the domestic sphere assisted in the memorialization and celebration of colonial women's martial roles.

An offshoot of ideologies of republican motherhood and feminine domesticity, resolute motherhood allowed authors to safely celebrate the war making of colonial women. Following the American Revolution, women's attempts to claim full citizenship in a republic founded on revolutionary ideals of equality and liberty soon seemed overly radical. Women in the new nation would find themselves offered exalted but nevertheless second-class positions as loving "republican wives" and "republican mothers." These women—who were almost exclusively white—might exercise their duties as citizens by supporting their husbands' ambitions and providing the republic with future generations of white republican sons.[9] Against this backdrop, the related discourse of resolute motherhood served as the most celebrated form of a remembered martial womanhood that also included resolute wives, daughters, and other women of the household. Reimagining colonial gender ideologies that had offered space for women to act within informal and formal public spheres, nineteenth-century chroniclers such as Benjamin Mirick argued that a woman's "sphere of usefulness, of honor and glory, was in the precincts of the domestic circle," a newer construct that simply did not exist in the seventeenth and early eighteenth centuries.[10]

As New Englanders sought to create new identities and ideologies in the early republic, remembering and reshaping their colonial pasts to secure a republican future would prove essential. To understand how this process unfolded, it is necessary to trace the cultural transmission of these stories. Writers had not discarded accounts of women's martial activities once those narratives lost their immediate wartime propaganda value. Rather, accounts of women's war making remained an integral part of local and regional histories throughout the eighteenth century. These stories would survive the colonial period and assist post-Revolutionary New Englanders in their construction of new local and national histories. The persistence of accounts of women's martial activities as well as how writers appropriated those stories testifies to their value as cultural tools. Authorial additions, subtractions, and substitutions illuminate how authors reworked colonial accounts so that the memory of the public martial woman, celebrated and rewarded for her wartime participation as a member of an expansionist vanguard, was slowly erased from later histories. By the early nineteenth century, she would be remembered as a resolute wife and mother—a preternaturally calm and determined last line of defense of hearth and home. A versatile model of devotion to family and colonialism, the resolute mother of the past became a vessel for future projects ranging from nation building, westward expansionism, and the promotion of ideologies favoring separate, gendered spheres of action.[11]

This chapter, which focuses on New England, does not have a French counterpart. The royal takeover of New France in 1663, the decline in missionary publications, the lack of a provincial press, and low literacy rates all resulted in a dearth of written sources suitable for this type of analysis. More important, France lost the vast majority of its North American land claims—including Canada and Acadia—to the English over the course of the 1750s and 1760s. As a result, French-speaking settlers abandoned to the British did not participate in a project of memory making and nation building parallel to the one so conspicuously present in New England's histories. Following a discussion of two French incidents that did remain culturally relevant, the chapter will investigate stories from New England.

IN FRENCH CANADA, figures such as Madeleine de Verchères essentially disappeared from written records in the mid-eighteenth century before Quebecois nationalists rediscovered them around the turn of the twentieth century.[12] There is evidence, however, to suggest that the story of her defense of the Verchères seigneury would have been included in a French "canon" of accounts related to colonial history and war. In 1722, Claude-Charles Bacqueville de la Potherie included a version of the incident in his broad history of French North America published for European consumption.[13] La Potherie was an acquaintance of the Verchères family, and his published account of the event is quite similar to the 1699 version that Madeleine de Verchères sent to the comtesse de Maurepas when requesting her assistance in securing a reward for the defense of her family's seigneury.[14]

Perhaps the most famous history of New France written during the colonial period, Pierre François Xavier de Charlevoix's *Histoire et description générale de la Nouvelle-France*, also mentioned Madeleine de Verchères's and her mother's separate martial exploits.[15] Drawing directly from La Potherie's account, Charlevoix's history, originally published in 1744, was based in part on letters written to the duchess de Lesdiguieres during Charlevoix's visit to New France in 1721; Madeleine de Verchères's story was contained in one of these published letters.

Court cases and letters from eighteenth-century New France suggest that Madeleine de Verchères's defense of her family's seigneury maintained a parallel presence in provincial memory. In a 1730 court case involving Madeleine de Verchères, a priest remarked that "'God fears neither hero nor heroine,'" indicating that colonists continued to remember her actions.[16] Further confirming that her story was culturally persistent during the later colonial period, a married, middle-aged Madeleine de Verchères wrote a second narrative of the attack no earlier than 1726 at the request of the colony's new governor, the marquis de Beauharnois.[17] This account, which scholars have noted is less believable than the first, attempted to enhance Verchères's bravery by increasing the element of danger. Injecting further dramatic tension into her story, Verchères told of previously unmentioned, imperiled relatives bobbing along the river in a canoe nearby and offered more details of her command of the men within the fort.[18]

Verchères also included a later encounter with a group of Abenaki, whom she claimed entered her home and threatened its inhabitants. According to the account, after a French man subdued one of the two Abenaki, she killed the second with a tomahawk before he could kill her husband. After dispatching the man, Verchères wrote that she "found myself in the hands of four Indian women" who "seized me by the throat and another by the hair, after tearing off my cap" before attempting to throw her "into the fire." Verchères noted that she "felt . . . like a victim in the grasp of these furies" who had been "driven to desperation" by the deaths of their relatives only moments before.[19] Eventually, Verchères, her husband, and her twelve-year-old son were able to gain the upper hand. Verchères placed particular emphasis on the rescue of her husband and her son's brave actions, seeming to argue that heroism ran in her own family line, not in that of her husband. To add authenticity to the account, Verchères noted that the previous governor of New France, the marquis de Vaudreuil, had looked into the matter and declared it genuine.[20]

Adding a sense of religious pathos to the scene, she wrote piously that "a painter, seeing me at that moment, could have made a picture of Mary Magdalen: bareheaded, my hair tossed and disheveled, my clothing all in tatters, I was not unlike the saint, except as to the tears, which never flowed from my eyes."[21] That Verchères compared herself to a tearless Mary Magdalen is particularly revealing. In her 1699 account of the defense of Verchères, she disdained "the lamentations of the women, whose husbands had been carried off."[22] She also noted that one of the women was from Paris, dismissing her as "extremely timorous, as is natural to all Parisian women." This intriguing sentiment implies a difference in popular perception that contrasted hardy, zealous Canadian-born women with their cowardly, perhaps even inconstant French-born counterparts. Possibly the most compelling aspect of Verchères's assumption of the mantle of Mary Magdalen is the saint's history as a complex figure, strong, faithful, and favored by Christ, but thought to be far from innocent. Whatever effect Verchères's biblically inspired self-promotional propaganda may have had in the eighteenth century, it would be wasted on later audiences. By the turn of the twentieth century, according to historians Colin Coates and Cecilia Morgan, the historical memory of Madeleine de Verchères had merged with that of Joan of Arc in Quebecois lore. She had been remade "from a woman warrior into a domesticated, if brave, young woman."[23]

Interest in seventeenth-century women's martial activities in the St. Lawrence region extended beyond Quebecois and Anglo-Canadian nationalist constructions. The story of the captive Algonquin woman who freed herself and escaped to safety after killing one of her Iroquois captors with a hatchet survived from the seventeenth century through the mid-nineteenth century.[24] The original Jesuit account of the incident simultaneously excited and reassured readers in France by evoking her supposed Amazonian nature while filling her story with biblical allusions—including an insect-plagued journey through the wilderness that lasted nearly forty days. She arrived naked and self-conscious at Trois-Rivières, seemingly eager for French clothing as well as Christian civilization. Her story persisted, transmitted to European and American audiences in both English and French in the eighteenth and early nineteenth centuries. One earlier retelling, largely faithful to the original version, appeared in Charlevoix's history of New France in 1744.[25] The narrative again surfaced in 1809, recounted in the published journal of Roger Lamb, a British soldier who traveled through the Trois-Rivières area during the American Revolution. Lamb wrote that he included the story "for the sake of many of my readers who perhaps have never read the following anecdote."[26] It is unclear where Roger Lamb first encountered the story, though it matches quite well with the major points of the account in the *Jesuit Relations* and in Charlevoix's history. Reflecting changes in attitudes toward Indians, Lamb's account replaced the more nuanced Jesuit imagery of the Algonquin Amazon with the simple explanation that her actions were the result of "her revengeful temper." Finally, nineteenth-century American nationalist historian Francis Parkman also included the story in his 1867 *The Jesuits in North America in the Seventeenth Century*.[27] It is possible that more of these French stories survived through written and even oral tradition; however, the sources necessary to conduct further historical analysis simply do not exist.

The Cultural Persistence of Women's War Making

In 1770, New England printers began publishing new editions of Mary Rowlandson's 1682 captivity narrative, *The Soveraignty & Goodness of God*. Although the work had been reprinted in 1720, the early 1770s saw at least five editions: three editions in 1770 alone, one in 1771, and another in 1773.[28] In addition to sporting a new title, *A Narrative of the Captivity, Sufferings, and Removes of Mrs. Mary Rowlandson*, these late-eighteenth century versions offered readers a very different portrayal of the pious reverend's wife. Nathaniel Coverly's and Z. Cowle's 1770 editions of the narrative featured identical stock illustrations of a woman representing Rowlandson wearing a tricorne hat and a gown that would have been far more at home in the 1770s than the 1670s. Rowlandson is holding a powder horn—correctly, so as not to spill the powder—and grasping a musket approximately her own height. In the background is an anachronistic fortified structure flying a flag. In John Boyle's 1773 version, Mary Rowlandson appears standing next to her house, musket trained, prepared to fight her attackers in defense of her Lancaster home. Dressed in cap and apron, Rowlandson is alone, stationed in the foreground, and appears to be using the home as cover. Four Indigenous men dressed in European clothing and armed with an assortment of tomahawks and muskets approach the other side of the house.

The militarization of Mary Rowlandson's image served an important cultural function in 1770s New England. Despite the fact that no contemporary source ever reported that Mary Rowlandson even held a gun, these newer images placed Rowlandson within a homegrown tradition of women brandishing firearms during a period of increased tension between colonies and metropoles.[29] Many women throughout the northeastern borderlands

Woodcut used to portray a martial Mary Rowlandson in 1770. Publishers selected this image to portray fighting women during the late eighteenth century. This version is from *Thomas's New-England Almanack; or, The Massachusetts Calendar, for the Year of Our Lord Christ, 1775*, 2nd ed. (Boston, 1774). (*Source:* Courtesy of the American Antiquarian Society.)

of the seventeenth and eighteenth centuries had access to guns and knew how to shoot them. Stories that portrayed women firing guns and providing essential munitions support in New England's wars, particularly from the period prior to 1713, were culturally persistent, retold throughout the eighteenth and nineteenth centuries. For instance, both Thomas Hutchinson and Samuel Niles included the 1692 defense of Storer's garrison in Wells, Maine, in their mid-eighteenth-century histories of the region, reporting that "the women not only tended the men with ammunition and other necessaries, but many of them took their muskets and fired upon the enemy."[30] Niles borrowed directly from Cotton Mather's 1699 account in *Decennium Luctuosum*, which described how the women of Wells "took up the Amazonian Stroke" and fired with "a Manly Resolution," when he wrote that the women "acted their part in this engagement with an Amazonian spirit and courage, not only in supplying the men with ammunition as they wanted, but firing off the guns as there was occasion."[31] The continued inclusion of such accounts, lifted from earlier histories in lengthening chains of transmission, hints at the importance of women's martial activities to the creation of public memory in New England during the late colonial and early national periods.

The three most significant histories of northern New England's political and military past penned in the mid-to-late eighteenth century wove accounts of colonial women's war making into their narratives, albeit with slight alterations.[32] The first volume of Thomas Hutchinson's *The History of the Colony and Province of Massachusetts-Bay*, published in the mid-1760s, Samuel Niles's 1760 *Summary Historical Narrative of the Wars in New-England with the French and Indians*, and Jeremy Belknap's *The History of New-Hampshire*, published from 1784 to 1792, all saw women's martial activities as integral to understanding and constructing regional histories and identities. Niles's history of New England's border wars was, in the author's words, "some account of all the slaughter and bloodshed committed by them [New England's adversaries] that I could find, from the beginning to this day." Writing during the Seven Years' War, Niles hoped his work would provoke his fellow New Englanders "to awaken, reform, and quicken us to our duty, civil and religious."[33] Niles's history did not cite—but often borrowed verbatim from—many of the sources featured earlier in this study. For example, Niles used author Benjamin Doolittle's language when he wrote that "the women also assisted in charging the guns" in an attack on Fall Town in 1746.[34] Massachusetts Lieutenant Governor and future Loyalist Thomas Hutchinson's history of Massachusetts included more political events than Niles's military history of New England's wars. According to Hutchinson, he wrote the history "for the sake of [his] own countrymen," a history of a colony he saw "as the parent of all the other colonies of New-England."[35] As a more general history of Massachusetts, Hutchinson's work had fewer accounts of women's participation than Niles's military history, though Hutchinson did include some of these stories. Both works, however, served the purpose of creating a greater history of the region based on colonial events.

Despite the popularity of the image of a more militant Mary Rowlandson, few publications from the Revolutionary Era included accounts of women's participation during the colonial border wars, although this lacuna did not reflect a disapproval of their actions. After all, new editions of Rowlandson's narrative that portrayed her with weapons, as well as the acceptance of Revolutionary-era women's participation in that war, suggest that women continued to act as deputy husbands, camp followers, and even as combatants.[36] Major works published immediately after the American Revolution often focused on the former colonies as a whole, and the grand scale of these histories may have contributed to the absence of incidents involving colonial women.[37]

Jeremy Belknap had a different aim when he published his three-volume *History of New-Hampshire* over the course of the decade following the American Revolution: creating an identity for a state that had long been in the shadow of Massachusetts. Belknap, whom one writer dubbed "the American Plutarch," was a historian, scientist, Congregational minister, and constant correspondent.[38] Along with the histories of Hutchinson and Niles, Belknap's work drew largely from primary sources—principally earlier, written accounts of New England's history. Most of these sources, such as the histories of King Philip's War written by William Hubbard, Increase Mather, and Benjamin Church, as well as Cotton Mather's narratives of King William's War and Samuel Penhallow's work on Queen Anne's War and Dummer's War supplied material for Belknap's book.[39] In addition to these written sources, Belknap collected accounts from across New Hampshire in an attempt to preserve undocumented stories. Although the nature of his work as a history of New Hampshire prevented him from bringing in the many accounts of women's participation in Massachusetts and Maine, Belknap included all significant incidents from New Hampshire. Undoubtedly, Belknap saw the actions of these women as part of the history of his state and the state-based, nation-building process in which he participated.

Before further exploring these three histories, the importance of Samuel Penhallow's 1726 *History of the Wars of New-England, With the Eastern Indians* must be considered—both as a literary turning point and as a major influence on future histories. Penhallow's history was perhaps the final colonial military history written in the mold of Church, Hubbard, and the Mathers. Penhallow focused mainly on Queen Anne's War and the Anglo-Abenaki conflict, Dummer's War, which lasted from 1723 to 1726. He was also the last author to use the grand biblical or classical language of earlier writers when describing women's participation in the border conflicts. Although some authors in the early republic would rely on classical themes, their language more often referred to ideas about republican and resolute motherhood, not mythological warriors. Penhallow's book is also important as the last of the major narratives from the earlier period that historians from the mid-eighteenth century onward relied upon when crafting their histories of the colonial period. His work is also the principal reference on Queen Anne's War and Dummer's War for nearly all subsequent histories of the period.[40]

One incident recorded by Penhallow that appeared in all major eighteenth-century narrative histories of the region was the 1706 attack on Oyster River, New Hampshire. Its popularity offers unique possibilities for tracing changes in language over the eighteenth and early nineteenth centuries. To recap: in this incident, women in a fortified house pretended to be a large force of men, shooting muskets and successfully discouraging attackers who had already killed eight to ten people in an unfortified house nearby. Thomas Hutchinson's history of the attack borrowed directly from Penhallow's version, briefly noting that the women of Oyster River, "their husbands being abroad at their labor, or absent upon other occasions . . . put on their husbands hats and jackets, and let their hair loose, to make the appearance of men." He praised them for "firing briskly from the flankarts," an action that "saved the house and caused the enemy to retreat."[41] Samuel Niles's 1760 history also borrowed from Penhallow in its description of how "the women assumed an Amazonian courage; seeing nothing but death before them, they manfully ascended the watch-box and made an alarm."[42] Niles proceeded to repeat the rest of Penhallow's account nearly verbatim. Writing in the late eighteenth century, Jeremy Belknap's version of the incident was more subdued, perhaps reflecting a literary shift away from the portrayal of women as legendary warriors. In his retelling of the attack, Belknap unquestionably drew from Penhallow's 1726 account, even reusing the line, "the women . . . seeing nothing but death before them." Unlike

Penhallow and Niles, who both noted that the women fought with the courage of Amazons, Belknap made no mention of legendary warriors, contenting himself with observing that the women had fired "briskly" and fooled the enemy into thinking that the garrison was at full strength.[43]

Jeremy Belknap also recounted incidents involving two young women discussed in previous chapters, both from King Philip's War, in which a language of resoluteness appears more clearly. In the first, a young woman at Richard Tozer's house used her body weight against a door to allow more than a dozen women and children to escape through another door. Belknap drew from William Hubbard's account of the incident, which described the woman as "endued with more Courage than ordinarily the rest of her Sex use to be, (the blessing of Jael light upon her)."[44] Hubbard had also referred to her as a "Virago," a term that, like the character Jael, derived from a European tradition of acceptable warlike behavior for women. Belknap removed the most dramatic language from the account, hinting at the emerging language of resolute female defenders. Merely referring to the young woman's "intrepidity," a term that denoted calm bravery and action in the face of danger, he then simply noted that "the adventurous heroine recovered."[45] Borrowing from Belknap in the 1820s, Samuel Drake cited her "intrepidity," though he called her a "valiant heroine," rather than "adventurous."[46] Belknap also referred to Penhallow's account of Esther Jones, who "mounted guard" at an undefended garrison during an attack in 1712. Belknap approvingly wrote that her "commanding voice called so loudly and resolutely as made the enemy think there was help at hand, and prevented farther mischief."[47] Calm and determined, the Esther Jones of Belknap's work might serve as a model for future accounts of martial women, as images of feminine domesticity and women as resolute defenders of the private sphere began to infuse later local histories.

The transmission of these incidents through written accounts formed the foundation for their cultural persistence, yet some knowledge of the participation of New England women in the border wars survived solely due to oral tradition and the efforts of local historians to collect these stories during the early republic. Communities took pride in the actions of women they dubbed "heroic" and seemed to enjoy including such stories in the local histories that formed a basis for their new state and national identities. The story of John Minot's servant girl, who hid his children while she hurled hot coals, fired a weapon, and ultimately killed an intruder during King Philip's War in 1675, is one example of an incident that survived in oral tradition and in print. The original account appeared in Nathaniel Salton-stall's *The Present State of New-England*, one of several accounts Saltonstall penned during the war and published only in England.[48] Although Thomas Hutchinson's history of Massachusetts referred to Saltonstall's publication as a "letter to London" and related the encounter in a footnote, the story appears to have been passed along in a parallel, oral version. In this case, the oral tradition may add details of the incident missing from the con-temporary report.[49]

The first available written account of the oral version appeared in the English periodical *The Sporting Magazine* in 1802. The publication reached a wide audience in the English-speaking world and relied upon submissions from readers for some of its content. The use of specific and even obscure monikers and place names in the article suggests that the editor received it from an American reader or copied it from an earlier written source that is now unavailable. This version, either from the magazine or from an earlier source, formed the basis for all other nineteenth-century American publi-cations that referenced the incident. The basic narrative is comparable to Saltonstall's account, although this version is much more detailed. In the later version, Minot had refused a request from a group of Indians for food and drink the previous night. The attack the following day was in retalia-tion for the lack of hospitality. Minot had given his servant instructions be-fore he left for church services, which may explain her preparedness. The account ends with an intriguing—though unsubstantiated—claim that the "young maid was honoured" with the "approbation" of the government of Massachusetts and "presented with a silver wrist-band, on which her name was engraved, and this motto: 'She slew the Naraganset Hunter.'"[50]

Oral accounts add lost details and offer further evidence that such sto-ries possessed cultural staying power. In one instance, a confusing incident from King Philip's War only becomes clear when local tradition is taken into account alongside contemporary written chronicles. Two narrators of King Philip's War, William Hubbard and Increase Mather, reported on a battle that took place in Hadley, Massachusetts, in June 1676. At that point, the tide of the war had turned in favor of New England, although this par-ticular battle was fiercely contested, and the English fared poorly at the out-set. Much of the action of the battle took place on the south side of the town, which Mather claimed was a diversion. While English troops were engaged on Hadley's south side, a group of Indians—possibly the main assault force—attacked the north side, where, as Mather explains, they set a barn on fire and attempted to enter a house filled with "inhabitants." According to Mather "the inhabitants discharged a great Gun upon them, whereupon about fifty Indians were seen running out of the house."[51] Hubbard gave a similar account, noting that the firing of the "Ordnance . . . so affrighted the Salvages . . . that although they had just before surprized & possessed an house at the North end of the Town . . . they instantly fled, leaving some of their dead upon the place."[52] Both accounts describe the incident as if it had been relayed by someone watching the scene from a distance. The authors were unsure who had actually fired the "great gun." It was only after the war that the identities of the gun's operators were revealed. Nineteenth-century historian Henry Trumbull claimed that a group of Hadley's women loaded an eight-pound gun with "small shot, nails, &c." Trumbull wrote that after mounting the gun, the women delivered it to some English soldiers, who "discharged [it] with the best effect upon the enemy."[53]

Although Trumbull believed that the women turned the "great gun" over to English soldiers, Mather's seventeenth-century account hints that the women set off the gun. According to Mather, the blast came from within a house filled with inhabitants, who were likely taking refuge from the battle outside. The town records of Billerica, another frontier community besieged during King Philip's War, suggest that women and children sometimes gathered in a single garrison house when time permitted. During a town meeting in the summer of 1675, Billerica passed a resolution that "in case of need, the women and children shall be conveyed to the maine garison, if it may bee with safty."[54] In the case of Hadley, a more plausible scenario involves the town's women filling the gun with shot and nails to use if their sanctuary was breached. The story that the women left their refuge to deliver the gun to proper soldiers may have been an invention of later decades. As Trumbull later wrote, "thus it was that the English in a great measure owed the preservation of their lives to the unexampled heroism of a few women!"[55]

The story of Mary Woodwell, whose mother seized her captor's knife and attempted to run him through when the family was taken from their Hopkinton, New Hampshire, garrison in 1746, survived thanks to the efforts of New Hampshire scholars Jacob Bailey Moore and John Farmer.[56] The aging woman's interviewers dedicated their *Collections, Topographic, Historical, and Biographical* to "collecting and preserving what remains of the antiquities and curiosities of a country" with the hope of saving "those details, which alone may be unworthy of regard, but which in the aggregate form the most valuable sources from which to learn the exact condition of a people."[57] Moore and Farmer wrote that they aspired to continue the work of Jeremy Belknap, to seek out stories from rapidly aging survivors of the colonial period, and spur interest in the creation of historical societies similar to those in other new states.[58] Significantly, the authors' desire to preserve colonial history at the state and local levels in the early years of the republic necessarily included accounts of women's participation in the border wars as part of "learn[ing] the exact condition of a people."[59]

Of course, the construction of New England's local histories and new historical identity required selective historical memory and consensus regarding which historical actors to include and which to exclude. For authors writing about women's participation in the wars of the northeastern borderlands, the process of writing Native women's war making out of New England's history began early, in the eighteenth century. Both Hutchinson and Belknap largely wrote Indigenous women out of their histories of the region. Belknap did not discuss Weetamoo, Awashunkes, Matantuck, or any other prominent female sachems. In spite of the major role Native women played in King Philip's War, Belknap's only mention of an Indigenous woman was of a mother suffering from the death of her child, a role that would become increasingly important to the construction of the memory of women in warfare.[60] Hutchinson's history mentioned "the Squaw sachem" (Weetamoo) only briefly in a footnote that reproduced a short passage from a 1676 manuscript "narrative" of a Christian Indian, George, taken prisoner during the conflict.[61] Authors continued to write Native women out of earlier local histories, although these women occasionally reappeared later in the nineteenth century in books and poems as romanticized versions of themselves. But if excluding Indigenous women's participation offered a means of delineating the borders of the remembered body politic, memorializing and reworking the meaning of colonial women's war making would prove equally important in constructing the character of the new nation.

Of Amazons and Spartan Mothers

By the era of the early republic, a clear shift had emerged in the ways that local and regional historians applied classical and biblical allusions to women's war making. This is particularly evident in the work of New Hampshire's Jeremy Belknap, whose *History of New-Hampshire* was more likely to describe women as resolute or intrepid than as Amazons or viragos. His early references to a more sedate, respectable martial womanhood hinted at the discourses and debates shaping American conceptions of femininity and of women's roles as members of the new polity. The image of the resolute, martial mother as defender of the domestic sphere who appeared in nineteenth-century local histories would emerge from these conversations, drawing inspiration not from mythological Amazons but from the roles of historical women of the ancient world.

Spartan women captured the imagination of Americans in the early republic, proud mothers of warriors who also possessed some military training themselves. If the Amazon had lost the ability to inspire in the early republic, perhaps the women of Sparta might better reflect the ideals of proper womanhood. The nature of Spartan womanhood would serve as a focal point for questions about the martial roles of women in the new republic, provoking a debate over what historian Caroline Winterer has called the "double potential of the women of Sparta" as both mothers and fighting women. Determining the ideal manner in which to deploy the remembered Spartan woman was integral to the development of a usable past and to the evolution of the concept of republican motherhood as it related to the classical world.[62] One writer particularly intrigued by the idea of the Spartan mother was the American intellectual and women's rights pioneer, Judith Sargent Murray, best known for her work, "On the Equality of the Sexes."[63] Writing that "the character of the Spartan women is marked with uncommon firmness," normally a desirable quality in resolute women, Murray expressed discomfort over Spartan women who elevated militarism over maternal "affection." The determined Spartan females who raised heroic sons were far more acceptable models than the aggressively martial women who demonstrated that "the name of Citizen possessed, for them greater charms than that of Mother."[64] Despite some early intellectual interest in the most martial behavior of Sparta's women, this aspect of Spartan womanhood never attained widespread popularity. Women of the early American republic would contribute to the martial nation at home, as the image of the resolute Spartan mother preparing her sons for war won out as the preferred model of feminine behavior.[65]

For historians celebrating colonial martial womanhood, inscribing the idealized Spartan mother's restrained military readiness and maternal nature on earlier women's war making helped to neutralize its more disturbing aspects. The evolution of the story of a 1755 attack on the Kilburn garrison near Walpole, New Hampshire, illustrates the process of the transformation of the martial colonial woman to resolute classical mother in the early republic. The incident originally entered the historical record by way of a letter from Walpole's Reverend Thomas Fessenden to Jeremy Belknap in 1790. In his letter, Fessenden merely noted that John Kilburn, John Peak, "their two sons, with several women . . . bravely kept the enemy off, and obliged them to retire with several killed and wounded." From Fessenden's account, it appears that a large force attacked the "garrisoned house" and, as often happened, finding it to be defended and not worth the loss of further life, abandoned the assault.[66]

In 1827, the New Hampshire Historical Society printed an article from Walpole's *Cheshire Gazette*, fleshing out the women's actions at Kilburn's garrison while superimposing an intriguing, classically influenced narrative over the incident. In its reimagination of the attack, the *Cheshire Gazette* inflated the number of Indians to 197 from Fessenden's count of 170. Facing such long odds, it is unsurprising that the article portrayed John Kilburn as the Spartan leader, Leonidas, who "reap[ed] a . . . brilliant crown of laurels" that day. Thus, the attack on his garrison became an American Thermopylae— with a less tragic ending for the Kilburns. Crediting this "matchless defense" with "rescuing hundreds of our fellow citizens from the horrors of an Indian massacre," the article went on to describe "our intrepid Leonidas, not with 300 but only three followers."[67] The three male followers of Leonidas of New Hampshire did not include Ruth and Hitty Kilburn; however, the author did extend his classical allusion to them as Spartan women.

Rather than followers of Leonidas, the women of the Kilburn household assisted in the defense with "true Grecian firmness," a phrase suggesting the resolute and courageous quality attributed to women who took action in the border wars by authors of this later period. Ruth and Mehitable (Hitty) Kilburn showed admirable courage and "firmness" supporting John Kilburn, John Peak, and their sons in their colonial skirmish-turned-classical allegory. The article related that Kilburn's wife Ruth and daughter, Hitty, "contributed not a little to encourage and assist their companions, as well as to keep a watch upon the movements of the enemy." The author described how resolute mother Ruth Kilburn and the equally resolute Hitty Kilburn, "assisted in loading the guns" and recycled bullets by catching their opponents' shot in a blanket suspended underneath the roof of the house.[68] These women, although still described as heroic, were no longer associated with divine favor or biblical characters, nor were they portrayed as "assum[ing] an Amazonian courage" or "taking up the Amazonian stroke." Their heroics stemmed from intrepidness, courage, resolution, firmness, and a desire to act as the last line of defense of the domestic space.

The nineteenth-century language of resolute motherhood and its representative image, the woman as defender of the feminine private sphere, infuses an 1832 account of Susannah Swan's 1708 defense of her home with a fire poker or spit.[69] Appearing in Mirick's *History of Haverhill*, the story of Swan's war making survived through oral tradition, passed down through the neighboring Emerson family of Haverhill. The account implied that the Swans were not in a designated garrison at the time of the attack, and the overall success of the raid suggests that a number of families were surprised by the assault and not sheltered in safe structures. Emerson's report described the Swans' choice to stand together, "to save their own lives, and the lives of their children." After fending off the attack for a time, using their body weight to hold the door shut, the couple's energy began to flag. Responsibility for the failure of the defense fell on Mr. Swan, whom the narrator described as "rather a timid man" and who "almost despaired of saving himself and family." It was only after her husband's failure to play his role as a man, husband, and father that Susannah Swan took command of their home, realizing that "there was no time for parleying." At this point, "the heroic wife . . . seized her spit, which was nearly three feet in length, and a deadly weapon in the hands of woman" and "collecting all the strength she possessed, drove it through the body" of the first intruder. Seeing their dead companion, the other men left the Swan home. The basic narrative of the assault on the home, the Swans' defense, and the attackers' retreat, though perhaps more peculiar than some, does fit a standard pattern of an Indian raid. In this type of attack, a small group of Native men approached an unfortified home and attempted to break through the feeble defenses. Although successful in wearing down the defenders, the death of a comrade, combined with the promise of lower-hanging fruit elsewhere in the town, likely prompted the retreat.[70]

Susannah Swan's astute decision to allow the men to enter through the narrow doorway of her Haverhill home in 1708 while she skewered one with a spit stemmed from "the fortitude and heroic courage of a wife and a mother" protecting her family, according to author Benjamin Mirick. The narrative employed language that, although not unusual for 1832, would have been out of place in an account from the seventeenth or early eighteenth centuries. When describing Indians breaching the narrow doorway, the author's language suggests a violent sexual assault of the space of the wife and mother, as one man was "crowding himself in, while the other was pushing lustily after."[71] Swan, the "resolute and courageous woman," twice described as "heroic," virtuously protected the home. Prior to the nineteenth century, however, reports of such incidents did not equate the defense of the doorway with the protection of a virtuous domestic space or sphere.

The combined accounts of expectant mother Hannah Bradley's failed attempt to successfully defend the domestic space provide one of the strongest examples of the persistent transmission and dramatic reworking of an incident of women's war making from the late seventeenth century through the 1830s. Hannah, the wife of Joseph Bradley, was captured in Haverhill during raids in 1697 and 1704. In the 1697 attack, Hannah Bradley was taken along with Hannah Dustan and Mary Neff. Although living with a different group of Indians during the march north from Haverhill, Bradley later deposed that she had heard of the actions of Dustan and Neff at her camp from survivors of the massacre.[72] Having lived through that earlier attack, Bradley was determined to resist captivity a second time when a group of Indians approached her Haverhill home in 1704. Bradley, who was standing near her doorway, used boiling soap to kill the first Indian who entered while using the remaining soap to maim a second man. Eventually subdued, the pregnant Hannah Bradley traveled north once again and was later redeemed by her husband.

Bradley's story, in which she gave birth on her trek and watched her baby die, illustrates how authors' emphases shifted over time, from martial woman to resolute mother. In Cotton Mather's account of her defense and captivity, the earliest surviving version of Bradley's experience, Mather focused on her qualities as a "Vertuous Woman" and described in a matter-of-fact manner how she poured boiling soap on the face of the intruder while one of the men in her house held him down.[73] Mather, known for his gruesome depictions of children's deaths in captivity, described her ordeal as she gave birth but spared little time on the eventual death of the child or Bradley's reaction to its passing.[74] Samuel Penhallow also mentioned her use of boiling soap as a weapon and noted that she gave birth on the journey.[75] As in Mather's account, Penhallow focused on Bradley's experience in childbirth. Although he contributed additional details to the newborn's decline and noted that the captors allegedly placed hot embers in the baby's mouth, he did not discuss her response to the child's death. Samuel Niles, who also mentioned the incident, borrowed heavily from Penhallow, retaining his details and emphases.[76]

When Mirick composed his version of Bradley's story for *The History of Haverhill* in 1832, he made a special effort to draw from Penhallow's account as well as from Rev. Pike's journal and local oral tradition. He also interviewed her surviving family members and borrowed from a manuscript written by Haverhill's recently deceased minister, Abiel Abbot. The account itself, though quite accurate in many of its details, was far more dramatic than any previous version in its description of Hannah Bradley's experience. Mirick described how Bradley "seized her ladle, and filling it with the steaming liquid, discharged it on his tawny pate—a *soap*-orific that almost instantly brought on a *sleep*, from which he has never since awoke."[77] Following this series of ghastly puns, Mirick turned his attention to Bradley's "delicate circumstances" and "slender health," lamenting that "no situation of woman would ever protect her from their demon-like cruelties." Romanticizing Bradley's pregnancy and resolute motherhood, Mirick noted that "they obliged her to travel on foot, and carry a heavy burthen, too large even for the strength of man."[78]

After firmly situating Bradley as a mother, her body a delicate yet dependable vessel, Mirick detailed her reaction to the "agonies" suffered by an "innocent and almost friendless babe." His account almost voyeuristically described Bradley's persistent attempts to protect the infant, offering a lengthy portrayal of resolute maternal anguish as she witnessed the gruesome events that led to the death of her child. Mirick laced his tale of the days leading to the infant's death with colonialist language and imagery. In doing so, he drew a clear distinction between the rightness of Bradley's earlier violence in defense of the domestic sphere and the gratuitous violence of her Indigenous captors in the wilderness. According to Mirick, Bradley agreed to allow her captors to "baptize [the baby] in their manner" in exchange for the infant's safety. It is possible that Mirick's version of Bradley believed that this would be a Catholic baptism, given the prominent connections between captivity and Catholicism. Instead, Mirick shocked the reader with a mock christening, as her captors "baptized it by gashing its forehead with their knives." At the climax of this disturbing moment of conspicuous colonialism, Mirick described the return of the injured baby to its mother, "with its smooth and white forehead gashed with the knife, and its warm blood coursing down its cheeks." Incongruously, given his penchant for hyperbolic narrative, Mirick concluded the scene by noting that "the feelings of the mother" at that moment "can be better imagined than described."[79]

Despite his seeming reluctance to offer speculation on Bradley's emotions following the alleged mutilation of her newborn, Mirick showed no such qualms when recounting Bradley's later discovery of the child's body "piked upon a pole." Again, he contrasted the dignity of the suffering but resilient Bradley with the cruelty of the "merciless savages," opining that the sight of the dead child was "shocking to a mother, and to every feeling of humanity." Appealing even further to the idea of Bradley as a resolute mother protecting her child in a hostile wilderness, Mirick noted that the infant "was born in sorrow, and nursed in the lap of affliction." Bradley, he wrote, "doted with maternal fondness" on the child and added that "its mother could only weep over its memory." With telling abruptness that confirmed Mirick's anti-Indian colonial project, he happily relayed in his next sentence that Bradley was sold to the French, by whom "she was treated kindly" and where she "eked out a comfortable subsistance [sic]."[80]

The construction of the image of Hannah Bradley as Indian-slayer and icon of resolute, suffering motherhood is also detectable in scholars' analyses of changes in Hannah Dustan's better-known narrative.[81] Some studies of Dustan have erroneously concluded that she faded into obscurity after her moment of celebrity; however, both Dustan and Bradley successfully petitioned the Massachusetts House of Representatives for land grants later in life. Dustan also appeared in Samuel Niles's history of New England's wars and in Thomas Hutchinson's history of Massachusetts. Hutchinson devoted two pages of the second volume of his work, first published in 1767, to Dustan, recalling that "there was a woman (Hannah Dunstan) a heroine, made prisoner at this time; whose story, although repeatedly published, we cannot well omit." Emphasizing the suffering of Dustan and Neff and their perilous situation, he opined that "the terror of the Indian gantlet seems to have inspired [Dustan] with resolution." Attempting to explain why their captors had not kept watch, Hutchinson proposed that "from women, ordinarily, attempts of this sort are not to be expected" and added that "the fame of so uncommon an action . . . soon spread through the continent."[82] Hutchinson's comparatively—almost disturbingly—understated retelling of this culturally persistent incident reveals much about the development of a new gendered language of colonial women's violence in the eighteenth and nineteenth centuries.

Writing before the American Revolution that he would famously oppose, Hutchinson was not a participant in the project of memory making that took place in the early republic. Instead, his account represented a transition, employing gendered language that drew on notions of the potential of women's natural fearfulness to "inspire" resolution. He was aware of Dustan's motherhood and the loss of her child, but the role of mother did not define Dustan in his narrative. Rather, Dustan's inspired violence was the natural reaction of a modest, frightened woman, "a heroine," who "prevailed upon the nurse and the English boy to join with her in the destruction of the Indian family." Hutchinson concluded his version with the group's return home, the trio bearing scalps across perilous terrain, before they finally "arrived safe with their trophies" to rewards from colonial governments and "many presents from their neighbours."[83] Most at home in the emerging discourses of resoluteness and domesticity, Hutchinson's Dustan anticipated subsequent iterations of the heroine as a resolute mother, though without the influence of later debates over women's roles in the republic.

The image of Dustan as a resolute mother would emerge in full form in the decades after the American Revolution. Authors of local histories from the 1820s and 1830s increasingly drew upon the language of resolute motherhood, the preservation of the home as a feminine space, and colonial and national virtue when crafting new versions of Dustan's story. Indeed, historian Barbara Cutter has suggested that Hannah Dustan became a symbol of a righteous, maternal, female violence that proponents of expansionism used to craft "a model of American identity in which violence committed by the United States was, by definition, feminine, and therefore justified, innocent, defensive violence." Unsurprisingly, this ideology—fostered by the literary transformation of Hannah Dustan—supported present and future acts of violence against Indians and aggressive territorial conquest.[84] When compared with changes to Dustan's story, alterations to accounts of the actions of the Kilburn women, Susannah Swan, and Hannah Bradley appear to have served a similar purpose. By employing these constructed memories of resolute colonial women who, in the words of Haverhill's Benjamin Mirick, "seem[ed] to possess, at times, as much courage and fortitude as the men," authors in the early nineteenth century created a new violent female figure to support ideologies of domesticity, separate spheres, and expansionism.[85] Intriguingly, the imagery associated with the violent Amazon may have persisted alongside the more "innocent" resolute motherhood, though primarily in captivity narratives set along a new national frontier.[86] In areas undergoing more overt colonization, women's more unrestrained violence as Amazons in captivity may have seemed appropriate in that colonial context. For local historians writing about New England, colonization had reportedly ended. The civilized yet determined resolute mother would justify women's violence and colonialism in states seeking a usable past and a genteel future even as she offered a vision of a domesticated frontier.

The continued popularity of Hannah Dustan's story throughout the nineteenth century extended to accounts of other women's participation in the border wars of the colonial period. Versions of these stories penned in the second half of the nineteenth century seem to have taken a more romantic—sometimes tragic—and overtly nationalistic approach to their subject matter. New Englander William Fowler's 1876 nationalist and hagiographical history, *Woman on the American Frontier*, illustrates the longevity of this ideology of resolute, maternal colonialism. In his celebration of continental conquest, Fowler included stories of these martial women, dubbing them "Pioneer Mothers of the Republic" in the book's extended title.[87] Women in the northeastern borderlands, in Fowler's words, "with muskets at their sides lulled their babes to sleep" and performed hybridized colonial and nineteenth-century gender roles, acting "as a soldier and laborer, a heroine and comforter." Rashly proclaiming the country's victory over nature and Indigenous people, Fowler argued for the centrality of women to the expansionist project, declaring that "it is precisely in her position as a pioneer and colonizer that her influence is the most potent and her life story most interesting."[88] Through this and other works, histories of women's war making remained culturally relevant, part of New England's shared memory of the colonial past as well as its vision of a colonial present and future.

Epilogue
Heroines, Saviors, and Curiosities

For well over one hundred years, women assumed active roles furthering the imperial and expansionist goals of dozens of polities in the northeastern borderlands. In the nineteenth and twentieth centuries, jubilant Anglo-American communities—as well as colonized Quebecois populations—found multiple meanings in the wartime actions of these women. Why, then, have scholars relegated the larger significance of women's war making in the northeastern borderlands to historical footnotes, singling out only the most extreme examples as curious anomalies? A fragmented source base certainly creates difficulties in piecing together a larger picture; however, the ways in which nineteenth- and twentieth-century authors and communities sought to memorialize women's roles is equally important in explaining their disappearance.

The monuments and stories of the nineteenth and early twentieth centuries added yet another layer of historical distance to early American women's war making. Representing a mere fraction of the women who contested the early American northeast, these plaques, memorial parks, statues, and even bobblehead dolls (of a nineteenth-century Hannah Dustan statue) simplify and obscure the ways women participated in and advanced expansionist and colonial policies in the seventeenth and eighteenth centuries. Statues of women who participated in these conflicts often depict their subjects as humble savior-heroines. The famous 1879 statue of Hannah Dustan in her hometown of Haverhill, Massachusetts, portrays a one-shoed Dustan in a simple nightdress wielding a tomahawk. Reliefs around the base depict her capture, the killings, and her journey home. A maternal figure in Haverhill's historical memory, Dustan became something of a civic patron saint of the defenseless, as schools and nursing facilities took on her name. In Quebec, fin-de-siècle monuments to Jeanne Mance in Montreal show her embracing the ill or the young, focusing on her role in establishing the city's first hospital rather than on her actions as a town founder who secured funds to fortify that critical French outpost. Coated with a Victorian veneer of domesticity and exclusively Euro-American, such memorializations project images of saviors who helped maintain—but never advanced—the margins of European territorial control.

This ideologically driven memorialization of a handful of more prominent women also masks the continued existence and contestation of the northeastern borderlands today. Although the end of the Seven Years' War famously provided a tidy (if surprisingly superficial) conclusion to this era of imperial warfare, colonial projects continue to thrive. Members of Native polities, such as the Abenaki, as well as French Canadians and members of the French Canadian diaspora, have rejected and survived colonizing efforts in both the United States and Canada. Yet, by locating physical and literary representations of Madeleine de Verchères and Jeanne Mance within Canadian—and Quebecois—borders while placing Hannah Dustan's statues firmly within the United States, nineteenth- and twentieth-century nationalists attempted to shore up the often porous boundaries and identities of the northeastern borderlands.

The act of deemphasizing and even removing Native women from these histories is also part of the larger effort to fully colonize and order the contemporary northeastern borderlands. This is particularly true of the region's interior, which has been transformed from a seventeenth-century wilderness that beguiled and frightened into a recreational haven. It is in these supposedly natural and empty spaces that vacationing twenty-first-century colonists encounter the names of Native women who fought in the region's wars, their memories fixed in a distant and unfamiliar past.[1] The most prominent example, Weetamoo of the Pocasset, was a particularly popular figure in local and regional histories from the nineteenth century, as well as in other forms of local lore.[2] Earlier generations of New Englanders appropriated Weetamoo's name for natural features and landmarks in both northern and southern New England. Although Weetamoe Street in Fall River, Massachusetts and Weetamoo Woods in Tiverton, Rhode Island lie in Pocasset land, the numerous sites bearing Weetamoo's moniker in the White Mountains of New Hampshire can only be attributed to a romantic and inaccurate 1845 poem by John Greenleaf Whittier.[3] Weetamoo Rock, Mt. Weetamoo, and Weetamoo Falls, all located near or in the White Mountains, take their name from Whittier's poem, "The Bridal of Pennacook," which portrayed Weetamoo as a Pennacook of the "wilder" White Mountain region, not a Pocasset of "civilized" southern New England.

The nationalist and colonizing impulses that underlie these local celebrations of female participation in the border wars—as well as the attempts to tame and geographically displace memories of Native women—ultimately render such commemorations deeply suspicious. The women involved appear worthy only of antiquarian interest. Yet, if we read between the lines of later stories, if we search for accounts of women's war making from the seventeenth and eighteenth centuries and place them within the social, military, and political conditions that produced these incidents, a substantially different history of the northeastern borderlands emerges.

Returning French, English, and Native women to the tumultuous borderlands of the early American northeast reveals surprising similarities between the contesting parties' political and military strategies and goals. Throughout the region, competing polities deployed women as part of the vanguard of their expansionist forces. Living on the perimeters of territory that linked the Atlantic world to the interior of North America, women participated in nearly every aspect of war making. Neither transgressive nor criminal, Native and European women's wartime activities supported preexisting gender ideologies that provided space for women of high rank to assume positions of leadership. Other women, who lacked access to more formal power structures, defended fortified communities, served as spies, and used group violence to determine the fate of captives while demanding changes in military policy. Men and women of the northeastern borderlands with access to pen, paper, and the press used these often violent accounts of women's war making to argue for specific expansionist policies and bolster morale in times of crisis. Even as the societies of New England and New France became increasingly intertwined with the military bureaucracies and imperial ideologies of Britain and France, respectively, women continued to contest the northeastern borderlands.

It would be a mistake, however, to assume that because women's wartime activities frequently supported patriarchies and wider imperial structures, women were either simple helpmates or victims of masculine colonial programs. This would, in essence, let women "off the hook" as often enthusiastic supporters of territorial expansionism in the northeastern borderlands. English women who demanded changes in colonial policy through violent mob action thought themselves more effective colonizers than the men they accused of lacking aggression. When an escaped Algonquin prisoner opted to kill her sleeping captor rather than slip away quietly, she chose to become a combatant and strike a blow on behalf of her nation. It is, perhaps, women's willingness to make war and support expansionism that later memorializations do correctly capture. Certainly, statues of a determined Hannah Dustan with hatchet in hand or of Madeleine de Verchères clasping a firearm as wind rustles her skirt helped construct heroines to promote ideologies of nationalism and colonialism in the nineteenth and twentieth centuries. For many of these memorialized women and the men they fought alongside, fear of death, fear of the Other, or even a desire for personal gain may have been more significant than pure patriotic sentiment. Yet, if women were necessary combatants in the contest for the northeastern borderlands, they were also highly invested participants, complicit in expansionist and colonial agendas.

Notes

Abbreviations

ARMB	*Acts and Resolves, Public and Private, of the Province of the Massachusetts Bay*, 21 vols. Boston: Wright & Potter, 1869–1922.
BANQ	Bibliothèque et Archives Nationales Québec
CMNF	*Collection de manuscrits contenant lettres, mémoires, et autres documents historiques relatifs à la Nouvelle-France*, 4 vols. Quebec, 1883–85.
DHSM	James Phinney Baxter, ed., *Documentary History of the State of Maine.* 24 vols. Portland: Maine Historical Society, 1869–1916.
EAI	Early American Imprints, Series 1: Evans, 1639–1800. www.readex.com.
EAN	Early American Newspapers. Series 1: 1690–1876. www.readex.com.
ECCO	Eighteenth Century Collections Online. www.gale.com.
EEBO	Early English Books Online. eebo.chadwyck.com.
HCPM	Thomas Hutchinson. *The History of the Colony and Province of Massachusetts-Bay.* Edited by Lawrence Shaw Mayo. 3 vols. Cambridge, Mass.: Harvard University Press, 1936.
JR	Reuben Gold Thwaites, ed. *The Jesuit Relations and Allied Documents: Travels and Explorations of the Jesuit Missionaries in New France, 1610–1791.* 73 vols. Cleveland: Burrows Brothers, 1896–1901.
JHRM	*Journals of the House of Representatives of Massachusetts.* 55 vols. Boston: Massachusetts Historical Society, 1919–90.
LAC	Library and Archives Canada, Ottawa.
LMMI	Marie de l'Incarnation. *Lettres de la Révérende Mère Marie de l'Incarnation: Première Supérieure du Monastère des Ursulines de Québec.* Edited by L'Abbé Richaudeau. 2 vols. Paris, 1876.
MDI	Marie de l'Incarnation
MG1 B	LAC. Fonds des Colonies. Manuscript Group 1. Series B: Lettres envoyées.
MG1 C11A	LAC. Fonds des Colonies. Manuscript Group 1. Series C11A: Correspondance générale (Canada).
MG1 C11D	LAC. Fonds des Colonies. Manuscript Group 1. Series C11D: Correspondance générale (Acadie).
MG1 G2	LAC. Fonds des Colonies. Manuscript Group 1. Series G2: Dépôt des papiers publics des colonies.
MG7 II	LAC. Fonds de la Bibliothèque de l'Arsenal, Archives de la Bastille. Manuscript Group 7. Series II: Prisonniers.
MHSC	*Collections of the Massachusetts Historical Society*, all series. Boston: Massachusetts Historical Society, 1792–.

MRGC   Nathaniel B. Shurtleff, ed. *Records of the Governor and Company of the Massachusetts Bay in New England.* 5 vols. Boston, 1853–54.

MSA   Massachusetts State Archives

NHHSC   *Collections of the New Hampshire Historical Society.* 15 vols. Concord, N.H.: New Hampshire Historical Society, 1824–1939.

NHPP   Nathaniel Bouton, ed. *Provincial Papers: Documents and Records Relating to the Province of New-Hampshire.* 7 vols. Concord, Nashua, Manchester, N.H.: 1867–73.

RCNP   Nathaniel B. Shurtleff and David Pulsifer, eds. *Records of the Colony of New Plymouth.* 12 vols. Boston, 1855–61.

SRCA   Édouard Richard, ed. *Supplement to Dr. Brymner's Report on Canadian Archives by Mr. Édouard Richard (1899).* Ottawa: S.E. Dawson, 1901.

WMQ   *William and Mary Quarterly*

Introduction

1. *JR*, 53:136–39. The French name for this important Mohawk village is "Gandaouagué." In 1674, Daniel Gookin described a longer siege and reported that Caughnawaga had made advance preparations for the attack. Gookin, "Historical Collections," 166–68.

2. John Pynchon to Gov. William Phips, August 1, 1693, in *ARMB*, 7:396–98.

3. N. S., *Present State of New-England*, 3, EEBO.

4. Marie Madeleine de Verchères à Mme de Maurepas, October 15, 1699, in *SRCA*, 6–7.

5. Morin, *Annales de L'Hotel-Dieu de Montreal*, 158.

6. Scholarly and popular awareness of women's participation in the wars of the northeastern borderlands persisted through the nineteenth and early twentieth centuries. For example, see Fowler, *Woman on the American Frontier.* Very few women who took part in these conflicts remain part of modern scholars' understanding of the region's history. Scholars of seventeenth- and eighteenth-century New England and New France have largely confined their studies of women's war making to two women: Hannah Dustan of Massachusetts and Canada's Madeleine de Verchères. Dustan slaughtered nearly a dozen of her captors on an island in New Hampshire in 1697, while fourteen-year-old Madeleine de Verchères successfully commanded the defense of her father's seigneury in 1692. In exploring the spectacle of these well-documented incidents, scholars have viewed these women as exceptional actors rather than as the most visible representatives of a tradition of women's war making. The only study that moved beyond Dustan to note women's active participation in New England, though on a much smaller scale, is Ulrich, *Good Wives*, 167–83. Other studies of Dustan include Derounian-Stodola, "Captive as Celebrity"; Strong, *Captive Selves*; and Toulouse, *Captive's Position.* On Madeleine de Verchères, see Coates and Morgan, *Heroines and History*; and Gervais and Lusignan, "De Jeanne d'Arc à Madelaine de Verchères." Our understanding of Native women's participation in these conflicts is similarly incomplete, limited primarily to women's roles in ritual torture and adoption and to the actions of two female sachems in King Philip's War. Works

that do address these issues include Little, *Abraham in Arms*, chaps. 2, 3; and Plane, "Putting a Face on Colonization."

7. On female criminality in New England and New France, see Ulrich, *Good Wives*, 184–201; Lachance, "Women and Crime in Canada"; Hull, *Female Felons*; Norton, *In the Devil's Snare*; and Norton, *Founding Mothers and Fathers*.

8. Louise Dechêne coined the term *guerre ambiante* in *Le peuple, l'état et la guerre*, 103. Other works that shed light on how this continuous warfare affected the region include Little, *Abraham in Arms*; and Norton, *In the Devil's Snare*. My use of the term "northeastern borderlands" to describe this region and these conflicts is influenced by Little, *Abraham in Arms*.

9. Studies of warfare in this region include Dechêne, *Le peuple, l'état et la guerre*; Haefeli and Sweeney, *Captors and Captives*; Crouch, *Nobility Lost*; Little, *Abraham in Arms*; Chet, *Conquering the American Wilderness*; Grenier, *First Way of War*; Zelner, *Rabble in Arms*; Pulsipher, *Subjects unto the Same King*; and Eames, *Rustic Warriors*.

10. Little, *Abraham in Arms*; Romero, *Making War and Minting Christians*.

11. The relationship between the "little commonwealth," order, and authority is supported by a large body of literature. Some early American examples include Norton, *Founding Mothers and Fathers*; Brown, *Good Wives, Nasty Wenches*; Little, *Abraham in Arms*, esp. chap. 3; and Demos, *A Little Commonwealth*. For England, see Amussen, *An Ordered Society*; Fletcher and Stevenson, *Order and Disorder*; and Stone, *Family, Sex and Marriage*.

12. On the masculinization of warfare in many Native polities, see Perdue, *Cherokee Women*; Ryan, *Mysteries of Sex*; Romero, *Making War and Minting Christians*; Little, *Abraham in Arms*; and Bragdon, *Native People of Southern New England, 1500–1650*.

13. Young, *Masquerade*; Cordingly, *Women Sailors and Sailors' Women*; Wheelwright, *Amazons and Military Maids*; Dugaw, *Warrior Women*; Mayer, *Belonging to the Army*; Rediker, "Liberty Beneath the Jolly Roger"; Dekker and Van de Pol, *Tradition of Female Transvestism*; Godineau, "De la guerrière à la citoyenne"; and Gervais and Lusignan, "De Jeanne d'Arc à Madelaine de Verchères."

14. A short list of studies on captivity in the northeastern borderlands might include Breitwieser, *American Puritanism*; Axtell, *Invasion Within*; Toulouse, *Captive's Position*; Little, *Abraham in Arms*; Burnham, *Captivity and Sentiment*; Strong, *Captive Selves*; Haefeli and Sweeney, *Captors and Captives*; and Derounian-Stodola, "Captive as Celebrity."

15. In particular, Ann Little and Juliana Barr have demonstrated the importance of gender as both a contested category and key component of contests for power in the borderlands of early America. Little, *Abraham in Arms*; Barr, *Peace Came in the Form of a Woman*.

16. On cultural misunderstandings and war, see Haefeli, "Kieft's War"; Lepore, *Name of War*; and Perdue, *Cherokee Women*.

17. Works that explore cultural similarities include Shoemaker, *Strange Likeness*; Little, *Abraham in Arms*; Barr, *Peace Came in the Form of a Woman*; and Romero, *Making War and Minting Christians*.

18. On public and private spheres in the early modern period, see, Goodman, "Public Sphere and Private Life"; Goodman, *Republic of Letters*; Klein, "Gender and the

Public/Private Distinction"; Boydston, "Gender as a Question"; Baker, "Defining the Public Sphere"; Brewer, "This, That and the Other"; and Longfellow, "Public, Private, and the Household."

19. Norton, *Founding Mothers and Fathers*; Norton, *Separated by Their Sex*.

20. Norton, *Separated by Their Sex*.

21. Norton acknowledges that her findings regarding the development of masculine public and feminine private spheres in England and British America during the eighteenth century likely did not apply to France (see Norton, *Separated by Their Sex*, 184n9). However, Canadian historian Jan Noel argues for the application of Norton's model to New France in *Along a River*. On the persistence of French women's public roles, see Goodman, "Public Sphere and Private Life"; Goodman, *Republic of Letters*; and Kale, "Women, Salons, and the State."

22. Smolenski and Humphrey, *New World Orders*, 14.

23. Scholars have successfully shown that borderlands were not confined to the familiar setting of northern New Spain. Nor did all middle grounds resemble the Great Lakes region described in White's *Middle Ground*. Indeed, continued research has revealed the stunning diversity of borderlands regions. Examples include Barr, *Peace Came in the Form of a Woman*; DuVal, *Native Ground*; Rushforth, *Bonds of Alliance*; Crouch, *Nobility Lost*; Lipman, *Saltwater Frontier*; and Grandjean, *American Passage*. On the blurring of boundaries between borderlands studies and Atlantic history, see Millett, "Borderlands in the Atlantic World."

24. Rowlandson, *Soveraignty & Goodness of God*, 48, 57, EAI.

25. On the nature of this plot, see Stanwood, *Empire Reformed*, 195–206.

Chapter 1

1. For statistics on raids in the northeastern borderlands and an excellent treatment of the Deerfield raid, see Haefeli and Sweeney, *Captors and Captives*, 190–93, appendix E. See also Demos, *Unredeemed Captive*.

2. Penhallow, *History of the Wars*, 32, EAI.

3. On "briskness," see Little, *Abraham in Arms*, 249n49.

4. "Frontier town" was a political designation that appeared in numerous colonial records.

5. "An Act to Prevent the Deserting of the Frontiers" [1695], in *ARMB*, 1:194–95; "List of the Public Acts," in *ARMB*, 1:767–87; "An Act for Reviving and Further Continuing of Several Acts Therein Mentioned that are Near Expiring" [1706], in *ARMB*, 1:585–86. These amendments were renewed along with the original act in 1707. Ibid., 1:605. The government of Massachusetts also passed a similar, temporary law banning the desertion of frontier towns in 1675 during King Philip's War, *MRGC*, 5:48, 51.

6. Although all towns had militias, colonists in designated frontier towns had additional responsibilities and restrictions. For examples of the settler-soldier's mandated duties, see "An Act for the Better Security and Defence of the Frontiers" [1711], in *ARMB*, 1:903–4.

7. Eames, *Rustic Warriors*, 29.

8. On the formal and informal public spheres, see Norton, *Founding Mothers and Fathers*; Norton, *Separated by Their Sex*.

9. Haefeli and Sweeney, *Captors and Captives*, 1.

10. Grandjean argues that food scarcity and a desire to control travel and exchange were of primary importance in instigating the war. Grandjean, *American Passage*, chap. 1.

11. On the Pequot War's influence on issues such as masculinity, power, and wartime violence, see Little, *Abraham in Arms*, chap. 1; Romero, *Making War and Minting Christians*, chap. 10; Grandjean, "Long Wake of the Pequot War"; Cremer, "Possession"; and Lipman, "'A Meanes to Knitt Them Togeather.'"

12. Grandjean, "Long Wake of the Pequot War," quotation on 383. Andrew Lipman also describes this period as far from peaceful in *Saltwater Frontier*.

13. The description of fortified structures and their development is indebted to Malone, "Indian and English Military Systems," 224–25.

14. Eames, *Rustic Warriors*, 28–29, 39.

15. *MRGC*, 5:48, 51. On the composition and function of New England's military in King Philip's War, see Zelner, *Rabble in Arms*. Volunteer armies began to replace the impressed forces of King Philip's War, providing more committed soldiers with pay and bounty opportunities in addition to government-provided uniforms, weapons, and supplies. Despite these changes, residents of frontier towns in Massachusetts, New Hampshire, and Maine were still expected to maintain and defend their fortified communities with help from troops assigned to their towns. Zelner, *Rabble in Arms*, 215–17. King William's War and Queen Anne's War, multiyear, intercolonial conflicts that followed King Philip's War, were substantially different from that Anglo-Indian struggle of the mid-1670s. These later conflicts, fought between the British, the French, and the region's Indians were American fronts of—or were otherwise related to—major European wars. See Chet, *Conquering the American Wilderness*; Haefeli and Sweeney, *Captors and Captives*; and Eames, *Rustic Warriors*.

16. "An Act to Prevent the Deserting of the Frontiers" [1695], in *ARMB*, 1:194–95; "An Act for Reviving and Further Continuing of Several Acts Therein Mentioned that are Near Expiring" [1706], in *ARMB*, 1:585–86. Massachusetts passed a similar law during the brief peace between King William's War and Queen Anne's War, although restrictions on leaving frontier towns went into effect only upon the resumption of hostilities. Laws requiring freeholders and non-freeholding men sixteen and older to stay in their frontier towns remained remarkably consistent until the Oyster River incident in 1706. "An Act to Prevent the Deserting of the Frontiers of this Province" [1700], in *ARMB*, 1:402–3.

17. "An Act to Prevent the Deserting of the Frontiers" [1695], in *ARMB*, 1:195.

18. On manhood, land, and military prowess, see Little, *Abraham in Arms*, chap. 1; Lombard, *Making Manhood*, chap. 1; and Wilson, *Ye Heart of a Man*, chap. 1.

19. *ARMB*, 8:432.

20. Joanna Cotton to Increase Mather, March 13, 1697, Massachusetts Archives Collection, 57:68–70, MSA.

21. Eames, *Rustic Warriors*, 39–40.

22. C. Mather, *Frontiers Well-Defended*, 4, EAI.

23. Petition of John Houghton, February 14, 1694, in *ARMB*, 7:445 (emphasis added).

24. Norton, *Founding Mothers and Fathers*, 38–39, 55, chap. 2; Demos, *A Little Commonwealth*.

25. The most famous description of the role of deputy husband appears in Ulrich, *Good Wives*. Ulrich rightly notes that several women in her study—including Hannah Dustan—may have been acting as deputy husbands when they defended their homes. Ibid., 178–79, 195. For a critique of the looseness this term has taken on, see Boydston, "Gender as a Question."

26. C. Mather, *Decennium Luctuosum*, 94, EAI.

27. Petition of Lydia Scottow, [1678?], in *DHSM*, 6:203.

28. On widows' roles in public spheres, see Norton, *Founding Mothers and Fathers*, chap. 3.

29. Petition of James Convers, February 26, 1696, in *DHSM*, 5:432–33.

30. C. Mather, *Decennium Luctuosum*, 33–36, EAI. The detail of how she was saved was not included in Mather's account. Jeremy Belknap, writing in the next century, believed that the Indian was a young man when Heard protected him during a massacre in 1676. The attack on Cochecho was a response to the 1676 massacre. Belknap, *History of New-Hampshire*, 1:250–52.

31. *MRGC*, 5:149.

32. Petition of Sir Bibye Lake, April 1731, in *DHSM*, 11:90–94.

33. Hubbard, *Narrative of the Troubles*, 83, EAI.

34. Penhallow, *History of the Wars*, 96–97, EAI; Belknap, *History of New-Hampshire*, 2:54–55.

35. N. S., *Present State of New-England*, 6–7, EEBO.

36. Little, *Abraham in Arms*, 27–28.

37. Nicholas Perryman Ledger B 1712–1754, Papers of the Emery Family, New Hampshire Historical Society, 7. On this ledger, see, Ulrich, *Good Wives*, 179.

38. Penhallow, *History of the Wars*, 104, EAI; Hutchinson, *HCPM*, 2:233.

39. Eames provides an excellent discussion of changes in military technology in *Rustic Warriors*, chap. 9.

40. Hubbard, *Narrative of the Troubles*, 20–21, EAI. Hubbard included this story in the supplemental section, "From Pascataqua to Pemmaquid."

41. Penhallow, *History of the Wars*, 10–11, EAI.

42. Mirick, *History of Haverhill*, 123–24. Mirick wrote that the story was passed down through the Emerson family of Haverhill. He heard the story from the grandson of Jonathan Emerson, who witnessed the attack.

43. Pike, "Journal," 136.

44. On literature related to scalping, see Lipman, "'A Meanes to Knitt Them Togeather'"; Axtell and Sturtevant, "Unkindest Cut."

45. "An Act for Encouraging the Prosecution of the Indian Enemy & Rebels, and Preserving Such as are Friends" [1694], in *ARMB*, 1:175–76.

46. "An Act for Encouragement of the Prosecution of the Indian Enemy and Rebels" [1697], in *ARMB*, 1:292–93.

47. Belknap, *History of New-Hampshire*, 1:140–45.

48. Gyles, *Memoirs of Odd Adventures*, 6, EAI. This story was also recounted in C. Mather, *Decennium Luctuosum*, 30, EAI.

49. Belknap, *History of New-Hampshire*, 1:246.

50. Gyles, *Memoirs of Odd Adventures*, 6, EAI.

51. N. S., *New and Further Narrative*, 4, EEBO.

52. Gookin, *Historical Account*, 503.

53. Ann Little rightly notes that such incidents "fed European stereotypes about Native savagery in general" and attributes much of the English repulsion to these actions to their belief that Indian women had "unnatural power" in their societies and lacked "family discipline." Little, *Abraham in Arms*, 101–2. On Native women's roles in stripping and clothing captives, a ritual meant to facilitate adoption, see ibid., chap. 2.

54. Although scholars of Native American women have made great strides toward understanding Indigenous gender roles, presenting sophisticated analyses of flexible, complex gender systems, our knowledge of Native women's authority—particularly as military leaders—is still incomplete. Scholarly emphasis on female sachems as diplomats and dealers of land in seventeenth-century northeastern North America has obscured their other roles in war making. Studies include Grumet, "Sunksquaws, Shamans, and Tradeswomen"; Strong, "Algonquian Women as Sunksquaws"; Plane, "Putting a Face on Colonization"; McCartney, "Cockacoeske, Queen of Pamunkey"; and Schmidt, "Cockacoeske, Weroansqua of the Pamunkeys."

55. On English leaders' abilities to shape Native leadership, see Plane, "Putting a Face on Colonization," 152.

56. N. S., *Present State of New-England*, 3, EEBO.

57. On Elizabethan constructions of gender and princely authority, see Montrose, *Subject of Elizabeth*.

58. N. S., *New and Further Narrative*, front matter, EEBO.

59. See Shoemaker, *Strange Likeness*, esp. chap. 2.

60. John Talbot to Richard Gillingham, November 24, 1702, in *Collections of the Protestant Episcopal Historical Society*, xxxii.

61. Bradford and Winslow, *Relation*, 57–59, EEBO.

62. *MRGC*, 1:201. On these land deals, see Cogley, *John Eliot's Mission*, 30–36.

63. On the gendering of gun ownership, see Little, *Abraham in Arms*, 27–28.

64. Records pertaining to the repair of the gun appear in *MRGC*, 2:36, 44. On this Massachusett sachem's identity, see ibid., 55–56; Cogley, *John Eliot's Mission*, 33.

65. *MRGC*, 4.5:357–59.

66. Ibid., 386.

67. Roger Williams to the General Court of Massachusetts Bay, May 7, 1668, Massachusetts Archives Collection, 30:147, MSA.

68. Land records confirm that this was the sachem known as Matantuck, Magnus, Matataog, and "the old queen" during King Philip's War. "The Trumbull Papers," in *MHSC*, 5th ser., 9:74–76. The phrase "old queen" in the treaty referred to Matataog (Matantuck), not Quaiapen, an alternate spelling of Weetamoo's husband Quinnapin's name. See treaties in Potter, *Early History of Narragansett*, 167–71. On her defeat, see Major John Talcott to the Connecticut War Council, July 4, 1676, in *Public Records of the Colony of Connecticut*, 2:458–59.

69. Pocasset was a member-nation of the Wampanoag Confederacy located on a large "neck" of land south of present-day Fall River, Massachusetts, in what is now Rhode Island.

70. Weetamoo appears under the names Tatapanum and Namumpum in the court cases discussed involving Wamsutta, Philip, and Pocasset land through 1668.

71. Deposition of Namumpum of Pokeesett, in Drake, *Biography and History*, 3:3–4. The volume is divided into five books. The deposition appears in the third book.

72. Worthington, *Rhode Island Land Evidences*, 1:188–89.

73. *RCNP*, 4:8, 16–17.

74. Ibid., 24–25.

75. *RCNP*, 5:77–79. The treaty stipulated that Philip submit to Plymouth's authority, pay one-hundred pounds, and turn over his weapons—among other conditions. On his motivations and the origins of the war, see Pulsipher, *Subjects unto the Same King*; Lepore, *Name of War*.

76. I. Mather, *Brief History*, 2–3, EAI.

77. Hubbard, *Narrative of the Troubles*, 109, EAI. Saltonstall estimated that Philip brought about five hundred men and that his local allies brought eight or nine hundred men combined. N. S., *Present State of New-England*, 4, EEBO.

78. N. S., *Present State of New-England*, 3, EEBO. Saltonstall's description of Weetamoo as a "Woman Prince, or Queen" as well as a prince—not to mention "potent"—is telling. His use of the masculine terms was neither mocking nor dismissive. Rather, his language and the details he provided regarding her holdings suggest that Saltonstall understood Weetamoo's importance and position in the region. Had Saltonstall hoped to diminish her importance, he might have employed the more violent, gendered language wielded by Major John Talcott when he boasted in July 1676 that the "ould peice of venum, Sunck squaw Magnus was slaine." Talcott's choice of the word "venom" conjures images of the poisonous old, female bodies that populated the literature of the day. Comparing Talcott and Saltonstall's language suggests that a female sachem receiving respect might be depicted in positive masculine terms. Talcott to the Connecticut War Council, July 4, 1676, in *Public Records of the Colony of Connecticut*, 2:458.

79. N. S., *Present State of New-England*, 4, EEBO. Weetamoo's assistance would have suggested that Philip was assembling a coalition capable of winning. It may have also signaled solidarity within the Wampanoag Confederacy, bringing the legitimacy of a leader and rival who had claimed power as sachem of the Pocasset and the former wife of Wamsutta.

80. I. Mather, *Brief History*, Postscript 5, EAI.

81. Church, *Entertaining Passages*, 3–4, EAI.

82. I. Mather, *Brief History*, 4, EAI.

83. N. S., *Present State of New-England*, 4, EEBO.

84. Easton, *Relacion of the Indyan Warre*, 12–13.

85. John Easton letter, May 26, 1675, to Josiah Winslow (Mss C 357). R. Stanton Avery Special Collections, New England Historic Genealogical Society, www.AmericanAncestors.org.

86. *RCNP*, 5:215–16. Southworth's son-in-law Benjamin Church—who purchased Saconet land from Awashunkes before the war—went on to benefit from the seizure of Pocasset land.

87. Easton to Winslow, May 26, 1675, Avery Special Collections. Although Easton appears to be double-crossing Weetamoo, he may have been trying to prevent a larger catastrophe. Easton, a Quaker, was known for his sympathetic stance on Native issues. Increase Mather wrote his history of the war as a response to Easton's history, which he claimed was "fraught with worse things then meer Mistakes." I. Mather, *Brief History*, i, EAI.

88. Josiah Winslow to Weetamoo, June 15, 1675, Winslow Family Papers II, 1638–1760, Massachusetts Historical Society.

89. Most sources refer to Weetamoo's husband at this time as Petananuet or a variation of that name such as Peter, though the name Ben also appears.

90. Josiah Winslow to Weetamoo, June 15, 1675, Winslow Papers.

91. "Narrative shewing the manor of the begining of the present Warr with the Indians of Mount hope and Pocassett," in *RCNP*, 10:362. Volume 10 of *RCNP* is the second volume of that series' two-part "Acts of the Commissioners of the United Colonies of New England."

92. James Cudworth to Gov. Josiah Winslow, July 20, 1675, in *MHSC*, 1st ser., 6:84–85. This volume was printed in 1798 and reprinted in 1835. Citations refer to the 1835 edition.

93. N. S., *Present State of New-England*, 9, EEBO; Mather, *Brief History*, 4–5, EAI; and Hubbard, *Narrative of the Troubles*, 25–28, EAI.

94. Easton, *Relacion of the Indyan Warre*, 14.

95. Pulsipher, *Subjects unto the Same King*, 124; N. S., *Present State of New-England*, 9, EEBO; N. S., *Continuation of the State of New-England*, 4, EEBO; and I. Mather, *Brief History*, 19, EAI.

96. Hubbard, *Narrative of the Troubles*, 16, EAI.

97. Weetamoo had experience working diplomatically with the Narragansett, as the 1662 court case shows.

98. N. S., *Continuation of the State of New-England*, 4, EEBO.

99. N. S., *Present State of New-England*, 9, 15, EEBO.

100. Ibid., 18.

101. Josiah Winslow to Increase Mather, May 1, 1676, in I. Mather, *Brief History*, Postscript, EAI.

102. On Narragansett motives, see Pulsipher, *Subjects unto the Same King*, chap. 5.

103. I. Mather, *Brief History*, 20, EAI.

104. Ibid., 18–21; N. S., *Continuation of the State of New-England*, 4–8, EEBO.

105. I. Mather, *Brief History*, 19, EAI; Church, *Entertaining Passages*, 14–17, EAI.

106. Church, *Entertaining Passages*, 17, EAI.

107. Pulsipher, *Subjects unto the Same King*, 127–28.

108. I. Mather, *Brief History*, 38, EAI; Hubbard, *Narrative of the Troubles*, 44, EAI. Pulsipher argues that Philip hoped to form an alliance with New York's Governor Andros against New England colonies that Philip viewed as violating treaties made with Charles II. *Subjects unto the Same King*, 129–32.

109. I. Mather, *Brief History*, 21–41, EAI.

110. Rowlandson, *Soveraignty & Goodness of God*, EAI. Rowlandson's narrative has been the subject of numerous studies, including Toulouse, *Captive's Position*; Burnham, *Captivity and Sentiment*; Arnold, "'Now . . . Didn't Our People Laugh?'"; Potter, "Writing Indigenous Femininity"; and Pauline Turner Strong, *Captive Selves*, chap. 4. Analyses have tended to focus on Rowlandson's experiences and assumptions as well as on conflicts between the two women. See Burnham, *Captivity and Sentiment*, 30–33; Strong, *Captive Selves*, chap. 4; Potter, "Writing Indigenous Femininity"; and Arnold, "'Now . . . Didn't Our People Laugh?'"

111. Rowlandson, *Soveraignty & Goodness of God*, 11, EAI. Michelle Burnham and Pauline Turner Strong have also suggested that Rowlandson was unaware of Weetamoo's political position. Burnham, *Captivity and Sentiment*, 30–33; Strong, *Captive Selves*, 100–101.

112. Little, *Abraham in Arms*, 109–11, 122–23. Chapter 3 of *Abraham in Arms* examines the relationship between gender, authority, and order in captivity.

113. Rowlandson, *Soveraignty & Goodness of God*, 47–48. See also: Arnold, "'Now . . . Didn't Our People Laugh?'"; Potter, "Writing Indigenous Femininity."

114. Rowlandson, *Soveraignty & Goodness of God*, 57, EAI.

115. Bragdon, *Native People of Southern New England, 1650–1775*, 132–38.

116. Hubbard, *Narrative of the Troubles*, 102–3, EAI; I. Mather, *Brief History*, 46, EAI.

117. Mather, *Brief History*, 46, EAI.

118. Ibid., 45–46.

119. Romero, *Making War and Minting Christians*, 167–68. In the Pequot War, Native societies exchanged body parts to build alliances, while colonists displayed heads as a reflection of mastery and to signal the end of a conflict. Lipman, "'A Meanes to Knitt Them Togeather,'" 4.

120. I. Mather, *Brief History*, 19, EAI.

121. Ibid., 45.

122. N. S., *Present State of New-England*, 3, EEBO.

123. Plane, "Putting a Face on Colonization," 149–57; Den Ouden, *Beyond Conquest*, 130–35.

124. Plane, "Putting a Face on Colonization," 149–57.

125. Ibid., 155, 157.

126. Norton, *Separated by Their Sex*, 2–3. Norton has attributed this shift in the Anglo-Atlantic world to developments in response to the Glorious Revolution of 1688–89. Ibid., 7–8.

127. Ryan, *Mysteries of Sex*, chap. 1. Scholars have shown that many Native women preserved older and created new forms of influence. See Shoemaker, *Negotiators of Change*; Shoemaker, "Rise or Fall"; Sleeper-Smith, *Indian Women and French Men*; Devens, *Countering Colonization*; Perdue, *Cherokee Women*; and White, *Wild Frenchmen and Frenchified Indians*.

128. Plane, "Putting a Face on Colonization," 155; Bragdon, *Native People of Southern New England, 1650–1775*, 114; and Den Ouden, *Beyond Conquest*, 130–35.

129. Den Ouden, *Beyond Conquest*, 71.

130. Ibid., 132.

131. John Walter has argued that women acting in mobs or crowds in England often "operated on behalf of, and drew support from, the wider community." In England, women may have enjoyed some measure of legal protection when acting as a mob, an unintended benefit of coverture, the legal doctrine that placed responsibility for women's actions on their fathers and husbands. In some instances, women even taunted officials with the knowledge that they were unable to prosecute female protesters in these chaotic episodes. Walter, "Faces in the Crowd," quotation on 120. On women's actions in early modern European mobs, see Shoemaker, "London 'Mob'"; Dekker, "Women in Revolt"; and Hurl-Eamon, *Gender and Petty Violence*, 107–22.

132. Deposition of Robert Roules, July 17, 1677, Massachusetts Archives Collection, 69:158, MSA. The initial attack was part of a larger strategy to capture fishing vessels, attack the islands in Boston Harbor, and burn Boston. Axtell, "Vengeful Women of Marblehead."

133. Deposition of Roules, July 17, 1677, MSA. Increase Mather reported that services had only just concluded. I. Mather, *Diary*, 48.

134. I. Mather, *Diary*, 48; Deposition of Roules, July 17, 1677, MSA.

135. Deposition of Roules, July 17, 1677, MSA.

136. Ibid. In a brief discussion of this incident, Ulrich notes that the women may have "acted as surrogates for the larger community." Ulrich, *Good Wives*, 194.

137. I. Mather, *Diary*, 48.

138. Cogley, *John Eliot's Mission*, 226–30.

139. On wartime anti-Indian sentiment, see Pulsipher, *Subjects unto the Same King*, chap. 6.

140. Gookin, *Historical Account*, 503, 494.

141. Ibid., 501–3.

142. John Winthrop to Fitz-John Winthrop, July 1707, in *MHSC*, 6th ser., 3:387–89.

143. Pencak, Dennis, and Newman, *Riot and Revelry*. See also Davis, *Society and Culture*; Ingram, "Ridings, Rough Music, and Mocking Rhymes."

144. Winthrop to Fitz-John Winthrop, July 1707, 387–89.

145. C. Mather, *The Deplorable State of New-England*, 34–35, EAI. Emphasis in original.

Chapter 2

1. Marie Madeleine de Verchères à Mme de Maurepas, October 15, 1699, in *SRCA*, 6–7.

2. Coates and Morgan, *Heroines and History*, 24.

3. Morin, *Annales de L'Hotel-Dieu de Montreal*, 158.

4. Studies that have examined women's wartime roles in continental Europe include Lynn, *Women, Armies, and Warfare*; Gervais and Lusignan, "De Jeanne d'Arc à Madelaine de Verchères"; Solterer, "Figures of Female Militancy"; McLaughlin, "Woman Warrior"; and Sandberg, "'Generous Amazons.'"

5. In the wars that followed, France's greater influence began to affect New France's war making, though, as in New England, its full impact would not become clear for

decades. Records from the late seventeenth century are even more fragmentary than those of the middle part of the century. Official correspondence from the emerging bureaucracy of New France increased during this time as other sources dwindled. The Jesuits ceased publication of their historically invaluable *Jesuit Relations* in 1673, and prolific letter writer Marie de l'Incarnation died in 1672. The lack of a press in New France and a dearth of chronicles from the period exacerbate the problem of piecing together women's roles in King William's and Queen Anne's Wars. In spite of this loss, it is still possible to glean patterns from the available sources.

6. Courville, *Quebec: A Historical Geography*, 51–52.

7. Harris, *Reluctant Land*, 66–67.

8. Courville, *Quebec: A Historical Geography*, 51–52.

9. The above paragraph is indebted to Dechêne, *Le peuple, l'état et la guerre*, 98–100.

10. *JR*, 38:51–53.

11. Laverdière and Casgrain, *Le Journal des Jésuites*, 174; MDI to Claude Martin, "Lettre CVI," September 1, 1652, in *LMMI*, 1:470.

12. Dollier de Casson, *History of Montreal*, 165–67.

13. Juliana Barr has argued that in regions where Indians had the upper hand, they often controlled how gender, power, and race intersected. Studies that have examined changes regarding race, gender, and power include Barr, *Peace Came in the Form of a Woman*; Gutiérrez, *When Jesus Came, the Corn Mothers Went Away*; Shoemaker, *Strange Likeness*; Brooks, *Captives and Cousins*; Spear, *Race, Sex, and Social Order*; Fischer, *Suspect Relations*; Brown, *Good Wives, Nasty Wenches*; Mumford, "Aristocracy on the Auction Block"; and Villella, "'Pure and Noble Indians.'"

14. MDI to Claude Martin, "Lettre CXXV," September 24, 1654, in *LMMI*, 2:68.

15. MDI to Claude Martin, "Lettre CXXXII," October 12, 1655, in *LMMI*, 2:90–93.

16. Ibid.; *JR*, 41:219–22.

17. *JR*, 58:161–65.

18. MDI to Martin, "Lettre CXXXII," October 12, 1655, in *LMMI*, 2:85–86.

19. MDI to Claude Martin, "Lettre LXXXI," 1647, in *LMMI*, 1:345–46.

20. MDI to Claude Martin, "Lettre CXL," October 4, 1658, in *LMMI*, 2:133.

21. *JR*, 46:209.

22. *JR*, 51:67.

23. *JR*, 8:23–25.

24. *JR*, 9:255.

25. Ibid., 257; Although Le Jeune's report was colored by his European perspective, ritual cannibalism was an important part of ceremonial torture among many polities. Consuming a captive warrior, particularly one who proved himself brave during torture, completed the group's triumph over a worthy adversary and may have allowed the victors to claim the captive's courage for themselves. Richter, "War and Culture"; Seeman, *Huron-Wendat Feast of the Dead*, 18.

26. *JR*, 9:257–59.

27. Ibid., 267–69.

28. For other discussions of Indigenous women's roles in torture in the *Jesuit Relations*, see *JR*, 5:29–31, 53 and 6:245.

29. On these changes, see Dechêne, *Le peuple, l'état et la guerre*, 157–58.

30. "Arrêt du Conseil Supérieur de Québec qui défend d'acheter, vendre ou troquer les armes des habitans, à peine de 50lbs. d'amende" [January 14, 1686], in *Arrêts et réglements*, 110–11.

31. Ibid.

32. Vachon de Belmont, "Histoire du Canada," 33. It is unclear when Vachon de Belmont wrote this work. His history ends in 1700, though Belmont did not die until 1732.

33. Anonymous, *Recueil de ce qui s'est passé en Canada au sujet de la guerre*, 52.

34. "Lettre du Conseil d'Etat au Sujet du Sieur de la Tour," March 6, 1644, in *Nouvelle-France: Documents historiques*, 1:99–102; Winthrop, *Journal*, 2:85, 105–16, 127–37, 178–208, 244–48, 254–56.

35. Denys, *Description géographique et historique*, 1:38–40. Denys, a resident of Acadia, provided the most thorough account in 1672, though the story was confirmed by Iberville in 1700. "Memoire du Sieur D'Iberville sur Baston et ses Dependances," in *CMNF*, 2:355.

36. Denys, *Description géographique et historique*, 1:38–39.

37. "The Case of William Crowne, Esq., Proprietor in part of Nova Scotia or L'Accady" [1668?], in Sainsbury, *Calendar of State Papers*, 596–97.

38. "Procès-verbaux et documents relatifs à la rébellion du sieur de La Tour et de sa femme contre le roi de France en Acadie," 1645, LAC, MG1 C11D, F-168, 72–79.

39. DeJean, *Tender Geographies*, chap. 1; Coates and Morgan, *Heroines and History*, 24–25; Ormerod, *Tracts Relating to Military Proceedings*, 155–86, 209–13.

40. MDI to Claude Martin, "CLXXVIII," November 12, 1666, in *LMMI*, 2:327–36.

41. Many of these early biographies were written by priests seeking to preserve and promote the work done by their colleagues. Additionally, as the administrators of institutions that required significant networking and correspondence with benefactors, female religious leaders produced a large number of sources about their lives.

42. Dollier de Casson, *History of Montreal*, 75, 79.

43. Ibid., 83, 149, 151–53.

44. Ibid., 159–61. Sister Marie Morin supports Dollier de Casson's claim that the Hôtel-Dieu's endowment paid for reinforcements. Morin, *Annales de L'Hotel-Dieu de Montreal*, 74.

45. MDI to Martin, "Lettre CLXXVIII," November 12, 1666, in *LMMI*, 2:327–36.

46. Examples of her numerous letters related to military affairs in both volumes of *LMMI* include "Lettre XLVI," 1:133–53; "Lettre LXVI," 1:237–60; "Lettre LXXIX," 1:324–25; "Lettre XCVI," 1:416–19; "Lettre CXIV," 2:10–12; "Lettre CXXXII," 2:84–93; "Lettre CXL," 2:128–37; and "Lettre CLXXVIII," 2:327–36.

47. MDI to Claude Martin, "CLIV," September 1661, in *LMMI*, 2:202–10; *JR*, 46:205–7.

48. Dollier de Casson, *History of Montreal*, 271–73. On Gabriel LeSel Du Clos's position in Montreal society, see "Ordonnances de Mr. Paul de Chomedey, Sieur de Maisonneufve, Premier Gouverneur de Montréal," in *Mémoires et documents relatifs à l'histoire du Canada*, 125–44; Tanguay, *Dictionnaire généalogique*, 1:109. The family was also known as Celles dit Duclos and other variations.

49. Dollier de Casson, *History of Montreal*, 271–73.

50. La Potherie, *Histoire de l'Amerique septentrionale*, 1:326–27.

51. An excellent study of the development of Madeleine de Verchères's personal narrative and its influence on Canadian nationalism is Coates and Morgan, *Heroines and History*.

52. On the composition of Madeleine de Verchères's letters, see Coates and Morgan, *Heroines and History*, 19–21. According to Coates and Morgan, La Potherie, who composed the earliest published version of the incident, may have either helped Madeleine write her first letter or used it as the basis for his own account first published in 1722.

53. Verchères à Maurepas, October 15, 1699, in *SRCA*, 6–7; Champigny au ministre, October 25, 1700, LAC, MG1 C11A, F-18, 102v–103.

54. Verchères à Maurepas, October 15, 1699, in *SRCA*, 6–7.

55. Ibid. On these imperial transformations, see Dechêne, *Le peuple, l'état et la guerre*; Crouch, *Nobility Lost*.

Chapter 3

1. Melzer, *"Relation de voyage,"* 37–42.

2. The phrase "early modern propaganda" is not anachronistic. Historians of early modern Europe have long noted the importance of the printing press in Luther's initial successes as well as in later struggles between confessions. The term "propaganda" originally referred to the propagation of the Catholic faith by two bodies established by the papacy in the early seventeenth century. Founded in 1622 by Pope Gregory XV, the Congregation of the Propaganda (Congregatio de Propaganda Fide) was a committee of cardinals that oversaw the Church's foreign missions, which were vividly described in the *Jesuit Relations*. Five years later, Urban VIII added a College of the Propaganda to train missionaries to spread the Christian faith abroad. For centuries, the term "propaganda" lacked the negative modern connotations associated with it. On early modern propaganda, see Eisenstein, *Printing Press*; Reinhard, "Reformation, Counter-Reformation"; Lake and Pincus, "Rethinking the Public Sphere"; Lake and Questier, "Puritans, Papists, and the 'Public Sphere'"; Cogswell, "Politics of Propaganda"; Edwards, *Printing, Propaganda, and Martin Luther*; Rice, "Cotton Mather Speaks to France"; Cooper, *Propaganda and the Tudor State*; Montaño, *Courting the Moderates*; Raymond, *Pamphlets and Pamphleteering*; and Jowett and O'Donnell, *Propaganda and Persuasion*.

3. On early modern Europeans' interest in Amazons, see Schwarz, *Tough Love*; Taufer, "The Only Good Amazon"; Denis, "Ces étranges étrangères"; and DeJean, *Tender Geographies*.

4. Taufer, "The Only Good Amazon."

5. For more on English perceptions of Native gender roles, see Brown, *Good Wives, Nasty Wenches*, chap. 2; Little, *Abraham in Arms*.

6. Bouvier, *Women and the Conquest of California*, chap. 1.

7. The above paragraph is indebted to Denis, "Ces étranges étrangères."

8. Joan DeJean has argued that beginning in the early 1620s, during the regency of Marie de Medici, authors and artists increasingly portrayed female leaders in heroic,

martial situations. According to DeJean, a number of aristocratic Frenchwomen took on military roles in conflicts from the 1630s to the 1650s. DeJean, *Tender Geographies*, chap. 1. On the femme forte and virago, see Craveri, *Age of Conversation*, 22–23; Maclean, *Woman Triumphant*, chap. 3; and Walker, *Crime, Gender, and Social Order*, chap. 3.

9. *JR*, 30:289.

10. Ibid., 291.

11. Ibid., 293.

12. Ibid., 293–95.

13. On this trope, see Greer, "Colonial Saints," 339–40.

14. MDI to Claude Martin, "Lettre CLXXVIII," November 12, 1666, in *LMMI*, 2:327.

15. Morin, *Annales de L'Hotel-Dieu de Montreal*, 158.

16. On the emergence of the ideal of a more active holy woman, see Deslandres, "Shadow of the Cloister." For Counter-Reformation reactions to these women and the implications for restricted activity in New France, see Choquette, "'Ces Amazones du Grand Dieu,'" 632. Ursuline missionaries in eighteenth-century Louisiana faced additional challenges in establishing a female religious order in a slave society. See Clark, *Masterless Mistresses*.

17. The above paragraph is based on Luria, *Sacred Boundaries*, chap. 5. Luria argues that these women "did not simply become 'men,'" but rather "were exceptional women." Ibid., 196. For discussions of other Jesuit and Ursuline uses of the femme forte with regard to their missions, see Harvey, *Figuring Modesty*, 116; Keller-Lapp, "Floating Cloisters."

18. On Jesuit fundraising and their relationships with female donors, see Hufton, "Altruism and Reciprocity"; Hufton, "Widow's Mite."

19. Few scholars have focused on the roles women donors played in the growth of women's orders and the mission in New France in the seventeenth century. One exception is Davis, *Women on the Margins*.

20. *JR*, 7:261.

21. *JR*, 38:97. According to Marie-Florine Bruneau, Marie de l'Incarnation wrote the biography of Marie de Saint Joseph. This biography was allegedly later slipped into that year's *Jesuit Relation* without Marie de l'Incarnation's knowledge. Bruneau suggests that this secrecy allowed Marie de l'Incarnation to anonymously praise a member of her order without appearing to promote it. Bruneau, *Women Mystics*, 83.

22. *JR*, 16:9. This biblical tone is also present in the original French, published side-by-side with the English translation.

23. *JR*, 18:77.

24. *JR*, 20:125–27.

25. *JR*, 30:275–77.

26. *JR*, 24:299 and 18:223–25.

27. *JR*, 9:296–99. The original French is "*une Megere*," while the English translation is "a Fury."

28. *JR*, 31:141.

29. *JR*, 44:153–71, quotation on 168.

30. Ibid., 167–69.

31. *JR*, 43:227–31.

32. Ibid., 231.

33. DeJean, "Violent Women and Violence against Women," 132–34; Walker, *Crime, Gender, and Social Order*, 96.

34. Hubbard, *Narrative of the Troubles*, 20–21, EAI. This story appears in "From Pascataqua to Pemmaquid," a separate section that follows the main narrative.

35. C. Mather, *Decennium Luctuosum*, 94, EAI.

36. Penhallow, *History of the Wars*, 32, EAI.

37. Oldmixon, *British Empire in America*, 1:75–76, ECCO.

38. This discussion of balladry and borrowing is based on Dugaw, *Warrior Women*, chap. 6.

39. Little, *Abraham in Arms*, 89; Ulrich, *Good Wives*, 178–79.

40. Penhallow, *History of the Wars*, 73, EAI.

41. C. Mather, *Decennium Luctuosum*, 122, EAI.

42. Tompson, *New Englands Crisis*, 30–31.

43. Ibid., 30; Shields, *American Aeneas*, 34.

44. Tompson, *New Englands Crisis*, 30–31.

45. On this shift in England, see Walker, *Crime, Gender, and Social Order*, chap. 3.

46. C. Mather, *Frontiers Well-Defended*, EAI; Petition of John Houghton, February 14, 1694, in *ARMB*, 7:445.

47. C. Mather, *Frontiers Well-Defended*, 21–23, EAI.

48. The association between a well-ordered New England family and a well-ordered frontier is supported by Ann Little's argument that English captives of Indians often complained about the "disorder" of Indian communities. Little, *Abraham in Arms*, chap. 3.

49. C. Mather, *Frontiers Well-Defended*, 45, 50, EAI. Mather's treatise was representative of an important cultural transition. Ann Little has argued that during the first Anglo-French war in the northeastern borderlands, King William's War, "English depictions of frontier warfare and captivity shifted dramatically," focusing less on threats posed by Indians and more on the dangers of "the French and their Catholicism as the chief threat to the New England way." Little, *Abraham in Arms*, 127–29.

50. Joanna Cotton to Increase Mather, March 13, 1697, Massachusetts Archives Collection, 57:68–70, MSA.

51. Little, *Abraham in Arms*, 164–65.

52. As Teresa Toulouse argues, captivity narratives promoted a female ideal that was "submissive, obedient, and loyal." Toulouse, *Captive's Position*, 9.

53. For another take on Dustan's celebrity, see Derounian-Stodola, "Captive as Celebrity."

54. Debates over Dustan's legacy have included attempts to explain how her experience fits into the model of a captivity narrative, Mather's role in shaping the story, whether her actions were deviant, and whether Dustan was a pawn in a conflict over political identity and autonomy in Massachusetts. Teresa Toulouse suggests that Mather may have used positive stories about active women such as Dustan and Elizabeth Heard in *Decennium Luctuosum* to chastise "certain colonial men's inabilities, cowardice and procrastination," failings that could lead to a breakdown of order on

the frontier. Toulouse also posits that stories of women's courage may have served "as a rebuke to other colonial mothers who let their children die." Toulouse, *Captive's Position*, 106, 113. On Dustan, see Ulrich, *Good Wives*, 167–72; Strong, *Captive Selves*; Toulouse, *Captive's Position*; and Derounian-Stodola, "Captive as Celebrity."

55. Mather published accounts of Hannah Dustan's exploits three times: C. Mather, *Humiliations Follow'd with Deliverances*, EAI; C. Mather, *Decennium Luctuosum*, EAI; and C. Mather, *Magnalia Christi Americana*, EAI.

56. Hutchinson, *HCPM*, 2:81.

57. Sewall, "Diary," 5:452–53.

58. C. Mather, *Decennium Luctuosum*, 143, EAI.

59. Lossing, "Hannah Dustin and Mary Corliss Neff Tankard," 4:339–40.

60. Marshall, *John Marshall's Diary*, 18.

61. Petition of Thomas Dunstan, June 8, 1697, in *ARMB*, 7:562. The petition records his name as Thomas Dunstan and Thomus Dustun.

62. *ARMB*, 7:153.

63. On intracolonial conflict during Dudley's rule, see Toulouse, *Captive's Position*, chap. 6.

64. C. Mather, *A Memorial Of the Present Deplorable State of New-England*, ECCO.

65. Ibid., 30.

66. Ibid., 33–36.

67. C. Mather, *The Deplorable State of New-England*, 34–35, EAI.

Chapter 4

1. Although women in rural Acadia did experience English raids throughout the eighteenth century, sources are scarce and insufficient to reach firm conclusions regarding their participation in these conflicts.

2. An excellent treatment of the life of Esther Wheelwright (1696–1780), a converted English captive who rose through the ranks to wield significant power with an international profile as the mother superior of the Ursulines in Quebec, is Little, *Many Captivities of Esther Wheelwright*.

3. Mascarene, "Memorial of Mascarene," 78.

4. Ibid., 76–78.

5. Ibid., 78, 82.

6. On population and migration, see Greer, *People of New France*, chap. 1.

7. Choquette discusses concerns regarding morality and fur traders in Montreal in *Frenchmen into Peasants*, 143–44.

8. Procès de Jacquette Moreau, August 21, 1688, BANQ, Fonds Prévôté de Québec, Registres et documents de la Prévôté de Québec, Registres de la Prévôté de Québec, M48/5, 2–2v.

9. "Instructions pour le Sieur Chevalier de Callières, Gouverneur et Lieutenant General pour le Roi" [May 25, 1699], in *CMNF*, 2:322. On Louis's morality, see Riley, *Lust for Virtue*; "Extrait des lettres particulières du Canada et des placets particuliers," 1698–99, LAC, MG1 C11A, F-121, 46v.

10. "Instructions pour le Sieur Chevalier de Callières," in *CMNF*, 2:320.

11. For an account of the king's efforts to reform France, see Riley, *Lust for Virtue*.

12. Griffiths, *From Migrant to Acadian*, esp. chaps. 5, 6; Faragher, *Great and Noble Scheme*.

13. Tanguay, *Dictionnaire généalogique*, 1:154; "Commission au sieur de Villeray pour informer de la vie, des moeurs et de la religion catholique apostolique et romaine de Mathieu Damours, sieur de Freneuse, nommé conseiller au Conseil Souverain en survivance à son père," July 10, 1690, BANQ, Fonds Conseil Souverain, Jugements et Délibérations, M9/3, 73–73v; "Relation d'une expédition anglaise en Acadie," 1697, LAC, MG1 C11A, F-14, 16.

14. Le sieur Degoutin au ministre, November 29, 1702, LAC, MG1 C11D, F-171, 200v. LAC dates the letter to 1702. According to the letter's author, it was composed in 1703.

15. Dion was an alternate spelling of Guyon. Registre de Port-Royal (1703), 19, Acadia, Canada, Vital and Church Records.

16. "Extrait d'une lettre non-datée de l'évêque de Québec," November 29, 1703, LAC, MG1 C11D, F-171, 316v–317.

17. "Extrait d'une lettre du frère Justinien Durand, récollet, faisant les fonctions curiales au Port-Royal," 1705, LAC, MG1 C11D, F-172, 197; "Extrait d'une lettre du père Félix Pein, aumônier du fort Royal," December 1705, LAC, MG1 C11D, F-172, 195.

18. "Mémoire du sieur de Brouillan pour réponse à la lettre que Monseigneur lui a écrite le 4 juin 1704," March 5, 1705, LAC, MG1 C11A, F-22, 135v-136; "Mémoire du roi à M. du Brouillan," June 3, 1705, LAC, MG1 B, F-207, 171–171v.

19. "Mémoire du sieur de Brouillan," March 5, 1705, LAC, MG1 C11A, F-22, 136v. In this letter, Brouillan denied living with Barrat, but did refer to her as a tavern keeper.

20. "Extrait d'une lettre non-datée de l'évêque de Québec," November 29, 1703, LAC, MG1 C11D, F-172, 317.

21. "Invasion des Anglois de Baston par Monsieur de la Bat," [1704], in *CMNF*, 2:417.

22. Brouillan later defended himself in a letter. "Mémoire du sieur de Brouillan," March 5, 1705, LAC, MG1 C11A F-22, 135.

23. M. de Bonaventure au ministre, November 30, 1705, LAC, MG1 C11D, F-172, 124v.

24. "Extrait d'une lettre du frère Justinien Durand," 1705, LAC, MG1 C11D, F-172, 197.

25. "Extrait d'une lettre du père Félix Pein," December 1705, LAC, MG1 C11D, F-172, 195.

26. Le ministre à M. Bégon, April 28, 1706, LAC, MG1 B, F-207, 343v–344.

27. "Ordre du roi pour faire sortir la Dame de Freneuse de l'Acadie," August 24, 1707, LAC, MG1 B, F-209, 237.

28. Le ministre à M. l'évêque de Québek, June 6, 1708, LAC, MG1 B, F-209, 380v; Le Ministre à Monsieur de Bonnaventure, June 30, 1707, in *CMNF*, 2:472–73.

29. Le Ministre à Monsieur de Subercase, June 6, 1708, in *CMNF*, 2:490–91.

30. Many of these letters are available at LAC on microfilm rolls F-209, F-213, and F-214 in MG1 B and on F-173 in MG1 C11D.

31. Le ministre à M. de Bonaventure, May 20, 1710, LAC, MG1 B, F-214, 96.

32. Tutelle aux mineurs de feu Mathieu Damours de Freneuse, May 16, 1714, BANQ, Fonds Cour supérieure. District judiciaire de Québec. Tutelles et curatelles, Dossiers, number 296.

33. Ibid., 1.

34. See for example, Le président du Conseil de Marine à M. Hocquart, April 1, 1732, LAC, MG1 B, F-259, 615; "Le Sieur Robert, qui va remplacer M. Bégon, a ordre," May 30, 1724, LAC, MG1 B, F-242, 1115.

35. Dechêne, *Le peuple, l'état et la guerre*, 147, 222–23. Another important study of changes in martial and imperial cultures in New France is Crouch, *Nobility Lost*.

36. Dechêne, *Le peuple, l'état et la guerre*, 223–24.

37. Arrêt du Roi pour la retenue des quatre deniers pour livre applicables aux Invalides de la Marine [May 1709], in *Édits, ordonnances royaux, declarations et arrêts*, 313–20.

38. Edit du Roi concernant les Invalides de la Marine [July 1720], in *Édits, ordonnances royaux, declarations et arrêts*, 405–25, quotation on 410.

39. The 1720 order suggests that in some cases, widows were also required to contribute to the new military order.

40. On this conflict over trade, see Preston, *Texture of Contact*, 54–60.

41. "Délibération du Conseil de Marine au sujet de la 'lieutenance vacante en Canada'," April 12, 1717, LAC, MG1 C11A, F-37, 170–170v.

42. See, for example, Aveu et dénombrement de dame Marie-Josephe Fezeret, April 23, 1723, BANQ, Fonds Intendants, Papiers terriers de la Compagnie des Indes occidentales et du Domaine du roi, Aveux et Dénombrements, M6/1.

43. "Mémoire de Mme de Thiersant au ministre," 1733, LAC, MG1 C11A, F-60, 410–13.

44. Ibid., 410v–411v.

45. Ibid., 411v–412.

46. Mme de Thiersant au ministre, October 15, 1731, LAC, MG1 C11A, F-55, 378–379v.

47. Mme Thiersant au ministre, September 5, 1731, LAC, MG1 C11A, F-55, 377v.

48. Ibid., 377–377v.

49. "Liste des personnes qui passent en France sur le vaisseau du roi le Héros," October 19, 1735, LAC, MG1 C11A, F-64, 138–138v.

50. "Mémoire présenté au cardinal de Fleury par Mme de Thiersant," June 1737, LAC, MG7 II, C-12869. Records show that Madame Thiersant continued her requests for assistance through 1743, though it is unclear why those requests ceased after that time. "Autre mémoire de Mme de Thiersant au cardinal de Fleury," 1743, LAC, MG7 II, C-12869.

51. Madame de Ramezay au ministre, September 25, 1731, LAC, MG1 C11A, F-56, 246–47v. This was not the first time Madame Ramezay submitted this type of petition. Mme de Ramezay au ministre, October 8, 1728, LAC, MG1 C11A, F-50, 353–54v.

52. "Succession du sieur Isabeau, entrepreneur des fortifications," 1725–31, LAC, MG1 G2, (Conseil Supérieur de Louisbourg), F-681, 616–87; Le président du Conseil de Marine à M. Verrier, June 20, 1730, LAC, MG1 B, F-254, 499. For additional context regarding widows such as Madame Planton, see Brun, *Vie et mort du couple*, 66.

53. In surveying these *lettres de change*, I did not include smaller, supplemental reports regarding payments made to a handful of people, often one or two recipients.

54. Samson, *Forges du Saint-Maurice*, 221–27; Miquelon, "Canada's Place in the French Imperial Economy."

55. "État de quarante-huit lettres de change premières et secondes tirées," October 30, 1743, LAC, MG1 C11A, F-80, 217–18v.

56. "État de 19 lettres de change tirées triples sur M. de Selle," October 31, 1744, LAC, MG1 C11A, F-82, 246–246v.

57. "État de 66 lettres de change tirées triples sur M. de Selle," October 31, 1744, LAC, MG1 C11A, F-82, 254–55v.

58. "État des lettres de change tirées triples la présente année sur M. Marcellin François Zacharie de Selle," October 30, 1745, LAC, MG1 C11A, F-84, 200–205.

59. On the Acadian expulsion, see Faragher, *Great and Noble Scheme*; Plank, *Unsettled Conquest*.

60. *Boston Gazette and Country Journal*, October 31, 1757, 1, 3, EAN.

61. Brendan McConville has identified the Glorious Revolution of 1688–89 as the origin of this new monarchicalism and offers 1740 as the approximate end date for this transformation, a date that coincides with the conclusion of a shift in policy and language regarding frontier families and women's participation in the border wars. McConville, *King's Three Faces*.

62. On eighteenth-century changes in masculinity, see Little, *Abraham in Arms*, 167. Little drew many of her conclusions from published "artillery sermons" preached to companies of active soldiers that did indicate such a transition in language. These same sermons suggest that settlers were not included in this rhetoric.

63. Norton places the culmination of this transition in the 1730s and 1740s. Norton, *Separated by Their Sex*, xi.

64. On British and American soldiers in eighteenth-century North America, see Brumwell, *Redcoats*; Anderson, *People's Army*; Chet, *Conquering the American Wilderness*; Grenier, *First Way of War*; and Eames, *Rustic Warriors*.

65. On Dudley's role in Queen Anne's War, see Chet, *Conquering the American Wilderness*, 86–99.

66. Eames, *Rustic Warriors*, 50–51, chap. 5.

67. Grenier, *First Way of War*, 47.

68. *Boston Gazette*, September 25, 1721, 3, EAN.

69. *JHRM*, 3:106–7.

70. *JHRM*, 3:173.

71. "An Act for Putting the Inhabitants of the Frontier Towns within this Province into a Posture of Defence" [1722], in *ARMB*, 2:259–60.

72. Coleman, *New England Captives*, 2:136.

73. Ibid., 1:99.

74. *JHRM*, 4:51, 55–56.

75. Coleman, *New England Captives*, 1:99.

76. *JHRM*, 5:8.

77. Ibid., 163.

78. Coleman, *New England Captives*, 1:149–53. On the Deerfield raid, see Demos, *Unredeemed Captive*; Haefeli and Sweeney, *Captors and Captives*.

79. "Resolve Allowing £20 to Christian Baker" [1722], in *ARMB*, 10:152.

80. "Vote Impowering Mrs. Christian Baker to Survey Lay Out and Sell 500 Acres of Land," June 26, 1734, in *ARMB*, 12:31; Coleman, *New England Captives*, 1:153.

81. *NHPP*, 4:677, 689.

82. "Vote Impowering Mrs. Christian Baker," in *ARMB*, 12:31.

83. On this development, see Akagi, *Town Proprietors*, 191–97.

84. *JHRM*, 10:332, 351.

85. Petition of Joseph Neff, June 1739, Massachusetts Archives Collection, 31:261, MSA.

86. "Vote Impowering Jos. Neff to Survey and Lay Out 200 Acres of Land" [1739], in *ARMB*, 12:620–21.

87. *ARMB*, 7:153–54.

88. Chase, *History of Haverhill*, 308.

89. Mirick, *History of Haverhill*, 112.

90. *JHRM*, 15:199, 201.

91. *JHRM*, 1:21, 86–87.

92. On this initiative, see Eames, *Rustic Warriors*, chap. 3.

93. McCormack, "New Militia."

94. *Boston Evening Post*, October 15, 1739, 1, EAN.

95. Ibid.

96. Symmes, *Historical memoirs*, 30, EAI.

97. Williams, *Martial Wisdom Recommended*, 26, EAI.

98. *Boston Weekly News-Letter*, August 29, 1745, 1, EAN.

99. "Orders and Votes Allowing Pay and Subsistence for Garrisons at Divers Points on the Eastern and Western Frontiers and Appointing Committees for Building New Blockhouses" [1747], in *ARMB*, 13:702–3.

100. "Vote Allowing a Premium for Indian Prisoners and Scalps" [1747], in *ARMB*, 13:712–13.

101. "Vote Granting Allowances for Fortifying Divers Towns in the County of York" [1743], in *ARMB*, 13:313.

102. *Boston Evening Post*, April 28, 1746, 4, EAN.

103. *Boston Evening Post*, May 26, 1746, 1, EAN.

104. Parsons, *Religion Recommended to the Soldier*, 6-7, EAI.

105. *Boston News-Letter*, June 5, 1746, 2, EAN.

106. Remarks appended to Doolittle, *Short Narrative Of Mischief*, 20–22, EAI.

107. Doolittle, *Short Narrative Of Mischief*, 22, EAI.

108. Ibid., 5.

109. Ibid., 4.

110. "Indian Attack at Walpole," in *NHHSC*, 2:49–58, quotations on 55, 57. This account will be discussed in greater detail in the next chapter. The volume's editor noted that the account was reprinted from an article in the *Cheshire Gazette*. See also, Thomas Fessenden to Jeremy Belknap, January 22, 1790," in *NHHSC*, 4:290–92.

111. "Captivity of Mary Fowler," in Farmer and Moore, *Collections, Topographical, Historical, and Biographical,* 1:284–87.

112. *Boston Evening Post,* July 28, 1755, 3, EAN.

113. *New-Hampshire Gazette,* June 24, 1757, 2, EAN.

Chapter 5

1. Mirick, *History of Haverhill.*

2. Pike, "Journal," 137.

3. Mirick, *History of Haverhill,* 64, 108.

4. On the creation of a usable past in the early United States, see Commager, "Search for a Usable Past"; Matthews, " 'Whig History.' "

5. O'Brien, *Firsting and Lasting,* xix–xx, 33–34. O'Brien has argued that these local histories also attempted to establish the claim that Indians had been removed from the region and replaced by a superior group. This removal allowed New Englanders to rewrite a more favorable history of the colonial era.

6. Of the many works that explore changes in gender roles, particularly the emergence of a more domestic, private role for (primarily) Anglo-American women in the eighteenth and nineteenth centuries, a short list might include Zagarri, *Revolutionary Backlash*; Kerber, *Women of the Republic*; Berkin, *Revolutionary Mothers*; Norton, *Liberty's Daughters*; Norton, *Separated by Their Sex*; Ryan, *Mysteries of Sex,* chaps. 2, 4; and Cott, *Bonds of Womanhood.*

7. My intent in coining the term "resolute motherhood" is to more accurately reflect the language of authors constructing the historical memory of colonial women's war making while situating this project within larger changes in ideologies of gender and political participation in the late eighteenth and early nineteenth centuries.

8. Mirick, *History of Haverhill,* 65. On gender borrowing, see Dugaw, *Warrior Women,* chap. 6.

9. On republican motherhood and related phenomena, see Zagarri, *Revolutionary Backlash*; Kerber, *Women of the Republic*; Norton, *Liberty's Daughters*; and Berkin, *Revolutionary Mothers.*

10. Mirick, *History of Haverhill,* 65.

11. Historians have increasingly appreciated the importance of the memory of these wars in the eighteenth and nineteenth centuries. Haefeli and Sweeney, " 'The Redeemed Captive' as Recurrent Seller"; MacNeil, *Emergence of the American Frontier Hero*; Burnham, *Captivity and Sentiment*; Derounian-Stodola, "Captive as Celebrity"; and Coates and Morgan, *Heroines and History.*

12. Coates and Morgan, *Heroines and History,* chap. 2.

13. La Potherie, *Histoire de l'Amerique septentrionale,* 1:324–28.

14. Marie Madeleine de Verchères à Mme de Maurepas, October 15, 1699, in *SRCA,* 6–7.

15. Charlevoix, *Histoire et description générale,* 5:183–85.

16. "Verchères-Naudière—Procès avec le curé de Batiscan" BANQ, ZQ27, 183, quoted in Coates and Morgan, *Heroines and History,* 37.

17. Madeleine de Verchères, "Relation des faits héroiques de Mademoiselle Marie-Madeleine de Verchères, âgée de quatorze ans, contre les Iroquois, en l'année 1696, le 22 octobre, à huit heures du matin," in *SRCA*, 7–12. The title of Verchères's account mistakenly placed the incident in 1696 rather than 1692. Coates and Morgan, *Heroines and History*, 20.

18. Coates and Morgan, *Heroines and History*, 20–21; Dechêne, *Le peuple, l'état et la guerre*, 161.

19. Verchères, "Relation des faits héroiques," 11.

20. Ibid., 11–12.

21. Ibid., 11.

22. Verchères à Maurepas, October 15, 1699, 7.

23. Coates and Morgan, *Heroines and History*, 41.

24. *JR*, 30:289–95.

25. Charlevoix, *Histoire et description générale*, 1:277–79.

26. Lamb, *Original and Authentic Journal*, 105–7.

27. Parkman, *Jesuits in North America*, 313–16.

28. Rowlandson, *Narrative of the Captivity, Sufferings, and Removes*, EAI.

29. Michelle Burnham suggests that the 1773 image of Rowlandson—and presumably the 1770 illustration—represent a desire to place Rowlandson in a Revolutionary context. Burnham, *Captivity and Sentiment*, 63–67. Noting that narratives such as Rowlandson's were important in creating "an appropriate image of colonial oppression," Burnham convincingly argues that the image "provided an effective rhetoric for imagining and justifying colonial resistance." Burnham also suggests that this "refiguration" was "grafted" on the "image of a more violently aggressive captive such as Hannah Dustan." Ibid., 65, 67. Although Dustan's story undoubtedly influenced Rowlandson's new image, Dustan was only one of many women remembered for defending their homes, themselves, and their families in earlier wars.

30. Hutchinson, *HCPM*, 2:51.

31. Niles, *Summary Historical Narrative* (1837), 230; C. Mather, *Decennium Luctuosum*, 94, EAI.

32. Hutchinson, *HCPM*. Niles, *Summary Historical Narrative*; Belknap, *History of New-Hampshire*. The volumes of Hutchinson's history all had slightly different titles. The title given above is to the 1936 edited version.

33. Niles, *Summary Historical Narrative* (1837), 154.

34. Niles, *Summary Historical Narrative* (1861), 368; compare to Doolittle, *Short Narrative of Mischief*, 4, EAI.

35. Hutchinson, *HCPM*, 1:xxviii–xxix.

36. Young, *Masquerade*; Mayer, *Belonging to the Army*; Wheelwright, *Amazons and Military Maids*; Dugaw, *Warrior Women*; and Norton, *Liberty's Daughters*, chap. 7.

37. Gordon, *History of the Rise*; Ramsay, *History of the American Revolution*.

38. Lawson, *American Plutarch*. See also Kirsch, "Jeremy Belknap," 35; Kaplan, "History of New-Hampshire," 37–38.

39. For example, see Hubbard, *Narrative of the Troubles*, EAI; N. S., *Present State of New-England*, EEBO; Church, *Entertaining Passages*, EAI; I. Mather, *Brief History*, EAI; C. Mather, *Decennium Luctuosum*, EAI; and Penhallow, *History of the Wars*, EAI.

40. Penhallow, *History of the Wars*, EAI.

41. Hutchinson, *HCPM*, 2:121.

42. Niles, *Summary Historical Narrative* (1837), 275.

43. Penhallow, *History of the Wars*, 32, EAI; Belknap, *History of New-Hampshire*, 1:338–39.

44. Hubbard, *Narrative of the Troubles*, 20–21, EAI. This story appears in a supplemental section, "From Pascataqua to Pemmaquid."

45. Belknap, *History of New-Hampshire*, 1:135.

46. Drake, "Appendix," 312.

47. Belknap, *History of New-Hampshire*, 1:357.

48. N. S., *Present State of New-England*, 6–7, EEBO.

49. Hutchinson, *HCPM*, 1:245.

50. *Sporting Magazine*, December 1802, 149–50. The December 1802 edition was published with several others in 1803 as "Vol. 21."

51. I. Mather, *Brief History*, 33, EAI.

52. Hubbard, *Narrative of the Troubles*, 94, EAI.

53. Trumbull, *History of the Discovery of America*, 66–67. Trumbull's account was supported—or perhaps repeated—by John Woodbridge, Hadley's minister, in a sermon celebrating the 200th anniversary of the founding of Plymouth. Woodbridge, *Jubilee of New England*, 10.

54. "Billerica Town Meetings, 1658–1685," Massachusetts County and Township Records, vol. 37, pt. 3: 59–60.

55. Trumbull, *History of the Discovery of America*, 66–67.

56. "Captivity of Mary Fowler," in Farmer and Moore, *Collections*, 1:284–87.

57. Farmer and Moore, *Collections*, 1:iii–iv.

58. Ibid., iv–vi.

59. Ibid., iv.

60. Belknap, *History of New-Hampshire*, 1:132–33.

61. Hutchinson, *HCPM*, 1:249.

62. On Spartan womanhood in the early republic, see Winterer, *Mirror of Antiquity*, 71–79.

63. Murray, "On the Equality of the Sexes," 3–14.

64. Murray, "Observations on Female Abilities," 236–37.

65. Winterer, *Mirror of Antiquity*, 76–79. Winterer notes that even Sargent Murray "recoiled from the most radical implications of the Spartan woman, embracing the Spartan mother instead." Ibid., 79.

66. Thomas Fessenden to Jeremy Belknap, January 22, 1790, in *NHHSC*, 4:290–92.

67. *NHHSC*, 2:55–57. Hamilton Child's 1885 *Gazetteer of Cheshire County* noted that the story of Kilburn's defense "forms an episode of Indian warfare familiar to every school boy." Child, *Gazetteer of Cheshire County*, 488.

68. *NHHSC*, 2:55–57.

69. Mirick, *History of Haverhill*, 123–24.

70. Ibid., 124.

71. Ibid.

72. Chase, *History of Haverhill*, 308.

73. C. Mather, *A Memorial Of the Present Deplorable State of New-England*, 33–36, ECCO.

74. Ibid., 35.

75. Penhallow, *History of the Wars*, 10–11, EAI.

76. Niles, *Summary Historical Narrative* (1837), 251–52.

77. Mirick, *History of Haverhill*, 108.

78. Ibid., 108–9.

79. Ibid., 109.

80. Ibid., 109–10.

81. Derounian-Stodola, "Captive as Celebrity"; Cutter, "Female Indian Killer Memorialized"; Humphreys, "Mass Marketing of the Colonial Captive Hannah Duston"; and Ulrich, *Good Wives*, 172.

82. Hutchinson, *HCPM*, 2:80–81; Niles, *Summary Historical Narrative* (1837), 240–41.

83. Hutchinson, *HCPM*, 2:80–81.

84. Cutter, "Female Indian Killer," 26. Cutter also observed that beginning in the 1820s and 1830s, authors began to emphasize Dustan's motherhood, to "erase" the children she killed from their accounts, and to reshape her "violent actions into a justified defense of the 'natural' ideals of motherhood." As Cutter pointed out, 1831 marked the appearance of the phrase "The Mother's Revenge," the title of a John Greenleaf Whittier poem as well as a prominent inscription on a statue later erected in Dustan's honor. Ibid., 19–20.

85. Mirick, *History of Haverhill*, 108.

86. Namias, *White Captives*, chap. 1.

87. The work's full title was: *Woman on the American Frontier: A Valuable and Authentic History of the Heroism, Adventures, Privations, Captivities, Trials, and Noble Lives and Deaths of the "Pioneer Mothers of the Republic."*

88. Fowler, *Woman on the American Frontier*, quotations on 81, 3–4.

Epilogue

1. As Jean O'Brien noted, appropriating Indian place names served to "situate Indians securely in the past, separating them neatly as part of nature instead of culture." *Firsting and Lasting*, 35.

2. The continued popularity of Mary Rowlandson's narrative has helped to keep Weetamoo in the public consciousness. MacNeil, *Emergence of the American Frontier Hero*; Burnham, *Captivity and Sentiment*.

3. Whittier, "Bridal of Pennacook," 537–51.

Bibliography

Primary Sources

Archival Materials

Boston, Massachusetts
  Massachusetts Historical Society
    Winslow Family Papers II, 1638–1760
  Massachusetts State Archives
    Massachusetts Archives Collection
  New England Historic Genealogical Society
    R. Stanton Avery Special Collections
Concord, New Hampshire
  New Hampshire Historical Society
    Papers of the Emery Family
Ottawa, Ontario
  Library and Archives Canada, Ottawa
    Fonds de la Bibliothèque de l'Arsenal. Archives de la Bastille.
        Manuscript Group 7
      Series II Prisonniers
    Fonds des Colonies. Manuscript Group 1
      Series B Lettres envoyées
      Series C11A Correspondance générale Series (Canada)
      Series C11D Correspondance générale Series (Acadie)
      Series G2 Dépôt des papiers publics des colonies
Quebec City, Quebec
  Bibliothèque et Archives Nationales Québec, Quebec
    Fonds Conseil Souverain. Jugements et Délibérations
    Fonds Cour supérieure. District judiciaire de Québec. Tutelles et curatelles,
      Dossiers
    Fonds Intendants. Papiers terriers de la Compagnie des Indes occidentales et
      du Domaine du roi. Aveux et Dénombrements
    Fonds Prévôté de Québec. Registres et documents de la Prévôté de Québec.
      Registres de la Prévôté de Québec

Online Databases

Acadia, Canada, Vital and Church Records (Drouin Collection), 1670–1946.
  www.ancestry.com.
Early American Imprints, Series 1: Evans, 1639–1800. www.readex.com.

Early American Newspapers, Series 1, 1690–1876. www.readex.com.
Early English Books Online. eebo.chadwyck.com.
Eighteenth Century Collections Online. www.gale.com.

Published Archival Collections

Acts and Resolves, Public and Private, of the Province of the Massachusetts Bay. 21 vols. Boston: Wright & Potter, 1869–1922.

Arrêts et réglements du Conseil supérieur de Québec, et ordonnances et jugements des intendants du Canada. Quebec, 1855.

Baxter, James Phinney, ed. *Documentary History of the State of Maine.* 24 vols. Portland: Maine Historical Society, 1869–1916.

Bouton, Nathaniel, ed. *Provincial Papers: Documents and Records Relating to the Province of New-Hampshire.* 7 vols. Concord, Nashua, Manchester, N.H., 1867–73.

Collection de manuscrits contenant lettres, mémoires, et autres documents historiques relatifs à la Nouvelle-France. 4 vols. Quebec, 1883–85.

Collections of the Massachusetts Historical Society, all series. Boston: Massachusetts Historical Society, 1792–.

Collections of the New Hampshire Historical Society. 15 vols. Concord, N.H.: New Hampshire Historical Society, 1824–1939.

Collections of the Protestant Episcopal Historical Society for the Year 1851. New York, 1851.

De l'Incarnation, Marie. *Lettres de la Révérende Mère Marie de l'Incarnation: Première Supérieure du Monastère des Ursulines de Québec.* 2 vols. Edited by L'Abbé Richaudeau. Paris, 1876.

Édits, ordonnances royaux, déclarations et arrêts du conseil d'État du roi concernant le Canada. 3 vols. Quebec, 1854–56.

Journals of the House of Representatives of Massachusetts. 55 vols. Boston: Massachusetts Historical Society, 1919–90.

Massachusetts County and Township Records. 126 vols. Series of bound manuscript photocopies held at Webster Library, Concordia University, Montreal.

Mémoires et documents relatifs à l'histoire du Canada. Memoires de la Société Historique de Montréal. Vol. 3. Montreal, 1860.

Nouvelle-France: Documents historiques; Correspondance échangée entre les autorités françaises et les gouverneurs et intendants. Vol 1. Quebec, 1893.

Ormerod, George, ed. *Tracts Relating to Military Proceedings in Lancashire During the Great Civil War.* London, 1844.

Richard, Édouard, ed. *Supplement to Dr. Brymner's Report on Canadian Archives by Mr. Édouard Richard (1899).* Ottawa: S. E. Dawson, 1901.

Sainsbury, W. Noel, ed. *Calendar of State Papers, Colonial Series, America and West Indies: 1661–1668.* London, 1880.

Shurtleff, Nathaniel B., ed. *Records of the Governor and Company of the Massachusetts Bay in New England.* 5 vols. Boston, 1853–54.

Shurtleff, Nathaniel B., and David Pulsifer, eds. *Records of the Colony of New Plymouth.* 12 vols. Boston, 1855–61.

Trumbull, J. Hammond, ed. *Public Records of the Colony of Connecticut.* 15 vols. Hartford, Conn., 1850–90.

Worthington, Dorothy, ed. *Rhode Island Land Evidences.* Providence: Rhode Island Historical Society, 1921.

Published Books and Pamphlets

Bacqueville de la Potherie, Claude-Charles Le Roy. *Histoire de l'Amerique septentrionale.* 4 vols. Paris, 1722.

Belknap, Jeremy. *The History of New-Hampshire.* 3 vols. Philadelphia: Robert Aitken, Isaiah Thomas, Belknap and Young, 1784, 1791, 1792.

[Bradford, William, and Edward Winslow]. *A Relation or Journall of the beginning and proceedings of the English Plantation Setled at Plimoth in New England.* London, 1622. Early English Books Online.

Charlevoix, Pierre François Xavier de. *Histoire et description générale de la Nouvelle-France.* 6 vols. Paris, 1744.

Chase, George Wingate. *The History of Haverhill, Massachusetts: From Its First Settlement, in 1640, to the Year 1860.* Haverhill, Mass., 1861.

Child, Hamilton. *Gazetteer of Cheshire County, N.H., 1736–1885.* Syracuse, N.Y., 1885.

Church, Benjamin. *Entertaining Passages Relating to Philip's War which Began in the Month of June, 1675.* Edited by Thomas Church. Boston, 1716. Early American Imprints.

Denys, Nicolas. *Description géographique et historique des costes de l'Amerique septentrionale.* 2 vols. Paris, 1672.

Dollier de Casson, François. *A History of Montreal, 1640–1672, from the French of Dollier de Casson.* Translated and edited by Ralph Flenley. London: J. M. Dent & Sons, 1928.

Doolittle, Benjamin. *A Short Narrative Of Mischief done by the French and Indian Enemy, on the Western Frontiers Of the Province of the Massachusetts-Bay.* Boston, 1750. Early American Imprints.

Drake, Samuel Gardner. Appendix to *The History of Philip's War, Commonly Called the Great Indian War, of 1675 and 1676,* 2nd ed., 287–353. Reprint of *Entertaining Passages Relating to Philip's War which Began in the Month of June, 1675,* by Thomas Church. Edited by Samuel Gardner Drake. Boston, 1827.

Easton, John. *A Relacion of the Indyan Warre* [1675]. In *Narratives of the Indian Wars: 1675–1699.* Edited by Charles H. Lincoln. New York: Charles Scribner's Sons, 1913.

Farmer, John, and Jacob Bailey Moore, eds. *Collections, Topographical, Historical, and Biographical Relating Principally to New Hampshire.* 3 vols. Concord, N.H., 1822–24.

Fowler, William Worthington. *Woman on the American Frontier: A Valuable and Authentic History of the Heroism, Adventures, Privations, Captivities, Trials, and Noble Lives and Deaths of the "Pioneer Mothers of the Republic."* Hartford, Conn., 1886.

Gookin, Daniel. "An Historical Account of the Doings and Sufferings of Christian Indians in New England in the Years 1675, 1676, 1677." In *Transactions and Collections of the American Antiquarian Society.* Vol. 2, 423–534. Cambridge, Mass., 1836.

———. "Historical Collections of the Indians in New England" (1674). *MHSC*, 1st ser., 1 (Boston, 1792), 141–226.

Gordon, William. *The History of the Rise, Progress, and Establishment, of the Independence of the United States of America.* 4 vols. London, 1788.

Gyles, John. *Memoirs of Odd Adventures, Strange Deliverances, &c. in the Captivity of John Gyles, Esq.* Boston, 1736. Early American Imprints.

Hubbard, William. *A Narrative of the Troubles with the Indians in New-England.* Boston, 1677. Early American Imprints.

Hutchinson, Thomas. *The History of the Colony and Province of Massachusetts-Bay.* Edited by Lawrence Shaw Mayo. 3 vols. Cambridge, Mass.: Harvard University Press, 1936.

Laverdière and Casgrain, Abbots, eds. *Le Journal des Jésuites.* Quebec, 1871.

Mascarene, Paul. "Memorial of Paul Mascarene, Nov. 6, 1713." *Collections of the Nova Scotia Historical Society.* Vol. 4, 69–85. Halifax, 1885.

Mather, Cotton. *Decennium Luctuosum.* Boston, 1699. Early American Imprints.

———. *The Deplorable State of New-England.* London, 1708, reprinted Boston, 1721. Early American Imprints.

———. *Frontiers Well-Defended.* Boston, 1707. Early American Imprints.

———. *Humiliations Follow'd with Deliverances.* Boston, 1697. Early American Imprints.

———. *Magnalia Christi Americana.* London, 1702. Early American Imprints.

———. *A Memorial Of the Present Deplorable State of New-England.* Boston, 1707. Eighteenth Century Collections Online.

Mather, Increase. *A Brief History of the Warr with the Indians in New-England.* Boston, 1676. Early American Imprints.

———. *Diary: March 1675–December 1676.* Edited by Samuel A. Green. Cambridge, Mass.: John Wilson and Son, 1900.

Mirick, B. L. *The History of Haverhill, Massachusetts.* Haverhill, Mass., 1832.

Morin, Marie. *Annales de L'Hotel-Dieu de Montreal: Rédigées par la soeur Morin.* Vol. 12. *Memoires de la Société Historique de Montréal,* edited by Æ Fauteux, E. A. Massicotte, and C. Bertrand. Montreal: L'Imprimerie des Editeurs Limitée, 1921.

Murray, Judith Sargent. "Observations on Female Abilities." In *The Neglected Canon: Nine Women Philosophers, First to the Twentieth Century,* edited by Therese Boos Dykeman, 233–61. Dordrecht, Neth.: Kluwer Academic, 1999.

———. "On the Equality of the Sexes." In *Selected Writings of Judith Sargent Murray.* Edited by Sharon M. Harris, 3–14. New York: Oxford University Press, 1995.

Niles, Samuel. *A Summary Historical Narrative of the Wars in New-England with the French and Indians, in the Several Parts of the Country.* [1760?]. Part 1: *MHSC,* 3d ser., 6 (Boston, 1837), 154–279. Part 2: *MHSC,* 4th ser., 5 (Boston, 1861), 309–589.

N. S. [Nathaniel Saltonstall]. *A Continuation Of the State of New-England.* London, 1676. Early English Books Online.

———. *A New and Further Narrative Of the State of New-England.* London, 1676. Early English Books Online.

———. *The Present State of New-England, With Respect to the Indian War.* London, 1675. Early English Books Online.

Oldmixon, John. *The British Empire in America.* 2 vols. London, 1708. Eighteenth Century Collections Online.

Parkman, Francis. *The Jesuits in North America in the Seventeenth Century.* Boston, 1867.

Parsons, Joseph. *Religion Recommended to the Soldier.* Boston, 1744. Early American Imprints.

Penhallow, Samuel. *The History of the Wars of New-England, With the Eastern Indians.* Boston, 1726. Early American Imprints.

Potter, Elisha R., Jr. *The Early History of Narragansett.* Vol. 3. *Collections of the Rhode Island Historical Society.* Providence, 1835.

Ramsay, David. *The History of the American Revolution.* 2 vols. Philadelphia, 1789.

Recueil de ce qui s'est passé en Canada au sujet de la guerre, tant des Anglais que des Iroquois, depuis l'année 1682. Quebec, 1871.

Rowlandson, Mary. *A Narrative of the Captivity, Sufferings, and Removes of Mrs. Mary Rowlandson.* Boston: T. Fleet, Z. Fowle, Nathaniel Coverly, John Boyle, 1720, 1770, 1771, 1773. Early American Imprints.

———. *The Soveraignty & Goodness of God.* Cambridge, Mass., 1682. Early American Imprints.

Symmes, Thomas. *Historical Memoirs of the Late Fight at Piggwacket.* Boston, 1725. Early American Imprints.

Thwaites, Reuben Gold, ed. *The Jesuit Relations and Allied Documents: Travels and Explorations of the Jesuit Missionaries in New France, 1610–1791.* 73 vols. Cleveland: Burrows Brothers, 1896–1901.

Tompson, Benjamin. *New Englands Crisis* [1676]. Edited by J. F. Hunnewell. Boston, 1894.

Trumbull, Henry. *History of the Discovery of America, of the Landing of our Forefathers, at Plymouth, and of their Most Remarkable Engagements with the Indians, in New-England.* Norwich, Conn., 1812.

Vachon de Belmont, François. "Histoire du Canada." *Collection de mémoires et de relations sur l'histoire ancienne du Canada.* Quebec, 1840.

Whittier, John Greenleaf. "The Bridal of Pennacook." *The United States Magazine and Democratic Review* 16 (1845): 537–51.

Williams, William. *Martial Wisdom Recommended.* Boston, 1737. Early American Imprints.

Woodbridge, John. *The Jubilee of New England: A Sermon, Preached in Hadley, December 22, 1820, in Commemoration of the Landing of our Fathers at Plymouth; Being Two Centuries from that Event.* Northampton, Mass., 1821.

Published Journals and Diaries

Lamb, Roger. *An Original and Authentic Journal of Occurrences During the Late American War from Its Commencement to the Year 1783.* Dublin, 1809.

Marshall, John. *Extracts from John Marshall's Diary: January 1689–December 1711.* Edited by Samuel A. Green. Cambridge, Mass.: John Wilson and Son, 1900.

Pike, John. "Journal of the Rev. John Pike." In *Proceedings of the Massachusetts Historical Society, 1875–1876.* Boston, 1876, 117–52.

Sewall, Samuel. "Diary of Samuel Sewall: 1674–1729." 3 vols. *MHSC*, 5th ser. (Boston, 1878–82).

Winthrop, John. *Winthrop's Journal: "History of New England," 1630–1649*. Edited by James Kendall Hosmer. 2 vols. New York: Charles Scribner's Sons, 1908.

Newspapers and Periodicals

Boston Evening Post	*Boston News-Letter*
Boston Gazette	*Boston Weekly News-Letter*
Boston Gazette and	*New-Hampshire Gazette*
Country Journal	*Sporting Magazine*

Secondary Sources

Akagi, Roy Hidemichi. *The Town Proprietors of the New England Colonies: A Study of Their Development, Organization, Activities and Controversies, 1620–1770*. Philadelphia: University of Pennsylvania Press, 1924.

Amussen, Susan Dwyer. *An Ordered Society: Gender and Class in Early Modern England*. New York: Columbia University Press, 1988.

Anderson, Fred. *A People's Army: Massachusetts Soldiers and Society in the Seven Years' War*. Chapel Hill: University of North Carolina Press, 1984.

Arnold, Laura. "'Now . . . Didn't Our People Laugh?' Female Misbehavior and Algonquian Culture in Mary Rowlandson's *Captivity and Restauration*." *American Indian Culture and Research Journal* 21, no. 4 (1997): 1–28.

Axtell, James. *The Invasion Within: The Contest of Cultures in Colonial North America*. New York: Oxford University Press, 1985.

———. "The Vengeful Women of Marblehead: Robert Roules's Deposition of 1677." *WMQ* 31, no. 4 (October 1974): 647–52.

Axtell, James, and William C. Sturtevant. "The Unkindest Cut, or Who Invented Scalping?" *WMQ* 37, no. 3 (July 1980): 451–72.

Baker, Keith Michael. "Defining the Public Sphere in Eighteenth-Century France: Variations on a Theme by Habermas." In *Habermas and the Public Sphere*, edited by Craig Calhoun, 181–211. Cambridge, Mass.: MIT Press, 1992.

Barr, Juliana. *Peace Came in the Form of a Woman: Indians and Spaniards in the Texas Borderlands*. Chapel Hill: University of North Carolina Press, 2007.

Berkin, Carol. *Revolutionary Mothers: Women in the Struggle for America's Independence*. New York: Knopf, 2005.

Bouvier, Virginia Marie. *Women and the Conquest of California, 1542–1840: Codes of Silence*. Tucson: University of Arizona Press, 2001.

Boydston, Jeanne. "Gender as a Question of Historical Analysis." *Gender & History* 20, no. 3 (November 2008): 558–83.

Bragdon, Kathleen J. *Native People of Southern New England, 1500–1650*. Norman: University of Oklahoma Press, 1996.

———. *Native People of Southern New England, 1650–1775*. Norman: University of Oklahoma Press, 2009.

Breitwieser, Mitchell Robert. *American Puritanism and the Defense of Mourning: Religion, Grief, and Ethnology in Mary White Rowlandson's Captivity Narrative*. Madison: University of Wisconsin Press, 1990.

Brewer, John. "This, That and the Other: Public, Social and Private in the Seventeenth and Eighteenth Centuries." In *Shifting the Boundaries: Transformation of the Languages of Public and Private in the Eighteenth Century*, edited by Dario Castiglione and Lesley Sharpe, 1–21. Exeter: University of Exeter Press, 1995.

Brooks, James F. *Captives and Cousins: Slavery, Kinship, and Community in the Southwest Borderlands*. Chapel Hill: University of North Carolina Press, 2002.

Brown, Kathleen, M. *Good Wives, Nasty Wenches, and Anxious Patriarchs: Gender, Race, and Power in Colonial Virginia*. Chapel Hill: University of North Carolina Press, 1996.

Brumwell, Stephen. *Redcoats: The British Soldier and War in the Americas, 1755–1763*. Cambridge, U.K.: Cambridge University Press, 2002.

Brun, Josette. *Vie et mort du couple en Nouvelle-France: Québec et Louisbourg au XVIIIe siècle*. Montreal: McGill-Queen's University Press, 2006.

Bruneau, Marie-Florine. *Women Mystics Confront the Modern World: Marie de L'Incarnation: 1599–1672 and Madame Guyon: 1648–1717*. Albany: State University of New York Press, 1998.

Burnham, Michelle. *Captivity and Sentiment: Cultural Exchange in American Literature, 1682–1861*. Hanover, N.H.: University Press of New England, 1997.

Chet, Guy. *Conquering the American Wilderness: The Triumph of European Warfare in the Colonial Northeast*. Amherst: University of Massachusetts Press, 2003.

Choquette, Leslie. "'Ces Amazones du Grand Dieu': Women and Mission in Seventeenth-Century Canada." *French Historical Studies* 17, no. 3 (Spring 1992): 627–55.

———. *Frenchmen into Peasants: Modernity and Tradition in the Peopling of French Canada*. Cambridge, Mass.: Harvard University Press, 1997.

Clark, Emily. *Masterless Mistresses: The New Orleans Ursulines and the Development of a New World Society, 1727–1834*. Chapel Hill: University of North Carolina Press, 2007.

Coates, Colin M., and Cecilia Morgan. *Heroines and History: Representations of Madeleine de Verchères and Laura Secord*. Toronto: University of Toronto Press, 2002.

Cogley, Richard W. *John Eliot's Mission to the Indians before King Philip's War*. Cambridge, Mass.: Harvard University Press, 1999.

Cogswell, Thomas. "The Politics of Propaganda: Charles I and the People in the 1620s." *Journal of British Studies* 29, no. 3 (July 1990): 187–215.

Coleman, Emma Lewis. *New England Captives Carried to Canada between 1677 and 1760 during the French and Indian Wars*. 2 vols. Portland, Maine: Southworth Press, 1925.

Commager, Henry Steele. "The Search for a Usable Past." In *The Search for a Usable Past and Other Essays in Historiography*, 13–27. New York: Knopf, 1967.

Cooper, J. P. D. *Propaganda and the Tudor State: Political Culture in the Westcountry*. Oxford: Oxford University Press, 2003.

Cordingly, David. *Women Sailors and Sailors' Women: An Untold Maritime History*. New York: Random House, 2001.

Cott, Nancy F. *The Bonds of Womanhood: "Woman's Sphere" in New England, 1780–1835.* New Haven, Conn.: Yale University Press, 1977.

Courville, Serge. *Quebec: A Historical Geography.* Translated by Richard Howard. Vancouver: University of British Columbia Press, 2008.

Craveri, Benedetta. *The Age of Conversation.* Translated by Teresa Waugh. New York: New York Review of Books, 2005.

Cremer, Andrea Robertson. "Possession: Indian Bodies, Cultural Control, and Colonialism in the Pequot War." *Early American Studies: An Interdisciplinary Journal* 6, no. 2 (Fall 2008): 295–345.

Crouch, Christian Ayne. *Nobility Lost: French & Canadian Martial Cultures, Indians & the End of New France.* Ithaca, N.Y.: Cornell University Press, 2014.

Cutter, Barbara. "The Female Indian Killer Memorialized: Hannah Duston and the Nineteenth-Century Feminization of American Violence." *Journal of Women's History* 20, no. 2 (Summer 2008): 10–33.

Davis, Natalie Zemon. *Society and Culture in Early Modern France.* Stanford: Stanford University Press, 1975.

———. *Women on the Margins: Three Seventeenth-Century Lives.* Cambridge, Mass.: Harvard University Press. 1995.

Dechêne, Louise. *Le peuple, l'état et la guerre au Canada sous le régime français.* Edited by Hélène Paré, Sylvie Dépatie, Catherine Desbarats, and Thomas Wien. Montreal: Les Éditions du Boréal, 2008.

DeJean, Joan. *Tender Geographies: Women and the Origins of the Novel in France.* New York: Columbia University Press, 1991.

———. "Violent Women and Violence against Women: Representing the 'Strong' Woman in Early Modern France." *Signs: Journal of Women in Culture and Society* 29, no. 1 (2003): 117–47.

Dekker, Rudolf M. "Women in Revolt: Popular Protest and its Social Basis in Holland in the Seventeenth and Eighteenth Centuries." *Theory and Society* 16, no. 3 (May 1987): 337–62.

Dekker, Rudolf M., and Lotte C. Van de Pol. *The Tradition of Female Transvestism in Early Modern Europe.* New York: St. Martin's Press, 1989.

Demos, John. *A Little Commonwealth: Family Life in Plymouth Colony.* Oxford: Oxford University Press, 1970.

———. *The Unredeemed Captive: A Family Story from Early America.* New York: Knopf, 1994.

Den Ouden, Amy E. *Beyond Conquest: Native Peoples and the Struggle for History in New England.* Lincoln: University of Nebraska Press, 2005.

Denis, Françoise. "Ces étranges étrangères: Les Amazones." In *Étrange topos étranger: Actes du XVIe Colloque de la SATOR, Kingston, 3–5 Octobre 2002,* edited by Max Vernet, 89–102. Laval, QC: Les Presses Université Laval, 2006.

Derounian-Stodola, Kathryn Zabelle. "The Captive as Celebrity." In *Lives Out of Letters: Essays on American Literary Biography and Documentation, in Honor of Robert N. Hudspet,* edited by Robert D. Habich, 65–92. Madison, N.J.: Fairleigh Dickinson University Press, 2004.

Deslandres, Dominique. "In the Shadow of the Cloister: Representations of Female Holiness in New France." In *Colonial Saints: Discovering the Holy in the Americas, 1500–1800*, edited by Allan Greer and Jodi Bilinkoff, 129–52. New York: Routledge, 2003.

Devens, Carol. *Countering Colonization: Native American Women and Great Lakes Missions, 1630–1900*. Berkeley: University of California Press, 1992.

Drake, Samuel G. *Biography and History of the Indians of North America*. 5th ed. Boston, 1837.

Dugaw, Dianne. *Warrior Women and Popular Balladry: 1650–1850*. Cambridge: Cambridge University Press, 1989.

DuVal, Kathleen. *The Native Ground: Indians and Colonists in the Heart of the Continent*. Philadelphia: University of Pennsylvania Press, 2006.

Eames, Steven C. *Rustic Warriors: Warfare and the Provincial Soldier on the New England Frontier, 1689–1748*. New York: New York University Press, 2011.

Edwards, Jr., Mark U. *Printing, Propaganda, and Martin Luther*. Berkeley: University of California Press, 1994.

Eisenstein, Elizabeth. *The Printing Press as an Agent of Change*. Cambridge: Cambridge University Press, 1979.

Faragher, John Mack. *A Great and Noble Scheme: The Tragic Story of the Expulsion of the French Acadians from their American Homeland*. New York: W. W. Norton, 2005.

Fischer, Kirsten. *Suspect Relations: Sex, Race, and Resistance in Colonial North Carolina*. Ithaca, N.Y.: Cornell University Press, 2002.

Fletcher, Anthony, and John Stevenson, eds. *Order and Disorder in Early Modern England*. Cambridge: Cambridge University Press, 1985.

Gervais, Diane, and Serge Lusignan. "De Jeanne d'Arc à Madelaine de Verchères la femme guerrière dans la société d'ancien régime." *Revue d'histoire de l'Amérique française* 53, no. 2 (1999): 171–205.

Godineau, Dominique. "De la guerrière à la citoyenne: Porter les armes pendant l'Ancien Régime et la Révolution française." *Clio* 20 (2004): 43–69.

Goodman, Dena. "Public Sphere and Private Life: Toward a Synthesis of Current Historiographical Approaches to the Old Regime." *History and Theory* 31, no. 1 (February 1992): 1–20.

———. *The Republic of Letters: A Cultural History of the French Enlightenment*. Ithaca, N.Y.: Cornell University Press, 1994.

Grandjean, Katherine. *American Passage: The Communications Frontier in Early New England*. Cambridge, Mass.: Harvard University Press, 2015.

———. "The Long Wake of the Pequot War." *Early American Studies: An Interdisciplinary Journal* 9, no. 2 (Spring 2011): 379–411.

Greer, Allan. "Colonial Saints: Gender, Race, and Hagiography in New France." *WMQ* 57, no. 2 (April 2000): 323–48.

———. *The People of New France*. Toronto: University of Toronto Press, 1997.

Grenier, John. *The First Way of War: American War Making on the Frontier, 1607–1814*. Cambridge: Cambridge University Press, 2005.

Griffiths, N. E. S. *From Migrant to Acadian: A North American Border People, 1604–1755*. Montreal: McGill-Queen's University Press, 2005.

Grumet, Robert Steven. "Sunksquaws, Shamans, and Tradeswomen: Middle Atlantic Coastal Algonkian Women during the 17th and 18th Centuries." In *Women and Colonization: Anthropological Perspectives*, edited by Mona Etienne and Eleanor Leacock, 43–62. New York: Praeger, 1980.

Gutiérrez, Ramón A. *When Jesus Came, the Corn Mothers Went Away: Marriage, Sexuality and Power in New Mexico, 1500–1846*. Stanford: Stanford University Press, 1991.

Haefeli, Evan. "Kieft's War and the Cultures of Violence in Colonial America." In *Lethal Imagination: Violence and Brutality in American History*, edited by Michael A. Bellesiles, 17–40. New York: New York University Press, 1999.

Haefeli, Evan, and Kevin Sweeney. *Captors and Captives: The 1704 French and Indian Raid on Deerfield*. Amherst: University of Massachusetts Press, 2003.

———. "'The Redeemed Captive' as Recurrent Seller: Politics and Publication, 1707–1853." *New England Quarterly* 77, no. 3 (September 2004): 341–67.

Harris, Cole. *The Reluctant Land: Society, Space, and Environment in Canada before Confederation*. Vancouver: University of British Columbia Press, 2008.

Harvey, Tamara. *Figuring Modesty in Feminist Discourse across the Americas, 1633–1700*. Burlington, Vt.: Ashgate, 2008.

Hufton, Olwen. "Altruism and Reciprocity: The Early Jesuits and their Female Patrons." *Renaissance Studies* 15, no. 3 (2001): 328–53.

———. "The Widow's Mite and Other Strategies: Funding the Catholic Reformation." *Transactions of the Royal Historical Society* 8 (December 1998): 117–37.

Hull, N. E. H. *Female Felons: Women and Serious Crime in Colonial Massachusetts*. Urbana: University of Illinois Press, 1987.

Humphreys, Sara. "The Mass Marketing of the Colonial Captive Hannah Duston." *Canadian Review of American Studies* 41, no. 2 (2011): 149–78.

Hurl-Eamon, Jennine. *Gender and Petty Violence in London: 1680–1720*. Columbus: Ohio State University Press, 2005.

Ingram, Martin. "Ridings, Rough Music, and Mocking Rhymes in Early Modern England." In *Popular Culture in Seventeenth-Century England*, edited by Barry Reay, 166–97. New York: St. Martin's Press, 1985.

Jowett, Garth S., and Victoria O'Donnell. *Propaganda and Persuasion*. 3d ed. Thousand Oaks, Calif.: Sage Publications, 1999.

Kale, Steven D. "Women, Salons, and the State in the Aftermath of the French Revolution." *Journal of Women's History* 13, no. 4 (Winter 2002): 54–80.

Kaplan, Sidney. "*The History of New-Hampshire*: Jeremy Belknap as Literary Craftsman." *WMQ* 21, no. 1 (January 1964): 18–39.

Keller-Lapp, Heidi. "Floating Cloisters and Heroic Women: French Ursuline Missionaries, 1639–1744." *World History Connected* 4, no. 3 (June 2007). http://worldhistoryconnected.press.uiuc.edu/4.3/lapp.html.

Kerber, Linda K. *Women of the Republic: Intellect and Ideology in Revolutionary America*. Chapel Hill: University of North Carolina Press, 1980.

Kirsch, George B. "Jeremy Belknap: Man of Letters in the Young Republic."
New England Quarterly 54, no. 1 (March 1981): 33–53.

Klein, Lawrence E. "Gender and the Public/Private Distinction in the Eighteenth
Century: Some Questions about Evidence and Analytic Procedure." *Eighteenth-
Century Studies* 29, no. 1 (Fall 1995): 97–109.

Lachance, André. "Women and Crime in Canada in the Early Eighteenth Century:
1712–1759." In *Crime and Criminal Justice in Europe and Canada*, edited by Louis A.
Knafla, 157–77. Waterloo, Ontario: Wilfrid Laurier University Press, 1981.

Lake, Peter, and Steve Pincus. "Rethinking the Public Sphere in Early Modern
England." *Journal of British Studies* 45, no. 2 (April 2006): 270–92.

Lake, Peter, and Michael Questier. "Puritans, Papists, and the 'Public Sphere' in
Early Modern England: The Edmund Campion Affair in Context." *Journal of
Modern History* 72, no. 3 (September 2000): 587–627.

Lawson, Russell M. *The American Plutarch: Jeremy Belknap and the Historian's Dialogue
with the Past*. Westport, Conn.: Praeger, 1998.

Lepore, Jill. *The Name of War: King Philip's War and the Origins of American Identity*.
New York: Knopf, 1998.

Lipman, Andrew. "'A Meanes to Knitt Them Togeather': The Exchange of Body
Parts in the Pequot War." *WMQ* 65, no. 1 (January 2008): 3–28.

———. *The Saltwater Frontier: Indians and the Contest for the American Coast*.
New Haven, Conn.: Yale University Press, 2015.

Little, Ann M. *Abraham in Arms: War and Gender in Colonial New England*.
Philadelphia: University of Pennsylvania Press, 2007.

———. *The Many Captivities of Esther Wheelwright*. New Haven, Conn.: Yale University
Press, 2016.

Lombard, Anne. *Making Manhood: Growing Up Male in Colonial New England*.
Cambridge, Mass.: Harvard University Press, 2003.

Longfellow, Erica. "Public, Private, and the Household in Early Seventeenth-
Century England." *Journal of British Studies* 45, no. 2 (April 2006): 313–34.

Lossing, Benson J. "The Hannah Dustin and Mary Corliss Neff Tankard." *Potter's
American Monthly: An Illustrated Magazine of History, Literature, Science and Art* 4
(1875): 339–40.

Luria, Keith P. *Sacred Boundaries: Religious Coexistence and Conflict in Early-Modern
France*. Washington, D.C.: Catholic University of America Press, 2005.

Lynn II, John A. *Women, Armies, and Warfare in Early Modern Europe*. Cambridge:
Cambridge University Press, 2008.

Maclean, Ian. *Woman Triumphant: Feminism in French Literature, 1610–1652*. Oxford:
Clarendon Press, 1977.

MacNeil, Denise Mary. *The Emergence of the American Frontier Hero: 1682–1826,
Gender, Action, and Emotion*. New York: Palgrave Macmillan, 2009.

Malone, Patrick M. "Indian and English Military Systems in New England in the
Seventeenth Century." Ph.D. diss., Brown University, 1971.

Matthews, J. V. "'Whig History': The New England Whigs and a Usable Past."
New England Quarterly 51, no. 2 (June 1978): 193–208.

Mayer, Holly A. *Belonging to the Army: Camp Followers and Community during the American Revolution*. Columbia: University of South Carolina Press, 1996.

McCartney, Martha W. "Cockacoeske, Queen of Pamunkey: Diplomat and Suzeraine." In *Powhatan's Mantle: Indians in the Colonial Southeast*, edited by Peter H. Wood, Gregory A. Waselkov, and M. Thomas Hatley, 173–95. Lincoln: University of Nebraska Press, 1989.

McConville, Brendan. *The King's Three Faces: The Rise and Fall of Royal America, 1688–1776*. Chapel Hill: University of North Carolina Press, 2006.

McCormack, Matthew. "The New Militia: War, Politics and Gender in 1750s Britain." *Gender & History* 19, no. 3 (November 2007): 483–500.

McLaughlin, Megan. "The Woman Warrior: Gender, Warfare and Society in Medieval Europe." *Women's Studies* 17 (1990): 193–209.

Melzer, Sara E. "The *Relation de voyage*: A Forgotten Genre of 17th-Century France." In *Relations and Relationships in Seventeenth-Century French Literature*, edited by Jennifer R. Perlmutter, 33–52. Tübingen: Gunter Narr, 2006.

Millett, Nathaniel. "Borderlands in the Atlantic World." *Atlantic Studies* 10, no. 2 (2013): 268–95.

Miquelon, Dale. "Canada's Place in the French Imperial Economy: An Eighteenth-Century Overview." *French Historical Studies* 15, no. 3 (Spring 1988): 432–43.

Montaño, John Patrick. *Courting the Moderates: Ideology, Propaganda, and the Emergence of Party, 1660–1678*. Newark: University of Delaware Press, 2002.

Montrose, Louis. *The Subject of Elizabeth: Authority, Gender, and Representation*. Chicago, University of Chicago Press, 2006.

Mumford, Jeremy. "Aristocracy on the Auction Block: Race, Lords, and the Perpetuity Controversy of Sixteenth-Century Peru." In *Imperial Subjects: Race and Identity in Colonial Latin America*, edited by Andrew B. Fisher and Matthew D. O'Hara, 39–59. Durham, N.C.: Duke University Press, 2009.

Namias, June. *White Captives: Gender and Ethnicity on the American Frontier*. Chapel Hill: University of North Carolina Press, 1993.

Noel, Jan. *Along a River: The First French-Canadian Women*. Toronto: University of Toronto Press, 2013.

Norton, Mary Beth. *Founding Mothers and Fathers: Gendered Power and the Forming of American Society*. New York: Vintage, 1997.

———. *In the Devil's Snare: The Salem Witchcraft Crisis of 1692*. New York: Vintage, 2003.

———. *Liberty's Daughters: The Revolutionary Experience of American Women, 1750–1800*. Boston: Little, Brown, 1980.

———. *Separated by Their Sex: Women in Public and Private in the Colonial Atlantic World*. Ithaca, N.Y.: Cornell University Press, 2011.

O'Brien, Jean M. *Firsting and Lasting: Writing Indians out of Existence in New England*. Minneapolis: University of Minnesota Press, 2010.

Pencak, William, Matthew Dennis, and Simon P. Newman, eds. *Riot and Revelry in Early America*. University Park: Pennsylvania State University Press, 2002.

Perdue, Theda. *Cherokee Women: Gender and Culture Change, 1700–1835*. Lincoln: University of Nebraska Press, 1998.

Plane, Ann Marie. "Putting a Face on Colonization: Factionalism and Gender Politics in the Life History of Awashunkes, the 'Squaw Sachem' of Saconet." In *Northeastern Indian Lives, 1632–1816*, edited by Robert S. Grumet, 140–65. Amherst: University of Massachusetts Press, 1996.

Plank, Geoffrey. *An Unsettled Conquest: The British Campaign against the Peoples of Acadia*. Philadelphia: University of Pennsylvania Press, 2001.

Potter, Tiffany. "Writing Indigenous Femininity: Mary Rowlandson's Narrative of Captivity." *Eighteenth-Century Studies* 36, no. 2 (2003): 153–67.

Preston, David L. *The Texture of Contact: European and Indian Settler Communities on the Frontiers of Iroquoia, 1667–1783*. Lincoln: University of Nebraska Press, 2009.

Pulsipher, Jenny Hale. *Subjects unto the Same King: Indians, English, and the Contest for Authority in Colonial New England*. Philadelphia: University of Pennsylvania Press, 2005.

Raymond, Joad. *Pamphlets and Pamphleteering in Early Modern Britain*. Cambridge: Cambridge University Press, 2003.

Rediker, Marcus. "Liberty Beneath the Jolly Roger: The Lives of Anne Bonny and Mary Read, Pirates." In *Iron Men, Wooden Women: Gender and Seafaring in the Atlantic World, 1700–1920*, edited by Margaret S. Creighton and Lisa Norling, 1–33. Baltimore: Johns Hopkins University Press, 1996.

Reinhard, Wolfgang. "Reformation, Counter-Reformation, and the Early Modern State: a Reassessment. *Catholic Historical Review* 75, no. 3 (July 1989): 383–404.

Rice, Howard C. "Cotton Mather Speaks to France: American Propaganda in the Age of Louis XIV." *New England Quarterly* 16, no. 2 (June 1943): 198–233.

Richter, Daniel K. "War and Culture: The Iroquois Experience." *WMQ* 40, no. 4 (October 1983): 528–59.

Riley, Philip F. *A Lust for Virtue: Louis XIV's Attack on Sin in Seventeenth-Century France*. Westport, Conn.: Greenwood Press, 2001.

Romero, R. Todd. *Making War and Minting Christians: Masculinity, Religion, and Colonialism in Early New England*. Amherst: University of Massachusetts Press, 2011.

Rushforth, Brett. *Bonds of Alliance: Indigenous and Atlantic Slaveries in New France*. Chapel Hill: University of North Carolina Press, 2012.

Ryan, Mary P. *Mysteries of Sex: Tracing Women and Men Through American History*. Chapel Hill: University of North Carolina Press, 2006.

Samson, Roch. *The Forges du Saint-Maurice: Beginnings of the Iron and Steel Industry in Canada, 1730–1883*. Laval, Quebec: Les Presses de l'Université Laval, 1998.

Sandberg, Brian. "'Generous Amazons Came to the Breach': Besieged Women, Agency and Subjectivity during the French Wars of Religion." *Gender and History* 16, no. 3 (November 2004): 654–88.

Schmidt, Ethan A. "Cockacoeske, Weroansqua of the Pamunkeys, and Indian Resistance in Seventeenth-Century Virginia." *American Indian Quarterly* 36, no. 3 (Summer 2012): 288–317.

Schwarz, Kathryn. *Tough Love: Amazon Encounters in the English Renaissance*. Durham, N.C.: Duke University Press, 2000.

Seeman, Erik R. *The Huron-Wendat Feast of the Dead: Indian-European Encounters in Early North America*. Baltimore: Johns Hopkins University Press, 2011.

Shields, John C. *The American Aeneas: Classical Origins of the American Self*. Knoxville: University of Tennessee Press, 2001.

Shoemaker, Nancy. "The Rise or Fall of Iroquois Women." *Journal of Women's History* 2, no. 3 (Winter 1991): 39–57.

———. *A Strange Likeness: Becoming Red and White in Eighteenth-Century North America*. Oxford: Oxford University Press, 2004.

Shoemaker, Nancy, ed. *Negotiators of Change: Historical Perspectives on Native American Women*. New York: Routledge, 1995.

Shoemaker, Robert B. "The London 'Mob' in the Early Eighteenth Century." *Journal of British Studies* 26, no. 3 (July 1987): 273–304.

Sleeper-Smith, Susan. *Indian Women and French Men: Rethinking Cultural Encounter in the Western Great Lakes*. Amherst: University of Massachusetts Press, 2001.

Smolenski, John, and Thomas J. Humphrey, eds. *New World Orders: Violence, Sanction, and Authority in the Colonial Americas*. Philadelphia: University of Pennsylvania Press, 2005.

Solterer, Helen. "Figures of Female Militancy in Medieval France." *Signs: Journal of Women in Culture and Society* 16, no. 3 (1991): 522–49.

Spear, Jennifer M. *Race, Sex, and Social Order in Early New Orleans*. Baltimore: Johns Hopkins University Press, 2009.

Stanwood, Owen. *The Empire Reformed: English America in the Age of the Glorious Revolution*. Philadelphia: University of Pennsylvania Press, 2011.

Stone, Lawrence. *The Family, Sex and Marriage in England 1500–1800*. Abridged edition. New York: Harper & Row, 1979.

Strong, John A. "Algonquian Women as Sunksquaws and Caretakers of the Soil: The Documentary Evidence in the Seventeenth Century Records." In *Native American Women in Literature and Culture*, edited by Susan Castillo and Victor M. P. Da Rosa, 191–214. Porto, Portugal: Fernando Pessoa University Press, 1997.

Strong, Pauline Turner. *Captive Selves, Captivating Others: The Politics and Poetics of Colonial American Captivity Narratives*. Boulder, Colo.: Westview Press, 1999.

Tanguay, Cyprien. *Dictionnaire généalogique des familles canadiennes depuis la fondation de la colonie jusqu'à nos jours*. 7 vols. Montreal, 1871–90.

Taufer, Alison. "The Only Good Amazon Is a Converted Amazon: The Woman Warrior and Christianity in the *Amadís Cycle*." In *Playing with Gender: A Renaissance Pursuit*, edited by Jean R. Brink, Maryanne C. Horowitz, and Allison P. Coudert, 35–51. Urbana: University of Illinois Press, 1991.

Toulouse, Teresa A. *The Captive's Position: Female Narrative, Male Identity, and Royal Authority in Colonial New England*. Philadelphia: University of Pennsylvania Press, 2007.

Ulrich, Laurel Thatcher. *Good Wives: Image and Reality in the Lives of Women in Northern New England, 1650–1750*. 1980; reprint, New York: Vintage, 1991.

Villella, Peter B. "'Pure and Noble Indians, Untainted by Inferior Idolatrous Races': Native Elites and the Discourse of Blood Purity in Late Colonial Mexico." *Hispanic American Historical Review* 91, no. 4 (2011): 633–63.

Walker, Garthine. *Crime, Gender, and Social Order in Early Modern England.* Cambridge: Cambridge University Press, 2003.

Walter, John. "Faces in the Crowd: Gender and Age in the Early Modern English Crowd." In *The Family in Early Modern England*, edited by Helen Berry and Elizabeth Foyster, 96–125. Cambridge: Cambridge University Press, 2007.

Wheelwright, Julie. *Amazons and Military Maids: Women who Dressed as Men in the Pursuit of Life, Liberty and Happiness.* London: Pandora, 1989.

White, Richard. *The Middle Ground: Indians, Empires, and Republics in the Great Lakes Region, 1650–1815.* Cambridge: Cambridge University Press, 1991.

White, Sophie. *Wild Frenchmen and Frenchified Indians: Material Culture and Race in Colonial Louisiana.* Philadelphia: University of Pennsylvania Press, 2012.

Wilson, Lisa. *Ye Heart of a Man: The Domestic Life of Men in Colonial New England.* New Haven, Conn.: Yale University Press, 1999.

Winterer, Caroline. *The Mirror of Antiquity: American Women and the Classical Tradition, 1750–1900.* Ithaca, N.Y.: Cornell University Press, 2007.

Young, Alfred F. *Masquerade: The Life and Times of Deborah Sampson, Continental Soldier.* New York: Knopf, 2004.

Zagarri, Rosemarie. *Revolutionary Backlash: Women and Politics in the Early American Republic.* Philadelphia: University of Pennsylvania Press, 2007.

Zelner, Kyle F. *A Rabble in Arms: Massachusetts Towns and Militiamen during King Philip's War.* New York: New York University Press, 2009.

Index

Page numbers in italics refer to illustrations.

Denys, Nicolas, 72
Deputy husband role, 29–30, 32, 72, 168n25
Dismemberment, 49, 172n119
Dollier de Casson, Francois, 62–63, 73–74, 75–76, 175n44
Doolittle, Benjamin, 131, 143
Doorway fighting, 34–35, 92–93, 152
Drake, Samuel, 146
Dudley, Joseph, 56, 81, 100, 101, 105, 121
Dummer's War (c. 1723–26): and captive retrieval petitions, 123–24; and firearm use, 33; and memory making, 144, 145; and separate spheres ideology, 129; and settler-soldier/garrison house model, 121–22; terminology, 15
Dupuis, Claude-Thomas, 116
Durand, Justinien, 113
Dustan, Hannah: and Bradley, 153; and deputy husband role, 168n25; land grant request, 126, 155; memorialization of, 158, 160; and memory making, 185n29; and propaganda, 98–100, 178–79nn54–55; and resolute motherhood discourse, 155–56, 187n84; scholarly approaches to, 98, 155, 164n6
Dustan, Thomas, 99–100

Eames, Steven, 20–21
Easton, John, 44, 171n87
Edgar, Jane, 124
Elite women's war participation, 2, 71–79; and European tradition, 72–73, 176–77n8; and female religious orders, 73, 74–75, 80, 175n41; and femme forte image, 86; and inter-seigneurial conflict, 71–72; and memory making, 138–40; and seigneury defense, 76–79
Elizabeth I (queen of England), 39, 95
Emma (countess of Norfolk), 72
English Civil War, 72

English propaganda, 92–101; and Amazon image, 93, 95; and captivity narratives, 98–101, 178–79n54; and female mob action, 56, 101; and gender borrowing, 93–96; and order/disorder, 96–98; and settler-soldier/garrison house model, 93, 96–98, 178–79nn48–49, 54; and virago image, 81, 82, 92–93, 95
European imperial wars, 11–12, 105. See also Imperial integration
Expansionism: and King Philip's War, 44–45, 171n86; and memorializations, 160–61; New France, 59, 61; and propaganda, 96; and resolute motherhood discourse, 156, 157; and settler-soldier/garrison house model, 20, 23

Farmer, John, 148–49
Female criminality, 3
Female mob action, 51–56; in England, 173n131; Marblehead incident, 51–53, 173n132–33, 136; Marlborough incident, 53–55; and propaganda, 56, 101; Scarlet's Wharf incident, 55–56, 81, 101
Female religious orders: and elite women's war participation, 73, 74–75, 80, 175n41; female donors, 177n19; and nonelite women's war participation, 63; and propaganda, 84–85, 87–88, 177n16. See also specific people
Female sachems: and cultural similarities, 39–40; European acceptance of, 39, 40–41, 169n68; and King Philip's War, 2, 10, 39, 41, 42, 43–47, 149; marginalization of, 49–50; and memory making, 149; ongoing influence of, 50; scholarly approaches to, 169n54. See also Weetamoo
Feminine private sphere. See Separate spheres ideology
Femininity. See Gender ideologies

War of the Austrian Succession. *See* King George's War

War of the Grand Alliance. *See* King William's War

War of the Spanish Succession. *See* Queen Anne's War

Watt, Margaret, 124

Weetamoo (Pocasset sachem), 2, 41–49; alternate names for, 170n70; death of, 48–49; dispute with Philip, 42–43, 170n79; European acceptance of rank, 39, 45, 50, 170n78; and King Philip's War, 43–47; and land deals, 42; marriage to Petananuet, 45, 171n89; marriage to Quinnapin, 46; and memory making, 149; in place-names, 159; and rank, 47–48; and Rowlandson, 47–48, 172n111, 187n2

Wells raid (1692), 29–30, 34, 93, 143

Wheelwright, Esther, 179n2

White, Richard, 166n23

Whittier, John Greenleaf, 159, 187n84

Widows' roles, 30–32, 72–73, 115, 168n30, 181n39

Williams, Roger, 41

Williams, William, 129–30

Winslow, Josiah, 44, 45, 46

Winterer, Caroline, 150, 186n65

Winthrop, John (1681–1747), 55–56

Woman on the American Frontier (Fowler), 157

Women's war participation, study of: chronological phases, 10–11; geographical context, 1, 7–8, 10, 166n23; linguistic choices, 14–15; scholarly approaches, 5–6, 158, 164–65nn6, 15, 169n54, 172n10; terminology, 14–15

Women's war participation, sources, 2, 9–10, 62, 173–74n5

Woodbridge, John, 186n53

Woodwell, David, 132–33

Woodwell, Mary, 132–33, 148